Charlotte Misselwitz, Cornelia Siebeck (eds.)
Dissonant Memories – Fragmented Present

Charlotte Misselwitz, Cornelia Siebeck (eds.)
Dissonant Memories – Fragmented Present
Exchanging Young Discourses between Israel and Germany

[transcript]

This book was printed with the support of
Stiftung für Erinnerung, Verantwortung und Zukunft

ConAct

Aktion Sühnezeichen Friedensdienste e.V.

Bibliographic information published by the Deutsche Nationalbibliothek
The Deutsche Nationalbibliothek lists this publication
in the Deutsche Nationalbibliografie; detailed bibliographic data
are available in the Internet at http://dnb.d-nb.de

© 2009 transcript Verlag, Bielefeld

All rights reserved. No part of this book may be reprinted or reproduced or utilized in any form or by any electronic, mechanical, or other means, now known or hereafter invented, including photocopying and recording, or in any information storage or retrieval system, without permission in writing from the publisher.

Cover layout & illustration: Schroeter and Berger
English Corrections: Timothy J. Gluckman
Proofread & Typeset by Charlotte Misselwitz and Cornelia Siebeck
Printed by Majuskel Medienproduktion GmbH, Wetzlar
ISBN 978-3-8376-1273-8

Distributed in North America by

Transaction Publishers
New Brunswick (U.S.A.) and London (U.K.)

Transaction Publishers	Tel.: (732) 445-2280
Rutgers University	Fax: (732) 445-3138
35 Berrue Circle	for orders (U.S. only):
Piscataway, NJ 08854	toll free 888-999-6778

Auschwitz in Four Languages
Hebrew: Meir Wieseltier

Translated by Nabil Armali, Maayan Lubel, Oren Kakun, Mieke Hartmann, Tomer Gardi
First published in "Mea Shirim", Gog Books, 1969

Auschwitz, ich hörte du bist jetzt in Mode.
Nette Leute sprechen von dir respektierlich.
Bald werden sie dich ganz polstern, Blätter Papier
Wie reiner Schnee wird es rascheln in dir.
Alles wird dann so weiss, nur die gedruckten Buchstaben,
Scharen in Marschtempo, mit hocherhobener Hand.

أوشفيتس، سمعتُ أنك في الموضة
باحترام يذكرك لطفاء الناس
عما قليل , ستغلفك صفحات ورقية بهذا القد
كأن حفيفها فيك كما في الثلج الناصع
سيغدو كل شيء أبيض أبيض، سوى الأحرف المطبوعة
طوابير باستعراض منظم وأياد مرفوعة

.אושוויץ, שמעתי שאת במודה
. מדברים בך נכבדות אנשים נחמדים
מעט ירפדוך עלי ניר כל כך עוד,
יהיה מרשרש בך כבשלג צח,
לבן, רק אותיות הדפוס הכל יהיה לבן
גדודים במועל יד ובמצעד קצוב

Auschwitz, I hear you have become trendy.
Nice people speak of you with respect.
Soon they will pad you leaves of paper all over,
All will rustle within you like the purest snow
Everything will be so very white, only printed letters
Will march on, pacing columns with elevated hands.

List of Content

Introduction	11
CHARLOTTE MISSELWITZ AND CORNELIA SIEBECK	

EXCHANGING THE "THIRD GENERATION"

Talking 'bout My (Third) Generation	17
SAMI KHATIB	
Why Do I Do What I Do. **On Interdependencies of Biographical Experiences and Academic Work in the Third Generation**	25
Phil C. Langer	
Holocaust at the Table. **Experiences from seven years of "German-Israeli Exchange"**	35
Roland Imhoff	
On "Mourning" and "Friendship" in German-Israeli Youth Encounters. **The Need to Address the Sensitive Issues**	45
MARTIN SCHELLENBERG	
Different Approaches to Collective Identity and Mourning: **Experiences from the Exchange Project "Beyond Memory"**	55
NIRIT BIALER AND TANJA KERSTING	
Israelis in Berlin. **Between History and Every Day Life**	65
ZOHAR MILCHGRUB AND YOAV SAPIR	

REVISITING NATIONAL MEMORY DISCOURSES

Humanize the Discourse!
Non-Academic Reflections of a Memory Researcher   75
CORNELIA SIEBECK

When "History" turns from a Fact into a Narrative.
Different Historical Perspectives in Israeli-Palestinian Encounters   85
DANNA BADER

Addressing the Ruins.
(A Postcard)   93
HAGIT KEYSAR

Wanderings   103
ALEXANDER BRUNGS AND DAVID KÖNIG

"The Kashuas".
A Palestinian Family Memory in Israel   111
SAYED KASHUA

No more Fascism – No more War!
East German Reflections on Political Remembrance
in Unified Germany   117
PAUL GRASSE

A Historical Narrative
as the Basis for Current Political Consciousness:
The Mizrachi Alternative   127
GALIA AVIANI

Colonialism and Holocaust Remembrance.
Disguising the Continuity of European History   133
MARC BELLINGHAUSEN

TRAVELOGUES

Plan B for Zionism "Medinat Weimar"   145
RONEN EIDELMAN

Meet the Migrants.
A Migrant Policy of Remembrance as Political Intervention   153
MASSIMO PERINELLI

Tonguerilla   163
TOMER GARDI

Between Individual Origin and Alien Territory:
On being a non-Jew working for a Jewish newspaper   169
MORITZ REININGHAUS

The Bureaucracy of the Occupation:
A Love Letter to Hannah Arendt   177
YAEL BERDA

On Filipina Caregivers and the Limits of Israeli Belonging, or:
Sentimental Zionism and the Solace of Southern Tel Aviv   185
CLAUDIA LIEBELT

Radical Pedagogy under the Migration Regime   195
URI ELLIS

From Both Sides, Now   203
ELAD ORIAN

A Yid iz in Goles. "For three Transgressions of Israel, yeah,
for four, I will not reverse it"   209
ELAZAR ELHANAN

GEGENWARTSBEWÄLTIGUNG.
Getting Drunk on the Past in Berlin
and Sobering up in Yiddishland   217
DANIEL KAHN

OUTLOOK

Easy-going Uneasiness   229
CHARLOTTE MISSELWITZ

Introduction

CHARLOTTE MISSELWITZ AND CORNELIA SIEBECK

In Israel and Germany we still live, one way or another, in the aftermath of the Nazi past and the Holocaust. Consequently, this book gathers young authors from both societies who reflect on how their perceptions of the past influence their present – and vice versa. They deal with this reciprocal relationship from very different angles. While none of them claims to speak for any "national collective", they all write from a subjective perspective, pondering their own experiences and life worlds. By embracing various positions within – and beyond – German and Israeli mainstream discourses, the book mirrors some of the actual fragmentations that exist in both societies. Added together, a transnational memory discourse emerges, exhibiting multiple tensions between memory and the present, both within German and Israeli society and in between them. Gathering various and at times controversial positions, it is a discourse that sounds dissonant. This dissonance, however, is the very message of this book.

It reflects the very reality of today's German-Israeli exchanges in the widest sense of this phenomenon. Within the past two decades, there have been countless exchange-projects, organized by schools, universities and memorial sites, or within the framework of German-Israeli municipal partnerships. Moreover, young Germans and Israelis do the individual "exchange". Hence, a growing number of Israelis live in Germany, especially in Berlin, studying or working. On the other hand, numerous Germans equipped with grants for research, journalism or other professional activities reside in Israel for a while. German civil servants do not only take care of Holocaust survivors in Israel, but also engage in Israeli educational institutions or organizations fostering social and minority rights. Not least, there is a vivid exchange between political and social activists from both countries. So inevitably, these multiple forms of German-Israeli exchange render a permanent encounter of different narratives and positions.

This book too, originates in exchange-projects between young adults, exploring the influences of the past on the present in both societies: *Beyond Memory – The Significance of the Nazi-Past and the Holocaust for the Younger Generations in Germany and Israel* (2004/2005) brought together young academics, educationalists as well as journalists to discuss remembrance cultures in both countries. In *AltNeuland – Third Generation Practice in Educational Work and Social Activism* (2006), young professionals and social activists from Israel and Germany (including participants with a migrant background and Palestinians with Israeli citizenship) dealt with remembrance politics and social and political issues in both countries.

As both projects debated the suggested notion of a "third generation" and raised many questions regarding "collective memory", the contributors to this book were invited to further elaborate on some of these issues. Hence, under the headline *Exchanging the "Third Generation"*, the very notion of a "third generation" is being challenged: does it not homogenize diverse approaches towards the past, not only between Germans and Israelis, but also among them? For example, there seem to be different results depending on whether in the context of organized exchange, participants conceptualize themselves in terms of differences – e.g. as "Germans" vs. "Israelis" dealing with the past – or rather as young people with shared concerns in the present. No certain formula exists about how the Holocaust should be dealt with in the context of German-Israeli exchanges, and how we define ourselves not only in relation to the historic event, but also in relation to the "other".

The question about who "we" are and who are the "others" in German-Israeli exchange directly relates to the notion of "collective memory" – or, more precisely, to national discourses of remembrance, telling us where we supposedly come from and what our "collective identity" therefore is. However, as becomes clear in the second chapter *Revisiting National Memory Discourses*, there is significant discomfort both among young Germans and Israelis regarding mainstream memory discourses in Israel and Germany. For example, the Israeli authors wonder about what happens to a rather monolithic "victim" narrative among the Jewish Israeli majority when being confronted with Palestinian perspectives and narratives. Another essay deals with the exclusion of Mizrachi memory – e.g. the Jews who immigrated to Israel from Arab countries – in dominant Zionist discourse, which is a thoroughly European discourse. The German authors, on the other hand, are somewhat wary of the German claim made with pride, to have "learnt from history", pointing at what in their view is disguised by official memory discourse, and how Holocaust remembrance is being functionalized in German politics. Taken together, the essays in this chapter highlight some of the many gaps in official German and Israeli narratives. Thereby they question unambiguous discourses of "collective memory", which also means challenging the very notion of a fixed "collective identity", whether "German", "Israel" or otherwise clearly defined.

Obviously, memories are never an end in themselves. It always also points to the present and the future. So the last chapter deals with what we call *Travelogues*. Looking for future paths between memory and the present, the authors disentangle from national or otherwise particularistic interpretations of the past. Whether depicting migrant discourses in Israel and Germany, Israeli thoughts on Palestine, German impressions of Israel or Israeli perspectives on Germany – each author looks back on a journey within memory and present discourses. They depict their points of departure, affected by familial, national, political or professional influences. They have encountered and (ex)changed perspectives and narratives, thereby permanently re-examining their own position. For none of them has this journey yet come to an end. All authors of this book will continue fathoming potential remembrance spaces in the present. New responsibilities and future memories will always stay ahead. The journey is its own reward.

***

First of all we owe many thanks to the *Foundation Remembrance, Responsibility, Future (EVZ)* and to *ConAct – Coordination of German-Israeli Youth Exchange*. They have not only made possible this present publication, but already generously funded the two initial exchange projects *Beyond Memory* and *AltNeuland*. Without *Action Reconciliation Service for Peace (ASF)*, specifically their financial coordinator Ronald Stöber, there would have been no administrative body for the project. Furthermore we thank everyone who contributed to realizing this publication – first of all to the authors for patiently enduring a sometimes protracted and controversial editing process via email. Tim J. Gluckman not only supported us with a thorough English proofreading, but also with critical questions and suggestions. Tomer Gardi helped editing some texts, especially the ones that were originally written in Hebrew. Phil C. Langer provided material and moral support in the final stages. Franziska Kast, Peter Carrier, Miriam Deutscher, Meredith Ziebart and Seanna Doolittle helped by translating various essays from Hebrew or German into English.

Exchanging the "Third Generation"

"Talking 'bout My (Third) Generation."
An Intervention in the Misuse of a Notion

SAMI KHATIB

"Generation": The Career of a Concept

In postmodern times, the notion of "generation" gained a great deal. Originally introduced to the field of sociology by theoreticians like Wilhelm Dilthey, Karl Mannheim and Marc Bloch, its significance in pop-culture, fiction and popular, academic writing has become almost omnipresent. A brief look at the German and the U.S.A. websites of the company amazon.com proves that the notion of "generation" is used in a wide variety of social domains ranging from the 1968 generation to Douglas Coupland's famous novel Generation X. In German public discourse, new generations are continuously being shaped, many of them with clear implications for remembrance politics: for example the Flakhelfer Generation, consisting of young men who by the end of World War II were drafted from the *Hitlerjugend* (Hitler Youth) to defy allied bombing raids; or the *Kriegskinder* Generation, considered to be a "forgotten generation" of Germans who experienced the war as small children, about whom claims are made that they are still collectively traumatized even nowadays, and so on and so forth.

Given this recent boom, it may not be surprising that "generation" has also been (re-)introduced to Cultural Studies, Sociology or Political Science as a hermeneutical concept. In line with this academic application, the term's common sense meaning of "individuals who were born at about the same period of time" has changed. "Generation" has become a symbolic concept suggesting that people of the same age share a similar social experience and, moreover, a "collective memory". Although the discourse on generation suggests an immediate common-sense understanding of what is meant by it, its subject-matter actually remains unclear.

In particular when it comes to historical periodisation, the generation term proves to be rather arbitrary, and closely connected to issues that each author wants to bring to the fore in public discourse. Politically and theoretically, the term is highly blurred by its very seemingly self-evident nature. Of course, the term necessarily lacks an exact definition since every historical periodisation is always overdetermined by the speaker's perspective, his or her social background, daily experience etc.. In the light of the general difficulty of periodising historical experiences, epochs or ages, the claim of a certain generational perspective is symptomatically problematic: it is never clear who is part of which generation.

Paradoxically, the pop-cultural and academic rise of the "generation" term might be best understood through the fact that there is no proper definition of its subject. Everyone who feels addressed can be part of it. Even in academia, the notion of generation is often used to label certain social groups and their supposedly pre-determined views, values and life-styles rather than to mark a parameter of age or generational relationship (father–mother/son–daughter etc.). And even though one cannot deny the importance of certain historical experiences based on significant historical events like the end of World War II, the fall of the Berlin Wall, 9/11 etc., the supposed analytical benefits of the concept "generation" in many cases remain diffuse.

"Post-ideological"? The Ideology of the "Generation" Concept

Given this environment described above, I am interested in the political shift of perspective that is implied when one talks about his or her own (political, social or whatever) experience in terms of a collective singular such as "generation". Instead of asking the theoretical question as to what might be gained from such a notion – which is, apart from the mentioned limitations, a lot– the question posed here is instead: what is theoretically excluded when we take part in "talking 'bout my generation"?

Hence, the crucial line of my argument addresses the ideological impact of the introduction of "generation" into the field of politics. If we remember good old leftist concepts like race, class, and gender which were traditionally relied on to explain one's "objective" socio-economic position within society, it becomes clearer what the notion of generation stands for today. With the decline of the terminology of critical thought and its analytical tools, we have been witnessing the rise of the nebulous and underdetermined notion of generation.

The lack of a theoretical approach to socio-economical subjectivity leaves a vacuum which can be filled by other allegedly "post-ideological" concepts. Here of course, "generation" comes into play providing a more undetermined or "post-ideological" narrative to grasp the postmodern Lebenswelt (literally lifeworld) rather than supposedly "outdated" social parameters like class, gender and race. However, according to Slavoj Žižek, this very claim of post-ideology is itself far from being post-ideological: it is in fact postmodern ideology par excellence.[1]

The "generation" term mixes biographical aspects of individual experience with a symbolic, political level of "collective memory" as well as "collective identity" and thereby functions as a kind of ideological "transmission-belt" to problematic collective concepts such as nation, culture, religion and so on. At first glance, this ideological mishmash establishes a supposedly "post-ideological" collective. On a second glance, however, the term "generation" thereby functions as an exemplary case of "mythologizing" (Roland Barthes).[2] In this process it ultimately turns political questions based on concepts, ideas, ideologies etc. into pseudo-natural/culturalistic narratives.

The Idea of a "Third Generation" in a German-Israeli Context

In the context of German-Israeli relationships, after we had a "Second Generation" (the children of Nazi perpetrators and Shoah survivors), it has now become fashionable to talk about a "Third Generation". Also in this case, "talking 'bout my (third) generation" implies a naturalisation/culturalisation of political standpoints as well as experiences, and vice versa mythologizes contingent, biographical circumstances. To make this point clear, we might take a brief look at the post-war history of the generation discourse in mainstream politics. Remember, for instance, the former German chancellor Helmut Kohl who in 1984 claimed the Gnade der späten Geburt (in a paraphrase: "the blessing of a more recent birth") in front of the Israeli parliament. Here we have a telling example of the conservative, old style use of the "generation" idea. Concerning Helmut Kohl, the conservative application of the generation term can be retrospectively described as a yearning hardly masked for a "normality" of German nationalism to be acknowledged by the rest of the world. And this line of argument has – with some variations – become the hegemonic narrative in German politics since then. In 1998, the Schröder government claimed to be a "Generation Berlin", socialized after the National Socialist period and therefore ready to rule a so-called "mature nation".

With the introduction of the notion of a "Third generation" to this field, however, we enter a different political discourse: rather than promoting an apologetic approach with regards to German history, the "Third Generation" discourse maintains a distance to revanchist or overtly nationalist positions. Moreover, the appeal of the "Third Generation" term can be read as a symptom for a postmodern re-defining of the political in terms of vague

---

1 See Žižek, Slavoj: The Spectre of Ideology, in: Id. (ed.): Mapping Ideology, London 1994, pp. 1-33.
2 See Barthes, Roland: Mythologies, New York 1972.

concepts like culture, biography and Gemeinschaft (community). Here the term functions as a surrogate for collective identity based on an alleged "post-national" concept like generational experience. And indeed, at first sight the basic assumption of this discourse seems quite plausible: once the Holocaust and its living memories fade away as ever more witnesses – victims as well as perpetrators – die off, the grandchildren might talk more freely about the past without feelings of resentment or guilt.

But if we look more closely at the feelings of "guilt" and "resentment", we quickly detect a certain phenomenon of transference from collective identity (nationhood) to generational experience i.e. belonging to the first or third generation in post-war Germany. In the case of the German discourse on the Holocaust, the individual feelings of "guilt" or "resentment" have always already been part of a (German post-war) collective identity. Introducing the concept of generation to this discourse, the construction of a collective identity – which in the case of nationhood already requires criticising – is transformed into a misleadingly self-evident matter of birth date. The crucial point here is not the denial of any historical differences between a generation born around 1920 and 1970; the ideological "twist" is caused by a transference from an ideological concept (nationhood as collective identity) to a contingent biographical incident. Therefore, "talking 'bout my generation" in this political arena is never "innocent", since the impact of this talk is overdetermined by a short-circuit of subjective identity and collective nationhood.

Although things become complex here, we should not rely on the post-modern reflex of hastily denouncing nationhood, collectivity etc. as merely "constructed". Of course, "German-ness" is an ideological construct – but a construction that supports the material gravity of the German national state.[3]

The political expression of this materiality can be seen in the "special relationship" between Germany and Israel as nation states, based upon an ethico-political agreement on "historical responsibility". Everyone shares this responsibility as a German citizen as soon as he or she acquires a German passport. But if we bear in mind the emergence of political subjectivity – the very act of criticising one's own collective identity by deconstructing it and/or search for a more universalist identity – then the ultimately contingent fact of citizenship has to be transcended and not be reproduced on a cultural or ideological level. In contrast, the concept of generation maintains a concept of collective identity as a de-politicizing surrogate for nationhood.

---

3 Concerning the materiality of ideology, see Louis Althusser's famous essay on Ideology and Ideological State Apparatuses, in: Žižek, Slavoj (ed.): The Spectre of Ideology, London 1994, pp.100-140 (first published in La Pensée, Paris 1970).

What is at Stake, or let's talk about real Politics

What is at stake here is the opening of the field of real politics or mésentente, as Jacques Rancière puts it,[4] understood as the act of becoming a political subject through political disagreement. However, this field of radical politics either becomes closed off, or re-integrated into mainstream politics by the discourse of "generation".

On the flipside of the self-evident and unavoidable belonging to a generation lies the unquestioned belief that generation provides a quasi-neutral standpoint of biographical age cleaned of all social, national or religious traces. On the contrary, the common-sense understanding of generation – no matter whether it is labelled as "Third Generation" or "Generation X" – derives from the very attributes which are believed to be excluded from the term i.e. race, gender, social background, political attitudes, class etc. For example, the so-called Generation 89, a German reference to the post-Cold-War generation, was coined in contrast to Generation 68. Of course, the bottom line of both terms does not only refer to objective historical or subjective biographical circumstances but to political standpoints: whereas Generation 68 is considered to be a critical, left-minded group of white European or North American intellectuals or culturally progressive middle classes, Generation 89 paints the picture of a "post-ideological", economically effective and efficient, new, German middle class that calls for economic reforms in order to get rid of the old, social-democratic welfare-state. Although both images are highly political, the idea of generation helps to transfer these political questions to the blurred field of culture.

Finally, the strange urge to point out one's "Third Generational Background" when it comes to Holocaust education, inner German-Jewish relations or the Middle East conflict, might be understood as the weakness or even lack of a truly political standpoint. Again, I am not arguing against the notion of "passively" belonging to a particular generational group that is defined by certain historical or biographical parameters. Nor am I denying the "active" relevance of historical experience conferred by generational belonging. What I am criticising concerns the political gesture of taking flight to a highly vague category when talking about issues that matter: the National Socialist past and the German present, the Middle Eastern conflict, anti-Semitism, questions of (post-/anti-) Zionism, and nationalism. Ultimately, the term "generation" should be understood as part of a general, postmodern tendency that turns political questions into cultural questions thereby avoiding political debate.

---

4   See Rancière, Jacques: Disagreement: Politics and Philosophy, Minneapolis 1998.

The End of History, or:
is there a real Meaning in the Term "Generation"?

Consequently, although there are profound reasons for sociologists, psychologists and other researchers focussing on Holocaust Studies so as to apply the term "generation" to their theoretical designs, in the political arena the use of the notion generation should certainly be rejected. Ultimately, the effect of an ongoing discourse of "talking 'bout my generation" contributes to an ideological procedure already at work in postmodern thought: redefining the political into a falsely natural set of factors i.e. culture, biography and collectiveness.

In contrast to this, an alternative concept of "generation" may also be possible, and it is one which I am sketching in conclusion. If the generation term were used to highlight the historical experience of certain events in history of major importance, a notion comparable to Kant's notion of a *Geschichtszeichen* ("a Sign of History")[5], a more "universalist" meaning could be attained. Whereas the generation term as criticised above always focuses on the "particular" or subjective side of history, a "universalist" meaning of generation could account for the impact of objective, socio-political relations crystallised in certain historical events, as for example the fall of the Berlin Wall which marks the end of the Cold War era. Instead of collectivizing, and as a result homogenizing people's individual experiences into an ideological concept, a universalist meaning of generation could focus instead on the irreducible conjunction of the active process of making history and suffering from it. Here we should revisit the "modern" or capitalist experience par excellence: the dialectic of being history's active subject and – at the same time – feeling impotently subjected to objectified historical

---

5 *Geschichtszeichen* relates to Kant's work Der Streit der Fakultäten (1794). With reference to the French Revolution, Kant introduces the notion of a "Sign of History" to mark or indicate a certain historical progress (Fortschreiten zum Besseren) of humanity as a whole which cannot be grasped on the level of the singularity of individuals or individual experiences. For Kant, this universal Fortschreiten or progression of humanity is to be addressed in terms of a roughly indicating (hindeutendes) sign of history expressing a certain historical tendency. Kant's crucial point resides in the irreducible conjunction of history as an inter-subjective or universal process and an ethical/political progress within society. As a result, in German the notion of *Fortschritt* has a double meaning implying a mere process within time as well as an ethical/political progress. As Walter Benjamin argued in his thesis "On the Concept of History", this (Kantian) claim of history as an ethical/political progress cannot be taken for granted and thereby objectified, since the historian himself is always already involved in a political struggle for the "true image" of the past. Consequently, Benjamin developed a different concept of history that is not based upon progress and the progression of "empty and homogenous time"(See: Benjamin, Walter: Selected Writings, Vol. 4 1938-1940, Cambridge, USA, London, 2003).

processes (e.g. social relations, historical transformations). So we could gain an understanding of the ambivalent nature of history in its objective impact i.e. objective historical processes like the end of the Cold War or the rise of global capitalism, and its subjective meaning i.e. historical or generational experiences which are always already inscribed in the symbolic field of culture.

In stark contrast to this proposed historico-political understanding of the term "generation", we are witnessing the decline of history as an epistemological approach. Ironically, with the rise of global capitalism the idea of history as a "universal history" has perversely come true in the capitalist world market. Hence, the outdated, historicist concept of history as a collective singular has now turned into the real (hi)story of a global capitalism acting like a universal matrix of history. Even more ironically, at the very moment of history becoming real *Weltgeschichte* (world history), Francis Fukuyama (1992) called for an "End of History": this opened up the postmodernist horizon for a plurality of histories, collective narratives, and of course generational stories. Once the concept of history is dropped, then the notion of generation seems to be one of its successors. In the meantime, history is being written.

Sami Khatib, born 1976 in Hamburg to a German mother and a Palestinian father; living as a freelance writer, lecturer and political activist in Berlin; currently writing his PhD on Walter Benjamin's messianic Marxism.

Why Do I Do What I Do.
On Interdependencies of Biographical
Experiences and Academic Work
in the Third Generation

PHIL C. LANGER

שימחה זאת התאפשרה על ידי יהונתן, הראי, שבתוכו לא ראיתי את עצמי.
עבודה זאת הוקדשה לו.
אולי היינו יותר מדי קרובים, וכתוצאה מכך יותר מדי רחוקים.[1]

Being identified as an HIV seropositive gay man, both my academic interest in the psychosocial aspects of this disease and my practical involvement in Aids prevention seem to be easily comprehensible.[2] As a personal approach to social phenomena, it is well conceptualized in emancipatory and participatory methodologies of social sciences.[3] But how can I, a German social psychologist, whose parents were small children when the Second World War ended, justify my work on autobiographies of Shoah survivors and Holocaust

---

1   For the Hebrew translation I would like to express my gratitude to Eik Dödtmann, Berlin.
2   See e.g. Langer, Phil C.: Paradoxes Begehren. Zur Bedeutung heteronormativer Männlichkeitsbilder in der Psychodynamik von HIV-Infektionen, in: Rainer Bartel et al. (Eds.), Heteronorrnativität und Homosexualitäten, Innsbruck/ Wien/ Bozen, pp. 65-83.
3   Kemmis, Stephen, McTaggart, Robin: Participatory action research: Communicative action and the public sphere, in: Norman K. Denzin,Yvonna S. Lincoln (Eds.): Strategies of qualitative inquiry, 3rd ed., Thousand Oaks 2008, pp. 271-330. Tolman, Deborah L., Brydon-Miller, Mary (Eds.): From subjects to subjectivities: A handbook of interpretive and participatory methods, New York 2001.

education?[4] Where is the connection between these apparently remote topics? And what does it have to do with the concept of the "Third Generation" that I was asked to outline briefly in this essay?

At conferences on issues related to National Socialism and Shoah/Holocaust,[5] questions about the personal links between past events and current work often come up at some point of discussion, especially if one belongs to a younger generation of scholars: e.g. what is your family background with regard to the Nazi era? Where does your interest come from? Why do you really want to study this topic? Somehow I have gained the impression that a grandmother-victim or a grandfather-perpetrator is not only seen as motivating, but is also often regarded as a legitimizing factor for research interests: dealing with the past as a matter of individual or collective trauma or responsibility.[6]

Of course I could contribute to the discourse of biographical Betroffenheit (concern) as well. In the preparation for my M.A. thesis on autobiographies of Shoah survivors, I experienced the counterfactual, family narration that Welzer empirically explored and significantly entitled *Opa war kein Nazi* (Grandpa was no Nazi).[7] While my family's myth regarded my grandfather as an ordinary deputy police officer who was said to have been murdered by a gangster in June 1944 during a night patrol in a small Polish village, my inquiries resulted in a totally different insight. The data in his police papers and the pictures of his burial are clear: performing his duties he died in the liquidation of the Łodz ghetto that led to the killing of the deported Jews in the gas chambers of the Chełmno concentration camp. Far from being the innocent victim the family narrative liked to perceive him as, he had played his probably small but for so many people still decisive part in the extermination process: another example of the "banality of evil" (H. Arendt).

---

4 Langer, Phil C.: Fünf Thesen zum schulischen Besuch von KZ-Gedenkstätten, in: Einsichten und Perspektiven, Themenheft 1, 2008, pp. 66-75; Kühner, Angela, Langer, Phil C.: Wie Geschichte zum Thema wird. Holocaust Education aus sozialpsychologischer Sicht, in: Psychosozial, 31, Vol. 114, 2008, pp. 34-49; Langer, Phil C.: Schreiben gegen die Erinnerung? Autobiographien von Überlebenden der Shoah, Hamburg 2002.
5 Although the terms Holocaust and Shoah are often synonymously used, they imply different connotations. See Heyl, Matthias: Von den Metaphern und der geteilten Erinnerung – Auschwitz, Holocaust, Schoah, Churban, "Endlösung", in: Helmut Schreier, Matthias Heyl (Eds.): Die Gegenwart der Schoah. Zur Aktualität des Mordes an den europäischen Juden, Hamburg 1994, pp. 11-32. In the following I refer to the historical events of the extermination of the European Jewry as Shoah or The Event, while Holocaust will signify the current public discourse about it, e.g. with regard to its pedagogical implications.
6 See Kühner, Angela: Trauma und Kollektives Gedächtnis, Gießen 2008.
7 Welzer, Harald: "Opa war kein Nazi". Nationalsozialismus und Holocaust im Familiengedächtnis, Frankfurt/M. 2002.

However, it would be misleading to think that it was this discovery that resulted in my work on National Socialism and the Shoah. Interpreting this preoccupation as an expression of a responsibility due to my grandfather's deeds overlooks two things: that the examination of my family's history was a consequence, rather than a starting point, of my relations to the Shoah which had begun much earlier in my life; and secondly, that it was the family reaction – or, more precisely its non-reaction – to my grandfather's crimes, rather than the crimes themselves, that has driven my work on the National Socialist era. Some of my early memories from kindergarten, later reinforced in primary school refer to a diffuse feeling of homelessness, of not belonging, of being recognized as a maverick, to experiences of stigmatization or even outright discrimination. Whether these feelings and experiences reflected an intuitive anticipation of a different sexual preference, my social status as an educationally deprived working-class child in a bourgeois Munich suburb, or the background of my mother (migration from Poland) in a traditional Bavarian context, or whether e extraneous; the significant point is that they indicate a very early development of a sensitivity and awareness of often subtle mechanisms of attribution and exclusion that in autobiographical terms engendered my engagement with social "others", one that has lasted to this day.

The psychological concept of secondary identification describes the predominantly unconscious process of assimilation of oneself with specific characteristics of another subject so that these subjective patterns become part of one's self.[8] From this viewpoint, personal identity is permanently shaped and re-shaped through identifications that occur during an entire lifetime. It is strongly associated with other psychological concepts like empathy. The perception of commonality which I had when I sought the friendship of other outsiders during my childhood, and my early – not yet academic – interest in the history of National Socialism and the Shoah can easily be explained by my identification with the Jews as victimized "others".[9] Hence, with my family's mythologisation of my grandfather not only the historic "truth" was at stake, but my adopted identity as well. This was because the family discourse implied an underlying, anti-Semitic drive that emerged at an Easter

---

8   Freud, Siegmund: Massenpsychologie und Ich-Analyse, in: Siegmund Freud: Gesammelte Werke. Band 13, Frankfurt/M. 1999.
9   Though it might be necessary to expand psychoanalytic theory at this point by assuming that all identification processes are preceded by projection mechanisms; identifying with someone or something basically requires the recognition (and, in its first meaning, the identification; see Laplanche, Jean, Pontalis, Jean-Bertrand: The Language of Psycho-Analysis, New York 1974) of it that can only be accepted as part of myself by reintegrating it as part of my self.

Sunday brunch: unfortunately not all Jews would have been exterminated, an uncle stated. Literally voiceless I left.

Writing up my M.A. thesis may have been an angry first attempt to reclaim my voice by giving space to the voices of the Jewish victims. And while I was looking for my own self in writing this thesis, in my current work on HIV infection dynamics among gay men I hope to uncover social discourses that drive my individual self: normative socio-cultural structures that constitute multiple burdens on gay identities and foster a certain sexual risk-taking behavior. By temporarily taking over the different perspectives of others something that scientific research enables, a process of self-reflection is signified, one that transcends those identifications. Becoming aware of the roots of one's own interest and of the underlying dynamics of one's work with regard to biographical experience, the identifications function as a tool for understanding. In this respect I would subscribe to Foucault's notion about writing as a means to become someone else than one presently is: he views writing as a medium of liberating a self, a practice of disengaging oneself from one's self.[10]

Based on the psychoanalytic concept of identification, I would therefore introduce the term identifiction to denote the process of reflecting upon these identifications and the biographical experiences they are based on – and therefore a certain need for projection of them – in order to use them productively: as a tool for deconstructing the discourses they are connected with; to playing with them performatively; and playing out one against the other. Hence, biography can be used as a catalyst of social comprehension: if social discourses are located and incorporated within the subject as the subject herself/himself is being constituted by them, then the conscious interplay of different identific(a)tion may lead to an analysis of prevalent discourses and subjectifying practices. Referring to Foucault again, it is a "thinking of the outside" that aims at recognizing its very limits, where all definite securities vanish.[11]

Some reflections on the project "Beyond Memory" may indicate how this might work in practice.[12] In our discussions within the "German" group, we soon came to acknowledge that the concept of identity plays a decisive role in the discourse about National Socialism and the Shoah, connecting topics like memory, mourning, and representation that were of importance for us. However, it was obvious that it was not something we could easily draw on:

---

10 Foucault, Michel: The History of Sexuality, Vol. 2: The Use of Pleasure, London 1990.
11 Foucault, Michel: Das Denken des Draußen, in: Michel Foucault, Schriften zur Literatur, Frankfurt/M. 1990, pp. 130-157.
12 I would like to thank everyone who was involved in this project for our intense, controversial, fruitful discussions that finally led to this essay.

most, if not all of us mentioned experiencing significant discomfort about personally relating to any labels of national – i.e. German – identity. So we tried to figure out how the category of identity functions in discourse, and in what ways we could make critical use of it by trying to deconstruct the complex academic debates in different disciplines (e.g. psychology, history, political sciences, cultural studies). This seemed somehow to constitute a very "neutral" approach – but wasn't the project meant exactly as an option to overcome cultural, historical, and national differences by pointing at a common, generational perspective?

Quite naturally it then too became a hot topic between the "German" and "Israeli" groups, when we first met in Jerusalem, and it determined the dynamics of the interaction process. Suddenly it was not possible anymore to rely on theoretical analyses, we were thrown back to our own situativeness in the identity discourse we aimed at getting rid of. The more we "Germans" tried to distance ourselves from any notion of a national identity that inescapably creates personal links to the Nazi past, and aimed instead to discuss the issue as a theoretical concept and discursive effect, the more it was emphasized and brought down to family matters by the "Israelis".

I do not think that in the end we, as a German-Israeli group, finally achieved much common ground on that topic. Among the "Germans" many perceived the highly emotional and conflict-ridden discussions as exhausting, sometimes frustrating, even annoying and possibly superfluous. In retrospect, our genuine surprise that this topic acquired such a prominent role, one that outweighed the planned thematic discussions and permanently underlay them, seems to be weird. We did not realise that the distinctions we had made between the academic and public debates we had tried to analyze and our critical position as researcher was a phantasmatic one. The Event which was the mirror we looked into, did not show our anticipated selves. The Israelis demanded disclosure of us who we were in this very position as Germans in Holocaust research.[13] What most of us – myself definitely included – did not understand was that this group reflection process could have been an excellent, one-off opportunity to gain insights into the discourses that constitute the field of knowledge about National Socialism and Shoah. It

---

13 As a footnote, it is quite interesting that questions, why young generation Germans would work on Jewish victims instead of "their" perpetrators, reflect the discussion A. and M. Mitscherlich tried to introduce by diagnosing an inability to mourn (about Hitler and the Germans' own victims). Moreover they identified philo-Semitic drives as an expression of rejected feelings of shame and guilt in post-1945 Germany (see Mitscherlich, Alexander, Mitscherlich, Margarete: Die Unfähigkeit zu trauern. Grundlagen kollektiven Verhaltens, München 1967).

pointed to the very centre of our project, but we just did not have the analytic tools to understand what was going on.

In her discussion of the significance of psychoanalysis for social psychology, Brockhaus emphatically argues against the application of psychoanalytic concepts to the analysis of social phenomena as it is usually done when talking e.g. about "collective trauma", "age of narcissism", or "death energy of the masses", especially with regard to frightening and violent events.[14] Apart from serious methodological challenges one faces when transferring clinical data derived from individual cases to broader or generalized social analysis, drawing analogies between psychic and social processes often serves highly problematic functions: "Psychoanalytic termini can be used as master keys to an apparent clarification that in fact only reinforces prejudices and observation of reality only to provide evidence for preconceived theses."[15]

On the other hand, she emphasizes the benefits of the psychoanalytic approach and therapeutic techniques for an understanding of social processes: in the reflection of one's own irrationalities and emotions; in the dynamics of resistance and transference; in the tolerance to uncertainty and ambiguities; in the awareness of the over-determinism of a phenomenon by the overlap of different causes; and in the permanent questioning of one's own basis. Brockhaus sees these as potent tools able to contribute to the understanding of social processes: "The analytic method – the connection between changing interventions and reflection of meanings – is the significant contribution of psychoanalysis to a critical social psychology."[16]

Bringing into play the concept of identifiction I have tried to concretize these remarks, for it points at the importance of the reflection of one's own identification processes and the underlying projections as tools of approaching the discourses that constitute social reality. For the Jerusalem workshop that would have meant to perceive the personalized debate on identity matters not as a delay of the "really" relevant issues and theoretical debates, but rather as taking the emotionality of the debate seriously because it hints at neuralgic points of one's own entanglement in non-reflected discourses and social practices. I, then, would have had to admit the various projections of otherness, victimhood, and martyrdom – and, at the same time, my family's history that I had rejected and my 'coming out' of a perpetrator's closet – that are at the root of my interest in the Shoah; my primary focus on the current society and politics and not The Event itself; and the individual

---

14 Brockhaus, Gudrun: Vom Nutzen psychoanalytischen Vorgehens in der Sozialpsychologie, in: Heiner Keupp (Eds.), Zugänge zum Subjekt. Perspektiven einer reflexiven Sozialpsychologie, Frankfurt/M. 1993, pp. 54-96.
15 Ibid., p. 56 (translation by PCL).
16 Ibid., p. 91 (translation by PCL).

way in which biographical experiences mirror self-fuelling, discursive aspects concerning National Socialism. Indeed those aspects seem to be – more or less dominantly and more or less obviously – inscribed in many other discourses: not only can the cited family story be taken as just another example substantiating Welzer's findings and, therefore, as paradigmatic for familial dissemination and the public discourse about the Nazi past in post-war Germany.

As a result they can become a starting point for a critique of ideological continuities and social memory discourses. As Herzog recently has shown, the discourse about sex after 1945 was as well a prominent place where conflicting ideological debates on National Socialism were carried out – the early public and political reactions as well as the media reports about Aids in the 1980s reflect this in a significant way;[17] hence it may be no coincidence that HIV prevention and Holocaust education have much in common with regard to the topics of stigmatization, discrimination, and the psychosocial dynamics of shame and projection.

If, then being consistent, identity is perceived as an effect of subjectifying practices, the subject herself/himself with his/her experiences function as a resonating body of social discourses;[18] reflections on the different identity fragments and identifications can be used for an understanding of present references to National Socialism and the Shoah. The focus of analysis shifts from questions about the transgenerational and mostly unconscious processes of transmission of memory or the unspeakable break of memory i.e. the trauma) to the (self) reflection on the incorporation of socio-cultural discourses, their socio-political operations and subjective consequences. From a political perspective, it becomes possible to strategically break up the enforcement of identity ("being" German) by calling into play other partial, disparate, fragmented identity narrations (living as a gay, coming from a working-class family, having HIV, working as an academic...) as Keupp et al. outlined in their concept of a "patchwork identity".[19]

Undoubtedly, the discourses on National Socialism and the Shoah constitute meta-discourse that intersect most of the governing social, political, and subject-related discourses. So it is crucial to come to terms with them so as to be able to get involved with current affairs in society and future visions

---

17 See Herzog, Dagmar: Sex After Fascism. Memory and Morality in Twentieth-Century Germany, Princeton 2005.
18 Hark, Sabine: Deviante Subjekte. Die paradoxe Politik der Identitäten, Leverkusen 1999.
19 Keupp, Heiner et al.: Identitätskonstruktionen. Das Patchwork der Identitäten in der Spätmoderne, Reinbek 1999.

of it.[20] Reflecting on subjective experience in other fields of social life may lead to a more complex understanding of the subtle mechanisms of this meta-discourse. In this respect common ground between the "Israeli" and "German" groups in the "Beyond Memory" project could have been achieved because the Shoah takes over this discursive meta-role in both societies. At least all the participants had stories to tell that went well beyond concrete personal/family links to The Event: disturbing feelings and experiences of uneasiness, and trouble with or even suffering from present social and political conditions due to their cultural backgrounds, political views, gender relations, sexual preferences and so on. These cause certain sensitivities towards social functions and political instrumentalisations of National Socialism and the Shoah and power relations in the exposure to them. The "Third Generation" was not the common ground where we had stood at the beginning of the project; we constituted it unnoticed as a discursive space within.

Finally, where do I see the potential of this "Third Generation"? It is quite obvious from the previous remarks that it cannot be understood in terms of biosocial ancestry, and only narrowly in its sociological sense as a point of reference of common experiences; rather it should be perceived as a programmatic concept to reflect critically on the discourses that constitute the field of knowledge about National Socialism and the Shoah. Subjective reflectivity is one of the decisive tools with which to come to new perspectives and insights – and a steady problematisation of one's own basis of argument. Although we do have quite different and disparate individual reasons for dealing with National Socialism and the Shoah, we know that the ethical paradigm of "Never Again!" requires critical analyses of current (social, political, academic...) discourses and practices (not only) about the Holocaust that are reflected in our experiences. To summarise, three common characteristics of the "Third Generation" may be outlined: a taking of own biographical experiences as a means of literally coming to terms with the topic; a deconstructivist reflection on the discourses that inescapably interconnect them; and a desire for active participation in these discourses in different ways (pedagogy, university, arts) so as to change current society and politics. As an invitation to participation, it opens up a new discursive space to carry out the Differend of discourses[21] without denying or resolving the differences that are constitutive for its very existence.

---

20 For a discussion of the influence of the discourse concerning National Socialism on the political debate about the Berlin Republic as a political concept see e.g. Langer, Phil C.: Kein Ort. Überall. Die Einschreibung von „Berlin" in die deutsche erzählende Literatur der neunziger Jahre, Berlin 2002.
21 Lyotard, Jean-François.: Differend. Phrases in Dispute, Minneapolis 1990. "Differend" as a "case where the plantiff is divested of the means to argue and

Phil C. Langer, born 1975 in Munich, literary scholar (PhD in German literature 2002) and social scientist (PhD in psychology, 2009); areas of research and academic teaching include National Socialism and Shoah, Gender and Queer Studies, Health Psychology (esp. HIV/AIDS and prevention); he worked as a guide at the Holocaust Memorial (2005–2006) and as head of youth prevention at the Berlin AIDS Aid Organization (2005–2007) in Berlin, where he currently lives.

---

becomes for that reason a victim. [...] A case of differend between two parties takes place when the regulation of the conflict that opposes them is done in the idiom of one of the parties while the wrong suffered by the other is not signified in that idiom"(p. 9).

Holocaust at the Table.
Experiences from seven years of
"German-Israeli Exchange"

ROLAND IMHOFF

The Cologne-based *Youth Club Courage* is a small and independent NGO. It is mainly active in the fields of education against racism, (neo-)fascism, National Socialism, and homophobia; furthermore it offers counselling for conscientious objectors to military service. Since 2002, we have been organizing an annual exchange between Israel and Germany of young professionals engaged in anti-racist and intercultural youth work. These groups consist of approximately ten people with an equal number of men and women, and diverse sexual identities. Whereas the Israeli delegation has a roughly equal participation from Israelis of Palestinian and Jewish descent, in the German group there is a proportion of mostly second generation migrants. All participants come from a leftist perspective within their own society, and are quite critical of their own society's discourses and hegemonic narratives.

In collaboration with *Beit Lohamei HaGetaot* (Ghetto Fighters' Museum and Memorial), the first part of the program brings German participants to Israel in order to visit various socio-political initiatives and institutions.[1] The idea is to learn about and discuss contemporary issues in Israeli society, most prominently the Israeli-Palestinian conflict, but also the situation of non-Jewish, Israeli citizens, Israeli memory politics, as well as issues of gender

---

1   These include among others intercultural dialogue initiatives like *Sadaka-Re'ut*, advocacy agencies for migrant workers like *Kav laOved* and the *Hotline for Migrant workers*, GLBT initiatives like the *Jerusalem Open House*, NGOs working on the conflict *like Peace Now Settlement Watch, B'tselem, Ta'ayush* as well as educational institutions like *Givat Haviva* and the *Center for Humanistic Education* at *Beit Lohamei HaGetaot*.

and sexual orientation. In the second part of the program, ten participants from different Israeli socio-political initiatives[2] come to Cologne for ten days.

In this essay, as a co-organizer of this program, I would like to focus on some aspects of German part of it. However, the following is not meant to be a comprehensive description of the seven years of these German-Israeli exchanges. I shall instead highlight some issues based on my own experiences during them. This will of course not do justice to the diversity and complexity of our programs; moreover, the essay will lack Palestinian perspectives because an analysis of the triangular relationships between Germans, Jews and Palestinians in respect of the past would go beyond the scope of this essay.

Stumbling over the Nazi Past in Germany

In the course of the period we spend together in Germany, we usually deal with many aspects of the current reality; among others these range from German memory politics to the rise of the extreme Right in Germany; from the situation of illegalised workers or minorities in general to political debates on integration; from HIV prevention for male prostitutes to sexual identity among gay adolescents.

Despite these mostly rather serious issues, the atmosphere of these encounters has been described by several participants as a school outing for grown-ups: individuals aged 22 to 40 in general sharing common values and political convictions, encounter each other in a packed ten-day program. During this period, the process of becoming one homogenous group of activists who are also having fun together gains the upper hand against the potentially divisive categories of history, gender, nationality and religion. However, periodically there were also certain limits to this process of bonding.

In Cologne, as in any other German city, historical issues tend to crop up regularly. Sometimes such incidents are coincidental as when passing by a *Stolperstein* (literally "stumbling stone",[3] or talking about a family history, and sometimes they are intentional, for example when visiting the El-De-Haus (a Documentary Centre on National Socialism in Cologne). In most of these situations, talking about history, entails above all talking about the

---

[2] Most of these initiatives and NGOs are informal groups of political activists on the far left of the political spectrum *like.g. New Profile, Zochrot, Sadaka-Re'ut, B'tselem* or the *Israeli Committee against House Demolitions*.

[3] A project to memorialize individuals killed by the Nazis by embedding small name plaques on pavements in front of the victims' former homes. The Cologne-based artist Gunter Demnig has by now installed over 4, 000 of these in more than 300 German towns and cities.

German National Socialist past and the Shoah,[4] and such discussions tend to create an awkward atmosphere immediately generating an uncomfortable distance between Germans and Israeli Jews. All of a sudden we became once again Germans and Jews – and suddenly we were grounded from our cosmopolitan class outing, seemingly arriving in historical reality with "inherited" victim-perpetrator identities.

Sometimes the signs of division were more subtle, as for example when the Jewish Israeli participants in a seemingly unplanned manner switched to Hebrew or formed exclusively Jewish sets while walking through the sites of former Nazi death camps. Sometimes the indications of separation were quite obvious, as for example when Israeli participants started joking about Nazi atrocities and Jewish suffering. Their behaviour very clearly drew attention to the formerly invisible boundaries; German participants were excluded because joking about the Shoah is for most Germans – unlike many Israelis – an absolute taboo.

Victimhood-Competition versus Perpetrator-Competition

During the years of our exchange programs, typical patterns amongst participants of attitudes to the past include Germans with strong feelings about the Third Reich and the Shoah. This position has led them to believe in the necessity of a strong Jewish state as a stronghold against global anti-Semitism. Such a pro-Israeli stance has become increasingly popular in the German left over the last ten years, culminating in the establishing of an outspokenly pro-Zionist, 'anti-German' faction within the radical left.[5]

On the other hand, our leftist Israeli participants would oppose this point of view for a number of reasons: as they see it *(a)* it negates any Palestinian perspective; *(b)* it is supposedly driven by a "typical German guilt complex"; *(c)* it ignores the alleged misuse by the Israeli state of the Shoah memory so as to justify its aggressive actions against the Palestinians both inside Israel and in the Palestinian territories; and *(d)* a syndrome is supposedly created of the eternally victimized Jews as if they were being kept in the position of helpless, persecuted victims which they are not in Israel nowadays. This rather sceptical attitude towards the actually existing Zionism has tended to be predominant amongst our Jewish participants. However, some Germans argued back against

---

4   Throughout the essay I use both expressions, "Shoah" and "Holocaust". I use Holocaust when I refer to the metaphorical personalization introduced in the title and where it is either part of a quote or a specific term (as in "post-Holocaust anti-Semitism"). In all other incidences I use Shoah. Both terms have been criticised and I am not arguing that they are ideal terminology. They are merely the ones I use for clarity and brevity.

5   For a characterization of this fraction from an Israel perspective see B. Weinthal: Lettter from Berlin: The anti-anti-Zionists in: Haaretz, 7.8.2007, www.haaretz.com/hasen/pages/ShArt.jhtml?itemNo=890853.

the Jewish Israelis, pointing out that the latter's attitudes towards Israeli's actions and its victims are no less guilt-ridden and their view of the Palestinians is usually one of people who are essentially poor victims as well.

There is a striking parallel here: the critical German stance outlined above resembles that of the Israeli right for the Israelis, whereas the critical Israeli viewpoint is not unlike anti-Israeli positions held by some German participants. So, in a sense a well-known pattern of dissent was not resolved but turned upside down: in mainstream, nationalist discourses there exists what is termed "competitive victimhood" e.g. Germans perceive their own suffering during bomb raids, flight and forced migration as the central tragedy of WWII, whereas Jews focus on the horror of the Shoah. In these lines of arguments, the suffering experienced by a group is refunctionalised so as to legitimise its own actions. During our annual exchanges, however, what I would term "perpetrator-competition" seemed to take place: people did not blame the "other" but instead their "own" country. German participants emphasized the necessity not only to remember the horror of the Shoah, but also to point out who was responsible for it as well as the continuities of the National Socialist past into contemporary German society. In contrast Jewish Israelis pointed to the alleged crimes of the Israeli occupation and the ongoing military engagements as much more pressing problems in their present reality.

Between the lines this was not only a question of German or Israeli perpetrators but also about the focus of our programs: whereas most of the Israeli participants were more interested in contemporary issues, the "German perspective" often involved reference to the importance in history of National Socialism – which remains a burning issue for them even as people who grew up in a post-fascist society.

In this context, especially a perceived German "overidentification" with Israel as the "state of Shoah survivors" sometimes alienated our Israeli participants. Mihal, one of our Israeli partners who has participated in several delegations, described her experiences in the following way: "I was bewildered when on my second visit I realized that a German woman sitting on the other side of the room was wearing a small Israeli flag on her shirt. A thing I wouldn't have dreamed of doing, and would have found foul and tasteless. Not because it is an Israeli flag, but just because it is a flag. I was further bewildered and somewhat irritated when the phenomenon was explained to me. I felt as if I had an old and persistent nanny who wouldn't let her children grow up, and become individual moral agents responsible for their own actions and misdeeds. I experienced as insulting the woman's historical obligation to support Israel, as if her guilt makes me, and Israel and Israelis in general, one-dimensional. It made me realize that I'd prefer to find a present perspective on the past than a past perspective on the present and the future."

Group-based Emotions as a Reaction to the Past

In this quote Mihal suggests that it is the experience of guilt that makes Germans over-identify with Israel. What caught my attention in this puzzling encroachment of the past into our present was the idea of group-based emotions towards history.

In the following section I shall address the question regarding these emotion-based reactions to historical atrocities committed by individuals with whom we share a social identity (e.g. German). One of my own key experiences was a scene rather typical among Germans in Israel. Lying on the beach in Tel Aviv, that beautiful, modern city on the Mediterranean, I was watching senior citizens go bathing or just sunbathing, and suddenly began to perceive the numbers tattooed on their arms, marking them as concentration camp survivors who once were nothing more than numbers for the German bureaucracy of death. I would argue that situations of this kind induce reactions specific to a German visitor. Probably it does not evoke the same kind of affect on Brazilians, Swedes or Taiwanese. I cannot be sure whether the subjective experience is the same for everybody. On the basis of conversations I have had with other Germans, I would argue that this experience includes the wish that one will not be identified as a German. At the same time a strong empathic reaction may be evoked towards that person, a sadness combined with feelings of helplessness. So for some people at least there seem to be strong affective reactions. And whether these are indeed termed guilt, or instead shame, regret, sorrow, embarrassment etc. may be more of a linguistic decision than anything else.

My own academic research has foregrounded exactly these "group-based emotions" as reactions to "historical representation" and what has puzzled me is how widely shared the assumptions are that the articulation of such ingroup-critical emotions has positive consequences. Adorno's conception of secondary anti-Semitism is one of the most influential theories in this field,[6] and it explains the potentially negative effects of feelings of guilt, whereas actually articulating that feeling serves as an indicator of positive intentions. In his theory of secondary anti-Semitism, he claimed that Germans projected their own guilt resulting from their complicity with the Shoah onto the Jews, and that they were blaming the Jews for their own feelings of guilt. He concluded that in this way a new, post-Holocaust, 'secondary' anti-Semitism had evolved. In academic writing today, the image of a secondary anti-Semitism still plays a pivotal role. Contemporary scholars argue that Germans still feel harassed by the reminders of Nazi atrocities and experience aversive

---

6   Adorno, T. W.: Schuld und Abwehr [Guilt and defense]. In F. Pollock (Ed.), Gruppenexperiment [Group Experiment], Frankfurt a. M. 1995, pp. 278-428.

feelings of guilt. As in the past, this guilt is denied and projected onto the Jews by a majority.

Moreover, Adorno went on to argue that some Germans were willing to accommodate and come to agreement (*"Verständigungswillige"*). In his view these were the ones who openly admitted their guilt. In other words, Adorno perceived the expression of guilt as a positive thing, an idea still resonating in modern conceptions of 'secondary anti-Semitism': those who willingly acknowledge guilt were and are the ones who are not anti-Semitic. In some studies the denial of an 'obligation' to feel guilty as a German actually serves as an indicator of (secondary) anti-Semitism. Not feeling guilty has been denounced as part of the *Schlussstrich* discourse i.e. the desire to draw a final line under the crimes of the past.[7] So, in a sense feeling guilty and talking about it may be regarded as a very positive factor.

Such a positive conception of guilt and its effects is also mirrored in the rather naïve view to be found in most psychological literature.[8] Group-based guilt is often celebrated as a very positive phenomenon, as it is claimed that feelings of guilt signal that intergroup relations have been damaged and that harm has been done. This in turn – as this theory has it – motivates reparation and compensation, leading to greater forgiveness on the part of the victim, which then initiates a process of healing and improved intergroup relations.

Adressing the Past in an Emancipatory Way
As the example with the Israeli flag already demonstrates, not everybody shares the conviction that feeling and admitting guilt leads to positive results, though. Especially in the context of international exchanges these emotional reactions seem rather to prevent people transcending the boundaries of two distinct nations, as one Israeli participant, Lily, a literature graduate and school librarian, pointed out: "This is also what I found in both groups (Israeli and German) that group-based feelings of guilt, shame and regret seemed to have reinforced national identifications. To put it more simply, group-based feelings seem to reinforce the 'us' as opposed to 'them' (German/Jewish, victimizers/victims)." I share these doubts and in fact, in my research I have found that guilt does not correlate at all with reduced prejudice, a willingness to engage in intergroup contact or other positive relations to the victim group. Instead, guilt was associated with mere verbal support for reparations rather than actual support in a resource distribution task); furthermore the

---
7   Frindte, W, et al: Neu-alte Mythen über die Juden: Ein Forschungsbericht. In R. Dollase et al. (Eds.): Politische Psychologie der Fremdenfeindlichkeit, Weinheim 1999, pp. 119-130.
8   For an overview see Imhoff, R. et. al: Collective Regret versus Collective Guilt: Different Emotional Reactions to Historical Atrocities and Their Consequences. Forthcoming.

expectation that guilt feelings would induce feelings of aversion about meeting a member of the victim group, thus further alienating them from the other group.

One could take these outcomes and the accompanying scepticism, and decide to try simply to ignore the past, especially in German-Israeli exchange programs. If it does not help us to overcome intergroup barriers, why confront it at all? In contrast to more recent conflicts like the ones in the Middle East, we – as Germans and/or Jews – actually are in an enviable position where we could just ignore the past and not come to terms with it at all. The Israeli participant Mihal voices such scepticism when she emphasizes: "We tend to look for glory in the past that might for us justify the present, and give a cosy feeling of legitimacy. But such glory is nowhere to be found, and maybe shouldn't be looked for at all." In line with this, social psychological research showed that in Jewish-Polish encounters, only when the two groups talked about contemporary issues did it lead to improved relations and less prejudice. In contrast, talking about the past and focusing in on historical crimes did not improve intergroup relations.[9]

However, despite there being good reasons to concentrate on the present, we chose a different approach for our exchange program. In 2006, after four years of dealing mainly with the present, we chose the exact opposite. Instead of avoiding the subject, we wanted to bring to the table as visibly as possible the past of the Shoah and the impact it has on us and our exchanges . So we decided to dedicate a whole program to the subject of the Shoah and Shoah memory in Germany and Israel, and entitled our encounter, "Looking back into the future". In our invitation we wrote: "Sometimes, some of our Israeli guests asked us prior to their stay, to avoid 'typical Jewish' themes and for sure they were also referring to all the issues connected to the Shoah. Well, this usually changes once we are together in Germany: whether during a 'normal' stroll through downtown Cologne, on a ride on a German train, the discussions about army service in Israel and Germany, or the question about our (grand-)parents. Whether in jokes told with a wink or in a shy statement: often the 'Holocaust' seems to sit at our table, too (whether we invited it or not)."

It seems noteworthy that the program dedicated specifically to the Shoah was the first program without any Palestinian participation. Despite our original aim to apply the usual diversity criteria to this program as well, it soon became evident that to do so would be a challenging task. In the event we had only one Palestinian application anyway. Not only was that

---

9 Bilewicz, M.: History as an obstacle: Impact of temporal-based social categorization on Polish-Jewish intergroup contact. In: Group Processes & Intergroup Relations, 10, 2007, 551-563.

problematic in itself, it turned out that he was rather new to the subject whereas the Jewish participants had dealt with the Shoah and remembrance almost exclusively either academically or in their artwork. Eventually, we decided not to invite him, as a result creating our first all Jewish Israeli delegation. At this meeting we chose a rather academic approach to questions of remembrance, identity and the National Socialist past. We discussed with each other if and why it was important for Germans and Jews to perceive themselves and meet each other as "descendants of victims and perpetrators". During this program we explored the Third Reich era very deeply, mostly on an intellectual level but at times also delving into feelings.

We talked about the history of German discursive shifts from 1945 until 1999 during a four hour session that ended with the Jewish participants complaining "Haven't we suffered enough?". Israeli participants talked about hegemonic Shoah discourses in Israel and how they function and to which ends. We visited the former concentration camp Bergen-Belsen, studied the Wewelsburg Castle as a pseudo-religious cult centre for the SS, and subjected the new exhibition concept for Burg Vogelsang, a former educational camp training cadres for the NSDAP elite to a critical examination.

We did not avoid the themes of guilt and emotional reactions: instead of avoiding these subject or waiting until we were once more overwhelmed by the impact of the past, we also discussed the questions of if and why and who should feel guilt, and for what. Despite initial strong convictions that Germans in particular should feel, acknowledge and articulate guilt for the crimes of the Shoah, we came to the conclusion that if they did so, it would merely reinforce lines of division instead of creating mutual understanding and less rigid identities. We tried to analyse how the guilt Germany supposedly has accepted was even used to bolster the image of the new, self-confident Germany in the mainstream discourse of the post-unification "Berlin Republic". The ideology behind this apparent acceptance of blame is as follows: when Germany ostentatiously accepts the original culpability and today's responsibility associated with the Nazi atrocities, it demonstrates that it has become a better, a more moral country that "faces up to its past", and has thereby become a "mature nation".

Instead of passively letting the past impact on us, we dissected it instead and the impact that it has on ideological discourses. Explaining our dilemmas to each other we created a new, a transnational, political identity. All this confirmed most of us in our conviction that if the Holocaust is among us anyway, we should invite it in, put the issue on the table, and reflect on emotional reactions to prevent them from generating boundaries between us invisibly. When I asked Lily how she remembered the program she said – and I shall let her words conclude – : "It became a kind of a 10-day network that transcended the boundaries of the 'Israeli' and 'German'identity from huge issues to small details... around the shared vegetarian meal in that charming little co-op, or around visiting different historical sites together while respecting each others' space, and then turning to each other for sharing emotions and thoughts or simply holding hands or waiting together for the bus to continue with this amazing journey to help us realize better our role in this world, as we tried to look back into the future with love."

Roland Imhoff, born 1977 in Bonn, will finish his social psychological dissertation on historical representations and group-based emotions at the University of Bonn in 2010. He is currently based in Cologne, where he is a co-organizer of the annual German-Israeli exchange by the Jugendclub Courage Köln e.V.. He has taken part in three delegations to Israel and Palestine, and has welcomed more than ten Israeli delegations in Cologne since 2004.

On "Mourning" and "Friendship" in German-Israeli Youth Encounters. The Need to Address the Sensitive Issues

MARTIN SCHELLENBERG

German public discourse often relates to the 'special relationship' between Germany and Israel due to the Holocaust – even on occasions when Israeli government policy is being criticized. Accordingly, many German-Israeli youth encounters take place in order to deepen this 'friendship'. But is the past not something that actually *separates* Germans and Israelis in the first place? Are there not numerous underlying questions, insecurities and, most notably, emotional conditionings on both sides as what concerns addressing the National Socialist past and the Holocaust? On the other hand: Do youngsters today still have access to those issues at all? In short: Can the Holocaust be communicated in the context of youth encounters, and if so, how?

Intercultural Happiness with a few Tears in between
Some years ago, together with a colleague I facilitated a group of 16-year-old German and Israeli students in the memorial site House of the Wannsee Conference.[1] I had talked to their tutor beforehand: they had four hours of time before lunch, and it was the only part of their programme in which the Holocaust was dealt with. He agreed that our proposal sounded very good: two separated lessons in German and Hebrew on the persecution of Jews

---

1 The Wannsee Conference on January 20, 1942, was a meeting of high-ranking civil servants and SS-officers chaired by Reinhard Heiydrich (head of the Reich Security Main Office) to discuss the organisation and implementation of the 'Final Solution'. Since 1992, the place has been a memorial and educational site offering diverse educational programmes on the Holocaust and the perpetrators' society. See: www.ghwk.de.

during the National Socialist past as well as on dealing with the Holocaust in the respective other country; to conclude a joint discussion on the participants' thoughts and impressions.

The Israelis that I tutored first of all wanted to know where they would be able to find the next H&M store afterwards.[2] But slowly they appeared to become more interested, questions were raised on the perpetrators of the Holocaust, and on German society at the time of National Socialism. They had not really talked about the Holocaust yet to their German counterparts. One student stated she would not dare to ask them what their grandparents had done, even though she was very curious about it – her grandmother was a survivor. In the following German-Israeli discussion, numerous questions were asked: was the Holocaust taught in German schools? What did the Germans do against Neo-Nazis? Another question was posed by a German student. She asked insecurely and bit aggressively at the same time: why didn't the Israelis treat the Palestinians better – after they had gone through the Holocaust themselves? Immediately, some Israelis interrupted each other with loud voices. Since there was not enough time to really go into this issue, I intervened: the Nazi camps had not been institutions of moral purification; moreover there was a difference between a racist policy of extermination and an occupation regime concerned with defending itself. Even so strong emotions were palpable in the room.

One of the Israeli teachers then asked how the German students felt about their grandparents? A German student took the opportunity to confess her guilt feelings towards the Israelis. She went on that she felt strange about standing together with Israelis in front of those pictures of persecution and killing of Jews ... In the middle of the sentence, she stopped, waited and started crying. Silence. An Israeli student then told her she was not guilty. As if to release themselves from the tension that was in the room, other Germans started crying too. Other students – most of them Israelis – hugged them to comfort them. The German teacher got nervous and cut the discussion without conferring with us before: this could not go on like that! How should he carry on with the situation? The Israeli teachers, however, were obviously content with the visit and thanked us for our work saying it was extremely important. At the same time, some of the students were already on their way out, partly in mixed groups. Probably their next stop was H&M.

In the context of my work in German memorial institutions to the National Socialist Past and the Holocaust, I have tutored already many such encounters. I have often asked myself whether it makes sense at all to touch the emotional level in this kind of group constellation especially if there is not

---

2 H&M is a Swedish fashion discounter very popular among youngsters that doesn't yet exist in Israel.

enough time to reflect upon the situation together with students and teachers. Even though usually the conversations were not that agitated, the situation described reveals some typical dynamics that I have often observed within such brief visits to memorial-sites in the framework of German-Israeli youth encounters: First of all, considerable caution on both sides may be noted. On other occasions, youngsters are curious and usually less hesitant to ask questions than adults. German participants are often interested in the significance of the Holocaust to their Israeli counterparts: do they have relatives who were killed or survived? How do they think about Germans in general? And first and foremost, they want to know from their Israeli exchange-partners what they think about Germans, and what they (the Israelis) expect from them.

Even though those questions are quite obvious, they are not necessarily asked – either in the group setting or in private conversations. Being aware of the delicacy of these topics, maybe the youngsters are afraid to break a taboo or drop a clanger. Perhaps they feel insecure because they do not yet have a sophisticated position regarding those questions, possibly they are merely concerned to avoid confronting the other with something unpleasant. This insecurity is shared on the Israeli side – they do not dare to ask the Germans about their family histories without being specifically invited to do so.

What is interesting to observe in those short-trips to remembrance sites is the obvious need for emotions: some Germans want to talk about their guilt feelings, partly to see how the Israelis react, a few of the Germans even want to show the former their tears. On the Israeli side, there seems to be a complementary need not only to listen to rational words of the Germans, but also to experience their unambiguous emotions concerning the National Socialist past. Hence, when some of the Germans cry, and Israelis comfort them – which by the way can also happen without any discussion – one might conclude that the Germans receive their absolution, while at the same times the Israelis can experience in a way the historical power relations upside down: once, the Jews were in the victim position towards the Germans, today, in remembrance discourse, the former are the more powerful. But does this lead to a deeper understanding of the underlying questions?

Here I am referring to concerns about the relevance of this history today: can we compare the Holocaust to other historical and current events? What relation is there between European history and the history and present in the Middle East? In Germany, there prevails the simplistic notion of the Palestinians as the "victims of the victims", while at the same time there is hardly any historical knowledge about Palestine before and after the foundation of the Israeli state in 1948. How does the Holocaust function in the context of Israeli national consciousness, and to what extent might Israeli needs for security also be related to the historical experience of the

47

Holocaust? In what way do anti-Semitism and racism still exist in Germany and the rest of the world? Most groups can agree on the formula 'Never again!', but this consensus disguises the actual questions: never again what? Never again anti-Semitism, war, Auschwitz, Holocaust, nationalism, genocide, violations of human rights, Germany?

Many youth encounters never touch on those questions but remain on the level of an intercultural exchange as there might be with any other country. An open dialogue with the 'other' in this case might offer possibilities not only to learn something about the other side, but also to understand better one's own notions through being mirrored by the 'other'. After a brief reflection on what 'mourning' could mean in German-Israeli encounters, I shall come back to the question of how a deeper understanding within a pedagogical framework of such encounters can actually be realized.

Derivative, but still different: German and Israeli mourning

In 2005, I had the chance to participate in a German-Israeli exchange of young professionals in which we wanted to explore and discuss how we – the so called 'Third Generation' – can come to an understanding on the National Socialist past and the Holocaust without strictly remaining within the respective national discourses.[3] Also in this constellation of young academics, artists, journalists and educationalists some dynamics evolved that reminded me of what I observed with the youngsters in German-Israeli youth encounters, albeit in a more reflected way. Consequently we chose a setting that was almost group-therapeutic in style. But it was not a joint 'generation' that expressed itself, but rather two national groups that were reproduced. Most symptomatic for this phenomenon is the following situation: during a discussion on the possibilities of mutual commemoration, an Israeli – let's call him Yuval here – had argued that there was no need for a German to mourn his Jewish grandfather who had been murdered in the Holocaust. It almost appeared as if Yuval would feel disturbed by a German mourning a Jewish victim. A German participant – let's call him Michael – countered that he was of course entitled to mourn the loss of individual human beings as well as the loss of humanity at large.

Freud defines mourning as a "reaction to the loss of a beloved person or of a substituted abstraction such as fatherland, freedom, an ideal etc." Mourning work is supposed to overcome this condition of memorizing a

---

3 The project *60 years later. On the Meaning of the Holocaust in the younger generation in Germany and Israel* involved ca. 25 participants from both countries and was funded by the Stiftung Erinnerung, Verantwortung, Zukunft. The project was concluded by the public conference *Beyond Memory - The Significance of the Holocaust and the Nazi Past for the Younger Generation* in the *Volksbühne* Berlin on Oct. 25, 2005.

certain loss by "withdrawing the libido from the beloved object"[4]. According to Freud, neither Yuval nor Michael can mourn for the loss of a loved one, since they have never met this person. Both know about this person only from posthumous stories or from other sources. In a strictly Freudian sense, their way of memorizing the loss even in an abstract way would not be considered mourning because the situation before the loss is unknown to both of them. But the process of commemoration is accompanied by emotions. Eventually, this emotional way of commemoration is adopted; it is mediated through the sense of belonging to a family, a nation, humanity or through people relating to yet more concepts like 'freedom' or 'human dignity'. However, even though both Yuval's and Michael's mourning has been adopted, there still is a difference in terms of what is implicated by their respective ways of mourning.

The descendants of survivors are carrying a different burden than those the children of the perpetrators' society do. Many Israelis conceptualize their society as an anti-thesis to the powerless victims: the strong Israeli has replaced the weak Jew of the Diaspora, who ultimately fell victim in the Holocaust. At the same time, the collective trauma of anti-Semitism and the sense of being existentially threatened by Israel's regional enemies is unconsciously omnipresent, and if only because these emotions are fuelled by a political functionalization of the Holocaust against the backdrop of the Middle Eastern conflict. For Yuval, it is a difficult decision to accept his grandfather as a 'weak' human being who was unable to defend himself. On the other hand, it is difficult for him to separate from the 'weak' history, since through the loss of his grandfather, it has affected his own life in a substantial manner. But in the very moment in which he adopts the 'weak grandfather' by mourning him, he opens up to the history on a new level. He does not suppress anymore the vulnerability of his own life through a fantasy of a strong Israeli army. The fundamental threat – that has affected his family – enters his life too.

Compared to Yuval's delicate brinkmanship, Michael's adoption of history is a relatively voluntary one, motivated by a humanist spirit as well as by empathy with the victims. He consciously opens himself up for the confrontation with this history. He exposes himself to his own perplexity when facing the National Socialist past, thereby admitting weakness, too, albeit a weakness different from that Yuval has to confront. Becoming aware that one's own grandfather was part of the *Tätergesellschaft* (the society of perpetrators), that he was involved in the National Socialist crimes or at least permitted these crimes to happen, is a disturbing experience and challenges all

---

4   Sigmund Freud: Trauer und Melancholie (1915/17), in: Id.: Studienausgabe, Frankfurt/M 2000, S. 197/8; my translation.

kinds of certainties: am I really different to him? How can I believe in humaneness, if my own grandparents have trampled on it with their feet? Perhaps the constant evocation of the formula 'not guilt, but responsibility' is so popular in contemporary Germany because we do not want to expose ourselves to the facts as to the serious extent we have been shaped by the thoughts and actions of our grandparents in our families and social surroundings. Against this backdrop, the obvious need of Germans to reinvent their forebears as resistance fighters or victims of the National Socialist regime should not be too surprising.[5] To consciously locate oneself in the direct aftermath of perpetrated crimes causes quite some shock and sadness. I would call this insight 'mourning' as well. It resists simplistic lessons that could be quickly formulated in responses, like 'human rights' or 'peace'. Instead, it causes constant irritation: there is no certainty about one's own moral integrity anymore.

At this point, I want to come back again to the combination depicted above of German tears and Israelis comforting the Germans. The German-Israeli ritual-like manner of forgiveness, the reduction of what could be a joint confrontation with history to a purely emotional level may appear authentic at a first glance. At a second glance, however, the symbolic emotional exchange seems to disguise underlying questions. Here, it may be useful to bring in a certain interpretation of the notion of 'mourning': 'mourning' is not to be translated as 'having sad emotions', but it is also linked to cognitive commemoration. Mourning can manifest itself in emotions but it also signifies definable losses in the life story of the individual, in the history of a group, or in the history of humanity. Hence, 'mourning' seems to me rather a consciously adopted attitude towards what was lost than a sudden sensation. 'Mourning' appears dysfunctional: it is best described by imagining the limp and bowed posture of a body with lowered gaze. Expressing helplessness, perplexity and powerlessness in view of what has happened, both body and mind are in another mode. Mourning work, however, is reflectively accepting of these notions of helplessness and lack of power. It is therefore not burying a chapter of one's story or history. It is instead an opportunity for rationalization of the relevant questions behind that specific loss in the past. So there are many implications as to what is mourning and how it can be

---

5 See Harald Welzer et.al.: Opa war kein Nazi. Nationalsozialismus und Holocaust im Familiengedächtnis [Grandpa was no Nazi. National Socialism and the Holocaust in family remembrance], Frankfurt a.M. 2002. By conducting qualitative interviews, Welzer et al. found out that circa 75% of the children and grandchildren generation narrate their ancestors as 'heroes' or 'victims', among them the granddaughter or a Gestapo member who was involved in the deportations of Jews.

expressed. However, the question remains as to how to include the issue of 'mourning' in the context of an educational program.

Addressing the present of the past

Most youth encounters, also German-Israeli ones, focus on sports, dancing, environmental protection or similar issues. Complex questions about the past are thereby left aside or reduced to a short obligatory trip to the next memorial site. In contrast to this tendency to neglect the past, a youth encounter between 16 year old students from Lower Saxony and the city of Ra'anana was supposed to explicitly address the Holocaust and its relevance today in both societies. In the framework of this programme called *Our past – our Future*, 15 Israelis and 15 Germans met for ten days in Germany, where they would stay in the guest house of the Bergen-Belsen memorial site, travel to Berlin and meet several *Zeitzeugen* (witnesses). During the German return visit to Israel, the group visited the Ghetto Fighter's Museum, Yad Vashem and other places.[6]

In the preparatory seminar for the German group, we focussed on questions like 'German identity?', 'Jews' and the history of the Middle Eastern conflict. For example, the youngsters were asked to express their associations regarding the term "Jewish", with various possible implications like 'race', 'religion', 'people' or 'curses'. In view of these notions, they were rather surprised about the multiple self-definitions of young German Jews in the documentary *Judenschublade*,[7] especially that many of them did not consider themselves to be religious.

Also during the actual encounters, we continued to hold meetings in separate groups and at times small mixed groups in order to exchange views and ideas about observations and thoughts without having the feeling that one had to mind one's words in order to not be misunderstood by 'the others'.

Regarding the encounter that started in the Bergen-Belsen concentration camp memorial site, we assumed that on both sides there was some basic knowledge about the past, but deficits as soon as it came to concrete details. In order to counter an often observable asymmetry of knowledge between the two groups, the first day was not for commemoration, but instead for historical learning. Pictures from the history of the concentration camp that did not explain themselves, but rather prompted questions, were used to activate what was already known and otherwise fill the gaps. Furthermore we

---

6 The project was funded by the Stiftung niedersächsische Gedenkstätten, the German Federal Ministry for Family Affairs, Senior Citizens, Women and Youth, ConAct and the city of Ra'anana.
7 In the film *Judenschublade* [Pigeon-holes for Jews] (2005), 12 young German Jews are portrayed, displaying different family backgrounds and different notions of their Jewish existence.

used Yiddish documents to let the group work together: in order to understand what was written there, Germans and Israelis had to cooperate: While Israelis were able to read the Hebrew alphabet, the Germans understood the contexts of most of the words. The documents originated in the period between 1945 and 1950, when Bergen-Belsen was the biggest camp for Displaced Persons in Germany, with thousands of survivors of concentration camps waiting for their life to start again, among them many Jews from Eastern Europe. The Yiddish culture displayed in these documents on the one hand was strange to both Israelis and Germans, while on the other hand it represents a bridge between European Jewry and Israeli culture. Only jointly, could the students decipher the cartoon of a survivor full of black humour regarding the National Socialist ideology. The Germans were amazed by this sarcasm while Israelis related that Holocaust jokes were quite common in Israel, which ultimately resulted in a discussion on whether one should joke about the Holocaust and to what ends.

At the end of the visit in Bergen-Belsen, a fierce debate took place as to how to depart from this place. In the end, the actual commemorative ceremony was kept even shorter than planned; instead, the students held discussions on questions like 'what do I want humanity to never forget?', or 'what do I think while memorizing?'. There was time for quiet remembrance and to write down wishes. There was an Israeli flag and the Kaddish was intoned,[8] however, the Israeli students somehow 'forgot' to sing the Israeli national anthem. Unlike the accompanying Israeli teacher, both the German and the Israeli students were content with this rather chaotic and undefined setting. During a joint trip to Berlin, the youngsters were then supposed to create mixed teams and visit several memorials to groups that were persecuted during the National Socialist period, to explore and document these places and to ask visitors and neighbours about their attitudes.[9] When the groups presented their results to the others, the Germans noted that while the Israelis obviously dealt rather emotionally and collectively with remembrance, the Germans tend to focus on historical facts and regard their emotions as a private affair.

When some months later the Germans travelled to Israel, a seminar was held in the Ghetto Fighter's Museum. The Center for Humanistic Education is also located there and consciously works not only on the issue of the Holocaust, but also addresses Jewish Israelis as well as Israeli Arabs in learning about universal questions today. Some of the Israeli students felt

---

8   The kaddish is a Jewish prayer said at mourning rituals like funerals or commemorative ceremonies.
9   I owe thanks to Lore Kleiber from House of the Wannsee-Conference for this idea; together with her I conducted similar seminars under the title 'Memorial Landscape Berlin'.

provoked by this teaching concept about the Middle East conflict with its explicit reference to the Holocaust and the National Socialist past. The Israeli facilitator resolved this conflict by inviting the Israeli group to explain their views on the Middle Eastern conflict to their German visitors. All the following night, some students continued their discussions on Israeli politics. So one may conclude from this that consciously bringing up also the sensitive and possibly painful; political issues resulted in an intensified understanding between the youngsters: during the last conflict in Gaza, students from both groups exchanged thoughts and feelings on the situation in Facebook. In my opinion it seems obvious that current political questions should be integrated into a joint German-Israeli process of learning – however, this can only happen in a reasonable way if beforehand some exchanges have taken place regarding the relevance for the participants of the Holocaust and the National Socialist past.[10]

Outlook

Of course, besides complex historical and political issues, other topics should not be neglected. But the youngsters are taking care of their leisure time themselves, for example by partying all the night and thereby slowing down the following day's program, or by doing a short shopping break while actually being supposed to explore Berlin's memorial landscape.

Connecting a confrontation with the history of the Holocaust, both from a learning and a mourning perspective, with current political issues in both countries, in my experience can lead to a deeper understanding of one's own as well as the other side's identities and positions. A prerequisite for this deepened learning experience, however, is openness and patience on the side of the facilitators, in order that they do not try to control the dynamics of the process and the individual positions represented. And such a difficult dialogue requires adequate preparation beforehand and support throughout the program on both sides, helping for example with the translation of culture in both directions. Such an experience can help provide the participants with an orientation beyond their belonging to a 'national collective'. Only by acknowledging their own emotional and political conditioning in their respective cultures, might they become empathetic and critical subjects, regarding the past as well as the present.

---

10 It may be that posing questions on political attitudes yet overtaxes youngsters in this age-group. The Israelis participate usually two years before their army service, where they will have to subordinate themselves also in terms of their political attitudes and at the same time will celebrate their being adult. For the Germans, it may as a result be easier to fundamentally criticize their own and the others' society. Perhaps the intensive discussions lead rather to even stronger perceptions of national differences instead of to a universalist orientation?

Martin Schellenberg, born 1972 in Wiesbaden, works at the memorial site of Bergen-Belsen, researching and developing educational programs, teacher trainings and international programs. He lived in Israel several times doing social volunteer work, studying at the Hebrew University, working in Yad Vashem and other places. He received his MA in history and philosophy at the Centre for the Study of Anti-Semitism at the TU Berlin.

Different Approaches to Collective Identity and Mourning: Experiences from the Exchange Project "Beyond Memory"

NIRIT BIALER AND TANJA KERSTING

This essay reflects our personal experiences, observations and discussions deriving from our participation in the project *Beyond Memory – The Significance of the Nazi Past and the Holocaust for the Younger Generations in Germany and Israel* which took place in the years 2004/2005. The participants in the *Beyond Memory*-project were aged 25 to 45, hence belonged mainly to the 'third generation', some to the 'second generation' after the Holocaust and the Nazi period. They were academics and students as well as young professionals of memorial sites and museums, and came from a wide range of various academic fields. Most of the participants in both groups had already gained some experiences in the field of German-Israeli exchanges in academic or professional activities or youth exchanges. In the German group the majority of the participants came from West German family backgrounds, while in the Israeli group the majority of the particpants came from European-Jewish family backgrounds.[1]

Initiated by the German participants, the idea was to create a joint meta-discourse on the memory of the Holocaust and the Nazi past in both countries along an interdisciplinary academic and professional input. The principal question therefore was whether we had or could develop a common perspective of young Israelis and Germans on the present and the future of

---

[1] Furthermore in the German group one participant came from an East German and one from a Polish-German family background. In the Israeli group one participant came from a Sfaradi family background and one came from a Non-Jewish German family background

55

memory in both societies. By unilateral as well as bilateral workshops in Israel and Germany, the participants intensively exchanged and discussed current commemoration of the Nazi past and the Holocaust in their own as well as in the other society.

In the following, we do not aim to assess this multi-faceted, interdisciplinary project in its entirety. Rather we want to present some of our personal experiences and impressions as participants, which do not only stem from the project itself, but also from further reflection and discussion between the two of us and other participants. Our central thesis is that this exchange did not result in common positions on memory in Germany and Israel but rather allowed us to understand that there are prevailing different approaches to the past. As a result, our interaction reflected rather two different cultures of memory and therefore enabled us to learn about the other's relations to the past and how they are very much influenced by our different socializations. However, the exchange-experience gave us not only a better understanding about the "other", it also functioned as a "mirror" enabling us to reflect upon ourselves and our own attitudes towards remembrance.

The 'Third Generation' Paradigm and its Limitations
The German group based its initiative for the exchange on the hypothesis that in both countries, a so-called 'third generation' could be distinguished from the 'first' and 'second generations' by displaying specific positions towards the Holocaust and the Nazi past. It was presumed that these positions could be even closer to the 'third generation' in the respective other country than to the ones of the 'first' and 'second generation' in the own society. Accordingly, the project was designed to look for similarities between the points of view of 'third generation' Germans and Israelis through self-reflexive discussion. Is the 'third generation' perhaps less involved or differently involved due to the temporal distance?

We observed that – regardless of the temporal distance – the differences between German and Israeli attitudes are still more relevant and therefore more fruitful to explore than potential similarities. In the course of the exchange, we found that different memory cultures of our respective societies deeply influenced our discussions, and that they obviously mirror genuinely different ways of dealing with the past. While initially it was presumed that we would have the same ideas in mind while we discuss terms like 'generation', 'collective identity' or 'mourning', it soon became clear that German and Israeli participants had very different associations regarding these terms, sometimes even diametrically opposed.

'Victim Society', 'Perpetrator Society': Different Memory Discourses
In our view, two major discourses of memory culture became apparent during the exchange, echoing different perspectives on the past in the two societies: a 'victim'- and a 'perpetrator'-discourse.

In the internal discussions of the Israeli group, it was obvious from the very beginning that for most of them the planned project was not only about creating a meta-discourse about memory culture, but that it would have a major personal and emotional component. As most participants were descendants of Holocaust survivors, it was important for them to bring in each family story to the group's knowledge to be considered in the general discussion, and to allow their family narrative or rather their personal relation to the matter, to influence the ideas of the Israelis as a group before meeting the German participants. Some of the Israeli participants did even not exclude the possibility that there would be a conflict with the Germans when discussing sensitive family stories and issues in an unsupervised frame. Others wondered about the motivation of the German participants to initiate this exchange as it was not at all obvious for the Israeli participants why Germans want to address Israelis with their discourse about memory culture of the Holocaust and the Nazi past. The Israelis asked themselves why they as 'descendants of victims' should talk to 'descendants of perpetrators' about these very delicate subjects at all. However, after all these questions the opportunity to enter into an exchange seemed to be even more intriguing.

Within the German group, the actual idea of an exchange with young Israelis on memory cultures in Germany and Israel was not questioned. But there were concerns that despite the reflexive and academic character of the project, a face-to-face discussion with Israelis could trigger feelings of guilt or shame which could make it difficult to speak out freely in the discussion. Questions concerning motivation and family stories were brought up too: how did the participants come to deal with subjects connected to the Nazi past or the Holocaust? Were there any key experiences in our life that effected their interest? To what extend does one feel affected by the personal involvement of our grandparents in the National Socialist regime? While in the beginning the hypothesis was brought up in the German group that in contrast to the 'second generation', the 'third generations' interests in the National Socialist past and Holocaust would not necessarily be influenced by the personal experiences or deeds of relatives during National Socialism, after the project it turned out that some of the participants ascribed their own motivation significantly much more to their own family story.

During the exchange both Germans and Israelis – though for different reasons – feared the personal component and did not want the encounter to end up as a "therapy group". But the more the Germans accentuated the cognitive and academic component of the discussions, the Israelis felt they had to emphasize their own emotional involvement in the subject. In our view, this very different general approach to the exchange became obvious especially while we were discussing – and performing – two themes: 'collective identity' and 'mourning'.

'Collective Identity' in Israel and Germany

A central issue brought up by Israeli participants was the question of 'collective identity' – what role did it play in our discussions? Most German participants were hardly interested by the issue of 'collective identity', being apprehensive about 'stereotyping'. However, the Israelis wanted the Germans to express their positions on this issue as a group, since among themselves they had discussed intensively if and how they would form a group, despite coming from a wide spectrum of professional fields and political directions. Furthermore, they discussed what the Israeli group wanted to represent in this project and what it wanted to represent when meeting Germans.

The Israeli participants wanted to represent one voice as a group to express their specific point of view on the issues discussed in the encounter with Germans. This 'one-voice' took into account the different family stories, perspectives and political and critical approaches of the various participants. It was important for the Israeli group to emphasize that although each one has his or her individual story, in a face-to face group exchange with Germans, they would as well represent the 'victim side'. They felt the need that this should be expressed, too. This additional subliminal component appeared to become stronger when the two groups met and worked togther.

Israel is still a young nation. Since it was founded in 1948 as a "Jewish state", it has had to integrate immigrants from all over the world and has strived to maintain a Jewish majority within its borders. At the same time, it is in a permanent state of war and has to provide for security on a daily basis. Accordingly, the Israeli Jewish educational system as well as the Israeli Army aim to create, maintain and strengthen the national collective, mainly via the emphasis on a collectively shared history and future. The socialization which is provided by these institutions in connection with a constant sense of threat creates a strong collective feeling among Israelis. Israelis often see themselves as 'us' against 'them' i.e. the 'enemies'. While seventy years ago it was the National Socialists who wanted to exterminate the Jews, today the threatening 'enemy' might be Iran or various terrorist organizations. A 'narrative of victimhood' seems to serve as a common ground for similarities between generations of Jews.

The most important days of public remembrance in Israel are dedicated to the memory of the Holocaust as well as to Israel's fallen soldiers and victims of terrorism: *Yom HaShoah*[2] and, one week later, *Yom HaZikaron*.[3] They are an offer to the population to connect collectively and emotionally to the traumatic events. While in the Diaspora, religion was the common category to keep Jewish people together, in Israel's secular culture, the ceremonial tradition of public remembrance days has a similar effect of establishing a common ground, especially the remembrance of the Holocaust. Ceremonies on *Yom HaShoah* are held in all possible contexts, so that the individual plays an active part in the nationwide commemorations. The Holocaust thus seems to be an important pillar of the social bonding of Israeli society and the creation of a collective.[4]

In Germany, however, the situation is very different when it comes to the question of 'collective identity'. Since after 1945, promoting an unambiguously positive 'national identity' was neither plausible nor necessary, until recently forming a traditional 'national identity' has not been a central element in German socialization. For 'third generation' Germans, it is typical to be critical of any form of national or collective belonging, because they were taught that nationalism and collective over-identification are features of Nazi Germany. Accordingly, the German participants felt uneasy during our meetings with terms like 'nation' or 'collective'. For them it was more attractive to refer to the term 'generation', because it allowed them to distinguish themselves in a critical and opposing position especially to their grandparents' generation. So while the Israeli participants before meeting the Germans had discussed how to form a group on a consensual basis, the Germans agreed from the beginning on not representing anything, and found that they could not even be representative for a 'German third generation'. Instead, they agreed that everybody stands for him- or herself as an individual.

In short: while for Israelis the Holocaust plays an important role for their 'collective identity', in Germany the Nazi past and the Holocaust rather deconstruct 'collective identity'.

---

2 *Yom HaZikaron laShoah ve-laGvura*, engl. Remembrance Day for the Holocaust and Heroism, Heroism refers to Jewish resistance, especially to the Warsaw Ghetto Uprising.
3 *Yom HaZikaron*, engl. Fallen Soldiers and Victims of Terrorism Remembrance Day.
4 Recently, however, also less national-oriented ceremonies have emerged, like an alternative memorial ceremony, which has been held for the past ten years at the Tmuna Theatre in Tel Aviv (in 2008, over a thousand people participated). Questioning the ritual character and the political instrumentalization of official ceremonial practice, it wants to enable people to relate to the Holocaust with their own point of view, and to leave space for narratives which are usually less represented publicly.

Memory and Mourning

For the Israeli participants, the subject of 'mourning' was a fundamental issue to deal with in the course of the project, emotionally as well as reflexively. In Israel 'mourning' is an integral part of Holocaust memory culture. There is an evident emotional connection to the collective past – and very often also to the family past. To the surprise of the Israeli participants, it turned out that 'mourning' is not at all a central part of the German memory culture. Even though the atrocities committed by the Nazis could also have emotional and tragical implications for Germans, memory culture in Germany seems to work on a rather rational and intellectual level. It is primarily associated with museums, exhibitions, memorial sites, literature, films, and public debates, which mediate, document and reflect the past. But is there space for mourning?

As an input, the issue of 'mourning' was brought up by the Israeli group while the German participants got very much interested in the subject and wanted to explore what role mourning would play for them in reference to the memory of the past. They approached the issue, however, in a rather academic way: By reading different authors like Alexander and Margarete Mitscherlich, Judith Butler, Sigmund Freud and others, they tried to find a concept of 'mourning' that could fit their discourse. In turn, they expected the Israelis to read texts as well, but the Israeli participants "did not do their homework". When the groups eventually came together in order to exchange on 'mourning', the Germans where disappointed by the fact that their Israeli partners had not read anything that could be discussed. The Israelis, on the other hand, were upset that the German side had only collected theoretical concepts for 'mourning' instead of dealing with its emotional dimension. To them, the Germans elaborating on different theories and types of mourning in an almost schematic way appeared to be very detached from an actual emotion of mourning. Why were the Germans "pretending" not to be personally involved? Why did they not express any emotional attitude?

For some of the Israeli group, the German cognitive approach seemed to be an "escape" from treating the subject on a personal and emotional level, as the Israelis felt it should be handled. In Israeli eyes, the mere fact to be born into a family of Holocaust survivors, or the mere fact that a person is born in Israel, makes one "a professional" in the field of mourning, so there is no reason to read or reflect. In contrast, the Germans wondered: why can they not speak with us about different concepts of mourning, without immediately involving their personal narratives? Some of the German participants found it impossible to speak on an academic level with the Israelis about the subject of mourning as long as they brought up their emotions.

For some Israelis, before conducting an academic discourse, it was crucial to explore firstly the personal dimension of mourning. For them, "mourning" signified the indispensable emotional side of remembering and the way the individual connects to the dead. When sitting for Pessach dinner and there are only fifteen relatives present instead of a hundred-fifty who might have been sitting there; or when reading a story about a young Jew prosecuted in Germany and imagining that this could have been oneself, they sense their personal connection to the past very strongly. Hence, the attempt of the Germans to find out about what 'mourning' could mean seemed in the eyes of the Israelis, almost too absurd to discuss.

Israelis mourn, of course, for the victims. The 'victim society' mourns the loss and the sufferings of victims, as they know what their families experienced in the past. Israeli youngsters are encouraged to learn their families' stories in order to understand their personal relation to the past. A major school project that takes place in the seventh grade is to write a family tree album, where pupils track back their family story to their great-great grandparents. Pupils are supposed to interview their relatives, to learn about their own family story in connection to major historical events. Finally a big, family tree album party is held, where each of the other students can read the others' family story.

On the 'perpetrator side', by contrast, many young people obviously hardly know their family's story. Some of the German participants had researched their familial backgrounds or taken up the dialogue within their families about the own family story. A study edited by social psychologist Harald Welzer "Opa war kein Nazi" ("Grandpa was no Nazi")[5] revealed that in many families, narratives of the Nazi period which are transmitted are actually completely different from the ones taught in schools or other institutions. The study constates a big gap between the "family album" and the "history book". While the atrocities committed by the Nazis are accepted and critically reflected, family stories very often tend to deal with the sufferings of relatives affected by the war, or – according to Welzer's findings – even convert actual Nazi perpetrator relatives into resistance fighters. Unlike the socialization in Israeli schools, in Germany tracing back family stories in connection to the Nazi period and to compare it to the same-aged, would also not be part of the school curriculum. The tracing back of family stories would rather be done on an individual basis.

So what could there be mourned in the 'perpetrator society', if people sometimes don't even know their family history? The German participants of the workshop would, of course, refuse to mourn their own relatives' suffering during the war, since they found it was illegitimate given that Germany had caused the war and the Holocaust. So they suggested that either they could

---

5   Cf. Harald, Welzer: Opa war kein Nazi. Nationalsozialismus und Holocaust im Familiengedächtnis. Frankfurt a. M., 2003 [2002].

mourn the victims of Nazi crimes, or the wrongly led German past itself. When some of them opted for mourning the victims, an Israeli participant objected that he would not want Germans to mourn his grandfather – the Germans should look for an object to mourn which is more closely related to themselves. To the German participants, this seemed rather offensive: why should they not mourn the victims? And what else should they mourn for then?

Mourning an object that – from an Israeli point of view – is more closely and personally related to them, implied for Germans to learn the story of their perpetrator relatives – and mourn. This is of course much more difficult and touched in our point of view a crucial point as it suggests an ambivalent way of mourning for the German side. Also, it obviously leads back to the question of 'collective identity': if the Germans do not feel they belong to a 'collective', but rather to a 'generation' that decisively opposes its grandparents, then why should and how could they feel the perpetrators to be closer to them than the victims? This question remained controversial and unresolved.

"Beyond Memory"
We only became critically aware of our own and the other's approaches to the memory of the Holocaust and the Nazi past through the exchange: in the 'mirror of the others' attitudes, it became easier to reflect our own ones. Consequently, the face-to-face discussion provided an experience which reveals and mirrors positions that in very central aspects seem to be diametrically opposed due to the different memory practices in our respective societies. This insight triggered unexpected new ways of perceptions and thinking. We achieved a deeper understanding of the relation to the past of the "other side". Engaging in the German-Israeli exchange about emotional and intellectual ways of relating to the past, we enabled ourselves to explore complex and intertwined social processes and discourses regarding our cultures of memory and collective identities'.

Last but not least, we believe this was a vivid and profound joint commemoration of the past – while raising important questions about our present and future.

Nirit Bialer, born in 1978 in Tel Aviv, studied International Relations and Middle Eastern Studies at Hebrew University in Jerusalem and Tel Aviv University. The project Beyond Memory, in which she took part as a participant in the Israeli group, has enhanced her interest in the subject of memory culture after being engaged for many years in German-Israeli exchange programs. Since 2006 she has lived in Berlin and works in the Israeli embassy. Parallel to her work she assists in different German-Israeli youth exchanges projects.

Tanja Kersting, born in 1978 in Paderborn, lives in Berlin. She studied Comparative Literature Studies, Political Science and Sociology in Berlin and Paris. The project Beyond Memory, in which she belonged as a participant to the German group, has deepened her interest in memory discourses and memory culture in praxis. Currently she is working as a research assistant in the project After the Survivors. Performing the Holocaust and the Jewish Past at the new Yad Vashem Museum and at the Jewish Museum, Berlin (University of Halle / Ben Gurion University). She is also an associate of the Kurt Tucholsky Museum in Rheinsberg.

Israelis in Berlin.
Between History and Every Day Life

ZOHAR MILCHGRUB AND YOAV SAPIR

"Why Germany?"

[**Zohar:**] "You can forget about me coming to visit you there, you know!" my mother scolded me, on hearing that I was going to spend one year of my Japanese and Political Studies course in Berlin. This must have been strongly connected to her acquaintanceship with my father's father: Moshe Rachmil Milchgrub, who had been wise enough to flee eastwards from Poland in the autumn of 1939, and who became the sole survivor of a large family. "Why Germany?", she wondered further "What's wrong with Italy or Spain, or any other normal place?"

The dry answer for this still recurrent question was that no place, as far as I know, encourages graduate students who are descendants of Holocaust victims to apply for a scholarship, as does the foundation *Erinnerung, Verantwortung and Zukunft* (Remembrance, Responsibility, and Future).* But it was much more than an attractive opportunity that brought me to Berlin. Actually, it had to do exactly with my mother's reaction. My decision to study German was originally an accidental one because out of boredom I joined a friend on an intensive German course at the Goethe Institute. Although I had neither my future studies in mind nor an extraordinary interest in German culture, it became, from the moment I began facing weird reactions about my studying the language, a kind of silent rebellion against prevailing conventions in my society and family.

---

* The scholarship is also available for other students interested in the subject of National-Socialism and the Holocaust. http://www.stiftung-evz.de/fonds_erinnerung_und_zukunft/stipendien/

[Yoav:] It is impossible to know how many Israelis – whether "young" or not – are living in Berlin at any given moment. The local institutions responsible for foreigners are able to record only those Israelis, who for lack of a European passport have no choice but to register with them; however, quite of a few of them have e.g. an American passport and do not necessarily use their Israeli one when applying for a visa.. But many Israelis do possess a passport of a member state of the European Union, which, as far as the German authorities are concerned, makes them "invisible" as Israelis. And then there are also those Israelis who possess a German passport. Article 116, Paragraph 2 of the Federal Constitution provides the legal basis, according to which descendants of German Jews can reclaim "their" German citizenship. There are many different incentives to come as a German citizen, such as financial support provided by the German state during one's studies. All in all, according to an Israeli engaged in the Israeli community in Berlin, Ilan Weiß, approximately 6,000 Israelis live in Berlin.

Many of the "German Israelis" are young people, probably some hundreds. Most of them go directly to Berlin, even if their roots are elsewhere in current Germany (or what once used to be the German Reich). Berlin has meanwhile (again) reached the status of an exciting metropolis, "the right place to be in", and this image of Berlin is conveyed also into foreign lands such as Israel, either by persons that have toured Berlin or, for example, by cinema movies, cf. for example the Israeli movie 'Walk on Water' by Eytan Fox (2004).

Somewhat different than those with a German (or, for that matter, other European passport) is the situation of those Israelis, who, like Zohar and myself, can only rely on their Israeli passport. Those Israelis may receive a visa for study purposes if they can prove their ability to support themselves financially during their studies, for example by transferring money from Israel, or as in the case of Zohar and myself, as scholarship holders. This in turn usually – although not always – means, that these students deal in one way or the other with German topics, and have completed at least some language studies. As in the case of Zohar, an interest that in Israel is usually eyed with suspicion.

This silent rebellion took me all the way to my first encounter with Berlin, on my way back from India – an attractive destination for Israelis out of the army – in the autumn of 2004. It might be for this reason then, that in addition to turning out to be a great city to live in, Berlin has endowed me with a strange feeling, one which has followed me since my first day in it, and still holds strong today, after having lived there more than a year; a somewhat childish pride of engaging in something prohibited, of having freed myself from the premises of a social disposition which is otherwise seen as natural, trespassing historically drawn borders, away to a fast unknown culture, from which I was "sheltered" all those years.

I remember myself as a child of the early 90's, watching a TV report about the freshly united Berlin, involving Jews, and – *oy weh iz mir!* – Israelis living in Berlin. The tone of the reporter was overtly sceptical, and I too could not for one moment imagine myself being there, not to mention living there, surrounded by bloodthirsty Nazis, who might jump on me at any moment. I remember how, sitting with my younger brother in the tub, he heard from me for the first time in his life, that there were once bad Germans, who wanted "us" killed, and came actually pretty close to doing that in our family's case.

The yearly Holocaust Memorial Day, known in Israel as *Yom HaZikaron laSho'ah ve-laGvura* (The Remembrance Day for the Holocaust and Courage), was for me, as for most Israeli youth, an unavoidable and essential part of growing-up in Israel. Once a year everything stops, both mentally and – for one minute of silence – physically as well. Ceremonies are held, songs are sung, stories told, and sad faces maintained. In such an environment, an instinctive disdain for anything German was almost a matter of course.

Things have evidently taken a sharp turn since those days, both for me and for many of my generation. I started studying German, visited Berlin twice and eventually stayed there for one year of studies, also thanks to the money of the German government. I am happy to have gotten this opportunity but to be sure – I am afraid this coming sentence will come out badly on all sides – I do not feel that Germany nor its people owe me anything other than an insistent maintenance of the holocaust memory. It might sound horrible, but I never actually "lost" any of my grandfather's siblings (all perished in the Holocaust), nor could I have really shared his grief. It is his life that has been destroyed not mine.

Berlin – another "Bubble" for Israelis?

It is no coincidence that many of the Israelis come from Tel-Aviv, the "bubble" of Israel as they call it. The "typical Tel Avivian" wishes to disconnect himself / herself from the (Jewish) national sphere in favour of a more global identity, finds their realization in the city most identified with the new, supranational and gradually unifying Europe. This unofficial "movement" has therefore a very clear and specific destination: Berlin, both as an image of a post-national Europe and as the reality of a promising metropolis.

In this constellation, the past is not nearly as important as the future. Although Israelis in Berlin like to describe the city as the "place where it all happened", most of them don't know and - more often than not - will also not really bother to find out what it is, exactly, that happened "here". They know when Israel commemorates the Holocaust, and might even refrain from going to a bar on that evening, but will not necessarily pay attention to January 27th, the official memorial day for the victims of National Socialism, and will scarcely attend the ceremonies on November 9th held by the Jewish community.

Humans are an adapting race, and tend to limit their thought to the daily and self-centred undertakings – carrying out daily chores, advancing in life, getting by, and having a good time. As I have already come to know extremely well from life in Jerusalem, one is capable of disregarding both the graveness of situations occurring around oneself – the misery in eastern Arab neighbourhoods like the Sho'afat refugee camp is unknown to an overwhelming majority of West Jerusalem citizens – and the historical meaning of surrounding places – although being a native Jerusalemite, I have visited in the past year the Church of the Redeemer for the first time in my 28 year long life!

So in my Berlin life, while that feeling of border-crossing described above has remained, the actual foundation of these borders has gradually become relatively marginal, and I have rarely found myself pondering about the history and memory of the holocaust. Interestingly enough, most times I was confronted with the city's past were by witnessing my visitors' experiences. For some of them – especially the older ones – it was really weird to be in Germany. Views similar to the ones mentioned above by my mother were uttered by my father just after he came to visit me in Berlin. Although having been raised by two tormented Holocaust survivors, my father bears no grudge, and is usually a man of good spirit. However, as of his second day in Berlin, he seemed to have succumbed to a gloomy mood.

The worst came when I took him to the new Holocaust Memorial in the middle of Berlin, close to the Brandenburg Gate and the Reichstag Building, a site which as it happened I had driven by with my bicycle many times, giving its emotional weight only a slight thought. We walked slowly through the big grey slabs, possibly even taking a couple of pictures, and went down to the information centre underground. He went out without me noticing, in the middle of the walk around it. When I found him outside, he looked horribly pale. "I can't stand this place", he told me, as if only by visiting it he was taking part in a crime. To my father, the city of Berlin for all its good features, will remain inaccessible, a stronghold of unspoken acts and merciless memories.

Whatever passport they carry, young Israelis in Berlin have, once they are in the city, several things in common. One of them is the generally speaking low level of "Jewishness", that is to say: active interest in Judaism. Religious Israelis are in general not attracted to Germany, not interested in moving here, and would not like to exchange their vivid, bustling community in Israel for the relatively pale substitute Berlin has to offer, not to mention other

German cities. Thus, one would hardly find young Israelis in Berlin's synagogues, unless it happens to be New Year or the Day of Atonement. This "avoiding" of Jewishness can also be seen on the campus of the Free University of Berlin as well as on that of the adjacent Potsdam, where Jewish Studies can be pursued, but only a handful of the numerous Israeli students in Berlin actually do that.

Yet for most young Israelis, so it seems to me, modern Berlin – with its dynamic artistic, party and activist scenes and youthful environment – is a city for itself, detached not only from National Socialist history but even from contemporary Germany, an island of some sort. Moreover, as I have come to understand, life in Berlin does not necessarily imply disregarding or downgrading Jewish and Israeli identity, but actually realising it.

I tried to explain that to my girlfriend, strolling on the Maybach riverbank one evening, at one of her visits (hoping for it to serve as some kind of excuse for me leaving her in Israel for a whole year). My life in Berlin, so I said, feels to me more Israeli than living in Israel. It is not only about some antagonistic approach of "proving to the Nazis" that a Jew can live here (although it does have its significance), nor is it some kind of abstract patriotic concept, by which being abroad and free counts for me as an emblem of "Israelitude".

It is a fact that almost everywhere I go (yes, just as my grandparents in Romania and Poland in different times), I am an Israeli\Jew. It is a mostly subtle feature that underlines most interactions I have in Berlin, and yet is not definitely negative. Why is that? Maybe, as an Israeli friend recently told me, because in interacting with Germans in Berlin, as opposed to the complicated situation in Jerusalem, I always "get to be the victim".

"Did you realise that it's the first time we've ever talked about the Holocaust?" I was told by a long-time German friend, as my recount of a short trip to Poland led to the story of my grandfather. No, actually I hadn't realised that, but it seemed that for her it was a significant moment.

Diasporic Community: Potentials and Dreams
As an Israeli in Berlin, I feel relatively free from the obstructions mentioned above, entitled to represent something, be it Israel, Israelis, Jews or simply me. What or how exactly do I represent – that is mostly left to me, and is not dependent on how I am being perceived. Thus, through interaction both with German and international friends, as well as with Israelis living here, who speak my language and share my background, I can enjoy the positive, intriguing sides of identity and culture, while hoping to spread some positive impressions about myself and my people, whoever they might be. I believe this feeling is not exclusively mine, but shared by many who come here.

And they do come. I might take pride of "discovering" Berlin relatively early, as the tide of Israelis is still yet to come, but it is probably on its way. More and more Israelis turn to me regarding an upcoming journey to Berlin – either for a visit or a fresh start. Many have German friends or even partners, and many do consider moving to Berlin, with the main obstacle being, surprisingly enough, not the terrible German past but the dreadful German language.

Most of the Israelis begin to learn the language only after their arrival: not immediately and quite often with only mediocre success. I have not yet heard of a new trend of Israelis moving to Paris or Rome. Surely there are some who do, even if no one writes a book about them as in the case of Israelis in Berlin (cf. Fania Oz-Salzberger, 'Israelis in Berlin', 2001).

I am confident however, that very few, if any, of those who move to Paris or Rome do so without speaking French or respectively Italian. Admittedly, Berlin is a city with a very high number of English speakers, the German population in the central and Western parts of the city often understands and speaks English, and the city is, in general, very friendly and hospitable towards people who do not speak German (in contrast, for example, to Paris). This makes it possible for many people, also for young Israelis, to live in Berlin without having to learn proper German.

Israelis coming to Berlin are of a slightly different kind. Many are very learned and open-minded, otherwise they might have not chosen Germany. They know where they are going to, but – whether out of ideological, academic or strictly egoistic reasons –simply rather live with the history of the city, or in-spite of it. "The worst day I have here", I was told by a high-school buddy whom I happened to run into on the street, "is still ten-times better than a good day in Jerusalem". Indeed, life in Israel for many is seen as a life of continual struggle with its daily pressures, with existential dangers, and with strict worldviews. While they definitely come expecting a good life, most do not come in search of money – other European capitals and German cities offer more lucrative chances for sure – but in search of a colourful, inspiring life.

In the western world, Berlin may be the farthest one can go from the perspectives of mainstream Israeli society, a society still traumatised by the holocaust, and from life with mentally or physically destroyed survivors, with their terrible, sometimes untold stories. Yes, most of the Israelis in Berlin do share some kind of individualism, which usually pulls them more apart than together. But they have still to discover the advantages and comfort of Diaspora community living: nicer housing opportunities, more familiar spots, better networking. I am no sociological expert, but in my humble estimation it is a matter of ten years or so till the loose ties close, and a both more self-conscious and apparent Israeli community, even a small one, comes together.

In recent years, the Israelis in Berlin have begun to organise themselves separately. The above-mentioned Ilan Weiß, an engineer from Haifa who now works as an insurance agent in Berlin, runs a newsletter for émigré Israelis, which in 2006 had around 800 subscribers. He provides his subscribers with important information sent to him by others regarding everyday life, such as renting a room, cultural events, and sometimes even a job offer or two. Most of Weiß's subscribers, though not all, live in Berlin, and a great number of them are indeed Israeli. For this circle Weiß organises a monthly Stammtisch, i.e. a regular meeting, in one of Berlin's kosher cafés. Another Israeli Stammtisch started not long ago and aims at getting the younger Israelis together. One should also mention the weekly radio broadcast in Berlin's channel open to all, which is run by the Israeli Aviv Russ and in which young Israelis interview other Israelis living in the city – or those who recently came to Berlin – and play some Israeli music.

As with almost any sociological change, this one too entails both positive and negative prospects. Facing growing friction with other communities might lead to unpleasant experiences. One could easily picture the day in which Israelis would be stopped at the door to an Arab restaurant, and the ensuing public shock. On the community level, neither side seems too anxious for contact: A German-Palestinian friend who has lived most of her life in Berlin once admitted to me that never before me had she really got to know either an Israeli or a Jew in the city.

Yet on the individual level, just as I have written above about the matter of representation inside and outside Israel, there is much more room for change. As a peace activist, who was somewhat disappointed by the current extent of activity in Berlin regarding the Israeli-Palestinian conflict, I was encouraged by the ability of some Israelis and Palestinians to maintain healthy communication, and even friendships. Riding back from the Humboldt University on my bicycle one day, for example, I stumbled upon a group of two Israelis I knew, who were sitting in the Mariannenplatz with a couple of Palestinian schoolmates. They were laughing and having a good time after school, and seemed remarkably unaffected by their national origins.

The emergence of such an Israeli community is therefore not a scenario Berliners need to fear, but instead one possibly to look forward to. Let me daydream about it for a while: with its broad historical awareness and generally advanced plurality, the city could provide the right conditions for the development of a gap-bridging dialogue between the diaspora Palestinians and diaspora Israelis, who in many countries tend to entertain relatively patriotic, not to say nationalistic views in regard to the conflict "back home". Not only are the Israeli residents of Berlin relatively open-minded, but so are other inhabitants. Through people such as the ones I have been meeting there,

Berlin might one day rise up to play an important role in relations between Arabs and Jews.

The same goes – it is almost needless to mention – for the integration of Israelis into German society. Once life together becomes a self-evident matter to all parties involved, so would the joint memory of the holocaust gain new perceptions. As much as I consider it the job of German society to maintain the remembrance of the Holocaust, it is through these additional perceptions that the memory stays alive.

Is this the "normality", that so many people long for? In a way, it is. But still, some aspects of the phenomenon called "Israelis in Berlin" might suggest the opposite: How normal is it, that young Israelis, who for the most part have neither much knowledge about Germany and its history nor speak its language properly, come to Berlin as German citizens and enjoy many legal and financial benefits that this country – in which they usually have never set foot before – has to offer? And how normal is it, that young Israelis expect to have an easy breakthrough in Berlin, just because they are (Jewish) Israelis? What we see today seems as a result not yet "normal", but maybe one of the many phases on the dialectical way towards this evasive "normality", which might just be possible at some time in the future.

Zohar Milchgrub, born in Jerusalem 1980, has recently finished his BA studies in Political Science and the Amirim Humanities Program in the Hebrew University in Jerusalem. These days he is travelling in China and studying Chinese. Since the end of his compulsory army duty in March 2002, he has been active in Yesh Gvul ('There is a Limit'), an Israeli peace organization dedicated to supporting Israeli soldiers who refuse taking part in the occupation, and to raising awareness in Israeli society regarding war crimes committed by the Israeli army.

Yoav Sapir, born 1979 in Haifa, studied German Literature and History in Jerusalem, Vienna and Berlin. He wrote his award-winning MA thesis on the representation of Jews in feature films of the GDR. Since 2007 he has been a rabbinical candidate at the Hochschule für Jüdische Studien (University for Jewish Studies) in Heidelberg and active in German-Jewish as well as Christian-Jewish dialogues. He has lived in Berlin three times up to now: 2006/7 as a scholarship holder of the foundation Remembrance, Responsibility, and Future; 2008 with a scholarship from the Heinrich Böll foundation; and 2009 as a scholarship holder of the German Bundestag.

Revisiting National Memory Discourses

Humanize the Discourse!
Non-academic Reflections
of a Memory Researcher

CORNELIA SIEBECK

Ten years ago, when still a student of history, I visited the Buchenwald memorial for the first time. I felt quite overwhelmed at the sight of this huge, grey sea of debris stretching down the mountainside, interrupted only by low-lying memorials and occasionally some historic buildings, most prominently the former crematory with its chimney. 'Regulations for visitors' at the entrances to the former prisoner's camp, countless signposts and explanatory plates as well as commemorative stones from various post-war periods, and, of course, several historical exhibitions, altogether aim at governing the visitor's gaze at a bygone concentration camp. However, at least on me, the impressive power of the actual wasteland acted much more intensely. It effectively subverted the regulatory efforts undertaken by the memorial institution to help me imagine a former concentration camp: I perceived some rather undefined space. An intriguing place not only with regards to its past, but also to its present form as a memorial site. A place to delve into and study: what was this wasteland all about?

The year after, I came back to do an internship in the educational department for half a year. Apart from my work, I studied the history of the camp and its post-war uses as a Soviet internment camp (1945-50) and, eventually, as a national memorial to anti-fascist resistance in the ex-German Democratic Republic (GDR).[1] Whenever I looked out of the window of my office, I observed visitors: individual tourists from all over the world clinging to their guide books, German school classes trying to figure out why they had

---

1 In line with the GDR's anti-fascist state doctrine, the *Nationale Mahn- und Gedenkstätte Buchenwald* [National Buchenwald Memorial] ostentatiously celebrated anti-fascist resistance and its ultimate victory over fascism.

75

to come here, trade union groups affirming their anti-fascist traditions, Neo-Nazis unobtrusively[2] celebrating their SS traditions, and so on and so forth. In this way I got to be confronted with a rather dissonant *spiritus loci*, which eventually I made the subject of my PhD. I do not only investigate about how Buchenwald has been produced, designed and performed as a memorial site after 1945, but in particular I try to collect as diverse attitudes towards the place as possible by participant observation. I have attended memorial ceremonies, meditated some days together with Zen Buddhists, or joint the annual *Antifacamp* (anti-fascist camp) in order to try to understand their fierce protests against 'historical revisionism' at the memorial site, repeatedly resulting in protest demonstrations held in front of the former camp's gate.[3]

Hence, in the meantime Buchenwald has become quite familiar to me. However, I have always refrained from mystifying this place. For me, Buchenwald never was by definition a strange location representing some remote past and reverberating with abstract concepts like a 'rupture in civilization'. Rather, I perceive Buchenwald as a place in the world – *this* world: loaded with multiple and often contradictory experiences, actions and interpretations, full of stories and memories, a historical and present complex of human interaction. In my understanding, nothing there is by definition 'absolutely other', 'unimaginable' and 'inexplicable', as is stereotypically repeated in global memory discourse. To construct an impermeable wall between 'us' and '*this* past' is nothing but creating as big as possible distance between today's allegedly 'better' world and 'Auschwitz' in terms of a metaphor for 'the absolute evil'.

Skipping this alleged distance, Buchenwald has become a prism for me: what I have learnt in Buchenwald has clearly reshaped the way I look at the world. Vice versa, I bring back what I have experienced elsewhere in order to then explore Buchenwald from new angles. So in some way, I change with the place, and the place changes with me. Not surprisingly, Buchenwald has cost me quite some illusions, about the past as well as about the present. Sometimes I felt burdened by this place, and wanted to get rid of it. But because one cannot rid oneself of something one has already internalized, the only viable way has always been to return and dig even deeper. So with time Buchenwald has become an inextricable part of my life.

---

2 As soon as Neo-Nazis display forbidden symbols (e.g. a swastika), perform forbidden actions (e.g. the Hitler salute) or explicitly provoke visitors, the memorial staff would call the police. As long as they behave inconspicuously, there is no means to banish them from the site.

3 The annual *Antifa Camp Weimar/Buchenwald*, consisting mainly of young anti-fascists criticizes several changes that have been made in the presentation of Buchenwald's history since the end of the GDR and the German unification as being 'anti-communist' and 'ideologically motivated'.

My Buchenwald

I can have diverse experiences in Buchenwald. Once, while living there for some time in a former SS barrack, I needed some relaxation after a long day. It was a beautiful summer evening. No tourists gazing around anymore, only me and the peaceful landscape. I was sitting on the lawn, smoking a cigarette and leaning towards a tree in the former zoo that the SS had placed adjacent to the camp. Looking at the silent wasteland stretching across the slope of the hill, only the chimney of the crematory standing out of the emptiness, I was enjoying the birdsong from the forests, feeling very much in harmony with myself and my surroundings. However, this was not at all a moment of forgetting or 'suppressing' what had happened here some decades ago. Rather, it was a sense of fully embracing the past, but at the same time stubbornly – even aggressively – feeling alive. More precisely: not agonized by Buchenwald, but ready to confront, and go on with this knowledge in a meaningful way.

But there were also less lofty experiences. Once I stood on the central watchtower at the top of the entrance to the former camp: from the wooden balcony, I glanced over the empty roll call square. Suddenly I imagined myself being a 17-year-old SS guard,[4] one of the guys on these old photographs, proudly wearing his uniform, laughing and playing with a dog. One of those pubescent teenagers being told day in and day out they were part of an Aryan elite, and that the men they guarded were nothing but scum. Down there on the sloping roll call square, I see nothing but an indefinite grey mass of elderly men, totally at my mercy. From here they appear dwarfish. They all look the same, shaved heads, filthy and tired. They are subjected to me, I have a gun... I felt weak in my knees, the smell of wood preservative became far too intense. Trying to escape my vision, I hardly managed to step down the stairs anymore.

These were rather extreme moments, most of my experiences in Buchenwald are far more trivial. After all it is a memorial site in the present, and the ghosts that 'haunt' us there are ghosts that we call up ourselves. However, one's own intuitions are obviously part of the game. I can talk on Buchenwald in a cognitive way for hours, and decisively argue that there is no other way to talk about it, at least if one wants to have a meaningful historical or political exchange. Nevertheless, cognitive concepts are indeed rooted in one's emotions and sensations. But at the same time, one's emotions are of course shaped by one's cognitive knowledge and conceptions. So after all

---

4   Before the war, most SS guards in Buchenwald were considerably younger than 21, see: Gedenkstätte Buchenwald (Ed.): Konzentrationslager Buchenwald 1937-1945, authored by Harry Stein, Göttingen 1999, p.37.

those years in Buchenwald, I came to believe in the banal truth that one only sees (and feels) what one 'knows'. There is nothing 'inherent' here.

Hence, I couldn't have felt exactly how I felt on the watchtower, had I not shortly before attended a lecture by Imre Kertész and been deeply impressed by his formula about being *erschießbar* anywhere and anytime.[5] Nor would this moment have shaken me so much, had I not recently studied photos of SS-teenagers whose clumsy posturing reminded me of any group of teenagers. Similarly, I could not have sensed a peaceful summer evening here, had I not long left behind extraterritorializing places like Buchenwald from what I conceptualize as 'normal', 'civilized' or 'humane'. Instead, I have adapted my notions of normalcy, civilization and humaneness. Hence I am aware that, while I am sitting there, looking at a disused crematory and enjoying the birdsong, the world bursts with phenomena that function by means of the same or similar mechanisms as the ones that were at work in Buchenwald. However, apart from sinking into despair – which also happens at times – the only thing I feel I can do right now is to try to understand these mechanisms, in the past as well as in the present. From there to try to think differently, talk differently, write differently; try to emancipate myself from my complicity in historical and political structures that created – and in all kinds of variations still create – ideologies resulting in places like Buchenwald. This, however, not only seems to be an ambiguous, but also a lifelong endeavour, and necessarily doomed to failure, as Adorno might suggest: "There is no right life in the wrong one."[6] I agree, but still it seems worth trying, and I anyway do not share Adorno's cultural pessimism. By the time I was born, paradise had long been lost. Moreover, I am not sure it ever existed. So there can only be something to gain.

A New World of Peace and Liberty?
Beside all kinds of particular monuments to specific places or victim groups, there is a memorial dedicated to "all inmates of the concentration camp"': a four square-meter metal plaque, located at ground level on the former roll-call square. It is placed exactly where liberated prisoners had erected a first temporary monument to their deceased fellow sufferers: a wooden obelisk with the inscription "K.L.B.", underneath a wreath enclosing the figure

---

5   Lit.: shootable (to death). There is actually neither an adjective *erschießba*r in German. In his novel Fiasco (1988) Kertész depicts himself as a 14-year-old boy caught in a collection camp together with other Jews from Budapest with the following insight: "I had grasped the simple secret of the world that was allocated to me: to be shootable anytime and anywhere." (my translation). This straight forward naming of fundamental human fragility and weakness when being confronted with blunt violence then deeply impressed me.

6   Theodor W. Adorno: Minima Moralia. Reflexionen aus dem beschädigten Leben [Reflections from damaged life], Frankfurt a.M. 2003 (orig. 1951), p.43.

"51,000".[7] On April 19, 1945, roughly a week after their liberation, 21,000 freed prisoners gathered around this monument to hold a first memorial ceremony. At this occasion, they swore the famous 'Oath of Buchenwald': "[...] The destruction of Nazism at its roots is our rallying cry. The creation of a new world of peace and liberty is our destination. This is what we owe to our murdered comrades and their relatives." I believe that this brief moment in history contained some profound and authentic meaning for the people who created it; some sense of determinedness and hope, for all their own recent experience of an excessively brutal lifeworld: an SS enforced community on the base of a merciless ideology of racial and social selection; hence a community in which hatred, stereotyping and ideological conflict became ever more existential not only in interaction with the SS, but also among the prisoners.

By taking the oath, the liberated prisoners (evidently) declared their radical opposition towards the system they had been ruled and tormented by for years. Since the notion of "peace and liberty" is entirely vague, the often quoted last two lines of the oath certainly do not outline any definite vision of the future.[8] They are a utopian vision, and utopias pre-eminently reflect what is wrong *in the present*, thereby making it discernible.[9] So in fact the survivors' positive statement about their "destination" mainly indicated how it was *not* supposed to be anymore: no war, no slavery, no exploitation, no repression. And this is exactly why this moment would have deserved a memorial, a constant reminder that this utopia has not been fulfilled: "Cognition has no other light than that which shines from redemption out upon the world,"[10] Adorno states, introducing another aporia, still worth being considered – I shall come back to it.

---

7 Short for: **K**onzentrations-**L**ager Buchenwald: KL was the contemporary abbreviation for concentration camp. 51,000 was the first estimation of the death toll, today it is approximated 56,000.
8 In the GDR, however, the oath was ideologically functionalized. There were slogans like: "In the GDR, the oath has been fulfilled!", or: "In the GDR, the legacy of the anti-fascists has become reality!".
9 Cf. a conversation between Ernst Bloch and Theodor W. Adorno on the paradox in utopian yearning: Etwas fehlt ... Über die Widersprüche der utopischen Sehnsucht. Ein Gespräch mit Th. W. Adorno und Ernst Bloch, in: R. Traub, H. Wieser (Ed.): Gespräche mit Ernst Bloch, Frankfurt/M. 1975, pp. 85-77.
10 Adorno (cf. 8), p. 283.

36,5 °C? – Anatomy of a memorial Plaque

However, instead of a memorial trying to grasp this momentum, there is the aforesaid metal plaque here today.[11] Quoting the mentioned historic epigraph "K.L.B", it then lists in the German language fifty 'national groups' in alphabetical order, from "Albanians" to "US Americans". "Stateless" are added to the end of the list, while "Jews", "Sinti" and "Romanies" are included in the alphabetical order. The plaque is constantly being heated to 36,5 °C human body temperature, so that one will always see people bowing down here, touching upon the surface, feeling for the contours of the engraved letters, thereby making other visitors curiously approach the plaque to follow their example. To tell the truth I find this haptic humanism rather kitschy, but I still like touching the plaque at times in order to warm up a bit, especially when it is cold and windy, as is often the case in Buchenwald.

I must have looked at this plaque already countless times, but again and again I feel uncertain about its inscription. At first glance, the list of 'nations' engraved in the plaque seems completely self-evident and easy to consume. Everyone of the estimated 250,000 inmates of Buchenwald appears accurately categorized according to his 'national belonging'. Furthermore the categories are put into a seemingly 'fair' alphabetical order: no one was forgotten here, not even the "Stateless". Moreover, heating the plaque to human body temperature suggests that apart from their national belongings, these people were all human beings. The alphabetical register implies that all are equally important, but suddenly the "Stateless" break the rule: they stand separately in the end of the list. Thereby a hefty dichotomy between people with and without a passport is being created, and suddenly the list discloses administrative connotations that reverberate rather eerily in a place like Buchenwald.

However, the plaque demonstrates inclusiveness towards "Jews", "Sinti" and "Roma". They are named as an extra set, but in the midst of "Canadians", "Yugoslavs", "Serbs", "Turks" or "Andorrans". Thus they are declared to be 'equally legitimate' national groups in a register that, however, in many ways represents the very same European ethno-nationalist carousel whose centrifugal forces have frequently expelled them. Hence, in this list they are ultimately being 'naturalized' in their being ousted by exclusive nationalisms, and allowed to form their own. Of course this is not implied here. In fact, the extra naming of "Jews", "Sinti" and "Roma" ostentatiously acknowledges a fact that had not been acknowledged for decades: their being persecuted in a specifically racist and eliminatory way. However, in this context this

---

11 The memorial, created by the German artist Horst Hoheisel, was inaugurated in 1995 on the occasion of the 50th anniversary of the camp's liberation as a "memorial to a memorial".

acknowledgement unfortunately results in an objectifying reproduction of Nazi categories, since in Buchenwald 'Jews' and 'gipsies' were defined according to National Socialist ideology – regardless of whether people defined themselves as a 'gipsy' or 'Jew' in cultural, religious, let alone in national terms.

But even if one agrees that the significance of National Socialist genocidal intentions are to be highlighted, then in turn all other categories in the list become completely unspecific. In fact, no one was in Buchenwald because of his nationality. Let alone "Germans", who are named as well. From a National Socialist perspective, people were hunted as political opponents, 'asocials', 'criminals', 'homosexuals', 'Soviet political commissars' etc. So if it is about the perpetrators' intentions, why not name these specific categories too? Whatever way one tries to make sense of this list, it does not really work out. If 'a list' is an adequate way of commemoration at all – which I am not sure about – then possibly to be consistent one should have reproduced the perpetrators' categories here, denouncing them as ideological concepts invented for the oppression and killing of human beings, regardless of which passports these people were carrying around (or not), or what they thought themselves they were.

Alternatively, one could have simply adapted the historical epigraph from the monument of April 1945: "K.L.B." and – since today's memorial is dedicated to all inmates of Buchenwald – the figure "250,000". From a pedagogical point of view, numbers are criticized as being 'abstract'. However, I assume a number would allow more space for imagination than a list of nations. Envisioning factories full of forced labourers, or a city of 250,000 inhabitants to me, however, seems far less abstract than trying to think of "Ukrainians" or "Egyptians". So what is this deliberate 'national' categorizing on the plaque about? I believe it aims at making people immediately *identify*. The way the plaque is conceptualized, I would automatically look for 'my' name in the list. If I read "French", and am French, I learn that there were people from 'my collective' imprisoned here, and that accordingly, I could have been victimized, too. Whether I myself am a racist or homophobic, does not matter in this moment.

Instead what matters here is some abstracted tribal sense of belonging, which in contemporary discourse is called 'collective identity'. Frequently, these 'collective identities' are transformed into particularist historical narratives, and then again these narratives are claimed to be 'collective memories' informing respective 'collective identities'. This way of thinking – which is by the way at the very root of phenomena like Buchenwald – is plainly reaffirmed here. And while the National Socialist regime and its victims remain historically defined for ever, national(ist) categories tend to change. Accordingly, the plaque is being updated at the moment:[12] seven more national categories have to be added, so for example the "Senegalese" will be separated off from their former colonial rulers. Afterwards, the plaque will again look innocently evident, as if it had never looked different before. And there will be another curious change: the "Stateless" will be complemented with "and other unknown prisoners." Consequently, all others are *known* to us because their *nationality* is written here?

Memorial to all inmates of Buchenwald concentration camp (Detail)
Cornelia Siebeck (2007)

Having Beer in Tel Aviv

"Do you consider me *a Palestinian*, or am I rather H. for you?", my friend H. suddenly asked me. We were sitting on the beach in Tel Aviv, having a beer together. What would have been a rather disconcerting question to me in another setting didn't irritate me at all after having lived in Israel/Palestine for some months already. There was no specific occasion for H.s question. He asked just like that, maybe to check whether I had already internalized the ethno-nationalist logic of the conflictive reality we were surrounded by, seemingly operating autonomously and hopelessly, sorting everyone into this and that category, thereby creating this and that consequence for his or her life. Truthfully, I responded that for me, he was unequivocally H. Of course I

---

12 March 2009; the new one is supposed to be installed in April 2009.

was aware he was 'Palestinian', as I had heard him calling himself a "Palestinian living in Israel". And I had learnt already that in a society that defines itself as 'Jewish' and at constant war with 'Palestinians', being 'Palestinian' is an objectified label that has an objective impact on one's everyday life.

Still, to me he was H., just as I envision myself as C., and not as 'a German', whether 'typically German' or 'different from other Germans'.

To many readers this may sound trivial, but it is absolutely not. By saying that H. is H. to me, I don't simply assert that we are all human beings, let's embrace each other. Facing the world as it is, this kind of naïve universalism would be nothing but self-betrayal. Even though being 'German' doesn't matter to me, I can fly back from Tel Aviv to Berlin with my German passport, living legitimately in a 'German' society, without anyone questioning it. H., on the other hand, carries an Israeli passport, has been living in Israel all his life, but still his mere presence there is constantly questioned. But nor could he simply decide to live in Germany, and even if he was 'permitted' to do so, he would remain a 'stranger' in the eyes of German mainstream society. So we are obviously not 'the same', and as a result I am not talking about happily dissolving objective differences into some glittering humanism.

Those differences have to be acknowledged as objective facts, however, in order to then figure out how they have come into being *historically* rather than essentializing them for identity politics – not even for sympathetic dentity politics. For this, I think, we will need a language different from the one that has actually created these differences: we must stop thinking and talking about political and historical realities in a way that implies the existence of fixed 'collective identities' determined by 'collective memories'. We must re-discover ourselves and others as human beings and political subjects, and resist perceiving ourselves and others as mere 'representatives' of some meta-historical body 'collectively' operating according to its own dynamics. The soothing truth is that history is being *made*. And whether in Germany, Israel or anywhere else, politics have always functioned along the lines of power, political and economical interests, and ideology. So we have to talk about our present and past in terms of power and ideology. And again: this certainly does not imply leaving behind historical realities and the objective differences they have created. On the contrary, in order to understand our present-day, it is crucial to examine them and take them into account.

But *what* we talk about should not determine *how* we talk about it. Hence in order to emancipate ourselves from what we are thinking and talking about, we have to find words and modes of expression that do not reproduce what we want to leave behind by analyzing it. "Cognition has no other light than that which shines from redemption out upon the world," says Adorno.[13] Hence, we have to consciously estrange ourselves from the world we live in to look at it from an utopian perspective (e.g. 'a new world of peace and liberty'). This seems to be the only way to release ourselves from this thick layer of determinism, essentialism and 'naturalness' that hitherto has informed our language and thinking. Whether talking about the past or about the present, we must stop adopting unchallenged labels and given categories, and instead begin questioning, exploring and analyzing. There is certainly nothing to loose.

So humanize the discourse, historicize the discourse, politicize the discourse!

Cornelia Siebeck, born 1975 in Munich, is a historian and publicist based in Berlin. During her work as a city guide on Jewish history and on German remembrance politics in Berlin urban planning as well as at several memorial institutions to the National Socialist past, she has collected broad experiences in every day German memory discourse. In 2004/5, she lived in Israel doing research on dissident Israeli-Palestinian memory initiatives. In 2006, she co-initiated the German-Israeli-Palestinian workshop AltNeuland – Third Generation Practice in Educational Work and Social Activism. Currently, she is working on her PhD on Buchenwald as a many-voiced memory site in past and present.

---

13 Adorno (cf. 8.)

When "History" turns from a Fact into a Narrative. Different Historical Perspectives in Israeli-Palestinian Encounters

DANNA BADER

Organized encounters between Jewish Israelis and Palestinians from the West Bank and Gaza Strip have been taking place since the 1980s. The aim of these initiatives is usually to bring about among the participants a better understanding regarding the Israeli-Palestinian conflict. Even though those encounters are varied, in this article I shall relate about a project, organized by a German NGO[1] groups usually consist of participants between the ages of 20 to 30. In this paper I shall discuss a critical thinking process which is experienced by Israeli Jewish participants in those encounters. Those meetings may increase the awareness of the Israeli Jewish participants not only of the reality as it is being experienced by "the other side of the conflict", but the encounters also make them explore and sometimes question their own society and themselves.

I started being involved in those meeting in the late 1990s when I was a 16-year-old, during the post Oslo period. After the outbreak of the second intifada, I felt that something had to be done in order to improve the situation. I joined an encounter organized by a friend of mine. Back then such projects were rather rare, however nowadays they are arranged by widely diverse organizations such as Reut Sadaka village, Nir School, the Peres Peace Center, Israeli political parties of all shades, and international NGOs such as ConAct (German). The encounter I participated in involved young adults; however in general all age groups are targeted by the various organisers.

---

[1] The name of the organization is not mentioned due to confidentiality.

During it I started realizing that there were still many things that I did not know regarding the current reality experienced by the Palestinians under the occupation regime as well as regarding the history of the place I was born and raised in. Afterwards, I myself started to facilitate and coordinate Israeli–Palestinian encounters in this initiative and in some others. I started doing so because I wanted to give people the same opportunity I had been given: understanding the reality I live in, dealing with questions that I have internalized and are part of the society through meeting directly with Palestinians.

One of the main issues dealt with in these meetings is the contrasting historical narratives of the two societies. These historical narratives are part of the daily reality of each one of us. The reality of the Palestinians, who still live under the Israeli occupation, and of the Israelis, changed dramatically in 1948. Back then, the Palestinians were turned into a refugee community and the Jewish Zionists obtained recognition for their own state.

In this paper I will discuss one aspect of those meetings; the new understanding that the Israeli Jewish participants usually experience regarding their concepts of history. This phenomenon of a new historical perception for the Israeli Jewish participants is a similar process to the one I went through. It is new understanding linked to their meeting directly with Palestinians. Hearing for the first time in my life things which were shocking for me such as the actual life experiences of the Palestinians under the occupation regime and the daily violence and restrictions which the Palestinians had to face opened me for a new understanding. Only through those direct meetings was I able to understand that there is more than one reality and more than one historical narrative.

By describing some experiences of Israeli Jewish women who attended a two-week long organised encounter which took place last summer in Germany, I want to demonstrate the complexity of this process. A few years ago I participated in two seminars organized by this project and later on I started to facilitate them. However, during this seminar, I was not facilitating but rather observing and interviewing the participants as part of my field research for my M.A. thesis at the Alice Solomon University of Applied Science in Berlin. The feelings and thoughts of the women who participated in this seminar are quoted here in order to demonstrate the processes they had gone through. Each woman had her own experience and went through her own process. However, for all of them hearing the daily stories of the Palestinians, realising that they were not aware of what "heir side"does in the occupied territories, understanding that they were not taught the full history is not an easy process. The history they had thought was a fact, in the course of the encounter turned into one narrative among many others.

Their new perceptions of the daily reality of the Israeli Palestinian conflict as well as about the historical narratives of the two nations and about history as a concept is a very unusual process within Israeli society. Apart from debates in leftwing Israeli forums belonging to organizations such as Achoti, Zochrot, The Mizrachi Democratic Rainbow or academic debates like the one between the "New Historians" questioning the Zionist monolithic narrative, there are hardly any critical spaces for people in their everyday lives.

Meeting with the other Side: Meeting with another Side of the Reality
The meeting with the other side of the conflict entails a confrontation with new information which raises many questions for the Israeli participants. For many of them the encounter is the first time in which they meet Palestinians from the West Bank and Gaza Strip as civilians. As most of the Israelis are doing their military service, those who met Palestinians before the meeting usually met them through their eyes as soldiers. In the actual meeting however, by listening to the experiences of the Palestinians, they realize Israeli occupation is experienced differently on the two sides of the wall. They understand that not only the Palestinians who 'have blood on their hands',[2] planning bus explosions or calling for the elimination of the Israeli State, are suffering from the occupation. While hearing how daily life is, they learn that all of the Palestinian civilians are being hurt every day by it.

A 25-year-old Israeli woman participated in the meeting:

"I am quite confused right now because I am in the middle of opening new things and discovering many more things about the other side. I am finding out that I really don't know anything about them and the stories they brought were really difficult so right now I am mostly observing and thinking."

Just as I did years ago in my first encounters, they realize what a checkpoint is for the Palestinians, what a closure is, a curfew, and what the Israeli soldiers represent for the other side. Soldiers that were seen by the Israelis as a symbol of Israeli Jewish morality are seen by the Palestinians as fighters, as occupiers, as those that directly hurt them and take away their basic human rights on a daily basis. Hearing the experiences of the Palestinians raises many questions and doubts for the Israeli participants. Those new thoughts are full of guilt feelings, since they realize that it's "their side", themselves, their own brothers and friends who are actually occupiers; that the society that is seen as frightening and full of evil by the Palestinian participants is actually their own society.

---

2 "People with blood on their hands" is a term which is used in Israel in order to describe Palestinians who killed or hurt Israelis.

A 22-year-old Israeli Jewish participant could not imagine her sister, who used to serve in checkpoints as one of the soldiers from the Palestinians stories:

"...my sister, she was in a checkpoint until today. I didn't know that the Palestinians really hate the guys there. But I know my sister wasn't like the soldiers in the stories we heard here. She always told me that they (The Palestinians) give food and cigarettes to the soldiers because the conditions of the soldiers are not so good in the checkpoints. She didn't want to be there. And she, I don't know, she has been treating them the way she should."

Their understanding that the knowledge they have is incomplete and lacking many facts that they did not know or perhaps did not want to know brings them to realize that they knew only parts of the current reality. So this exposure to the Palestinians' current reality also opens them up to another important process, in which Israeli history as it is told officially, previously perceived by them as a fact, reappears as a historical narrative amongst many others.

History as a Fact: The Israeli Jewish hegemonic historical Narrative
Entering the encounters, Israeli participants often perceive the historical narrative which they had internalized as Jews in Israel as a fact. Most of them internalized its hegemony as they had been taught it in schools, imbibed from their families and the Israeli media, and internalized as a part of Israeli Jewish society. It is permanently represented in textbooks and in national memorial days. I can hardly recall places where I was not exposed to the Israeli founding myth as a child.

Yet, the mainstream historical narrative is mainly driven by the experiences and perspectives of that section of the Jews which immigrated to Israel from European countries. Coming from an East European family with Zionist generations reaching back into the 19th century, I was integrated into this narrative without realizing the privilege I had. Many other narratives, like that of the Jews from the Arab countries, are not represented; not to mention the Palestinian narrative of the very region we all live in.

To make things clear, I would like to introduce this narrative, as it is usually presented by the Israeli Jewish participants in those encounters, in seven components[3]: first, the beginning of the Zionist movement which is explained by the participants as a movement that aimed to "bring back" Jews to the holy land of Israel. Second, the struggles of 1929 are described. In Israel they are called "the riots of 1929", and they are used in order to

---

3 Those were presented by the participants in the meeting in which I carried out my interviews for my thesis.

demonstrate that the Palestinians who lived in Palestine before 1948 were fundamentally hostile towards the peaceful Jewish residents. Third, the Holocaust is explained in order to emphasize that the Jews had to find another place to live in, a place of their own. Fourth, the decision of the United Nations to divide Palestine into a Jewish and a Palestinian state is mentioned. The "War of Independence", as it is called in the Israeli narrative, as well as the establishment of the State of Israel in 1948 is explained as a consequence of the disagreement of "the Arabs" with the UN partition plan. Fifth, after the establishment of the Israeli state, the main historical occasions which are being presented are the wars Israel was part of. Sixth, is the murder of the Israeli Prime Minister Yitzhak Rabin which symbolizes for them the repressiveness of the peace process. Last, the first and second intifada which are usually symbolized by bus explosions.

However, already for many Jewish participants this narrative actually does not fit. The historical narratives of the Mizrahi Jews (Israelis whose family emigrated to Israel from Asia and Africa) are often neglected in the mainstream historical narrative. As this short dialogue indicates, in the course of the encounters some Mizrahi participants often relate to their own history as individual stories, rather than "history":

A 27 years old Jewish woman from a Polish background:

"So why don't you tell the history of the Jewish who came from Arabic countries?"

A 22 years old Jewish woman from a Moroccan background:[4]

"Because I don't know the HISTORY, I know only my family story"

So Israelis find out that even in their own society there are variations of histories which the hegemonic Israeli narrative excludes. Often it is the first time for Israelis with European roots to hear experiences of Jews who immigrated to Israel from Arab countries. While meeting with the Palestinians, within the Israeli group there are discussions about how diverse the Israeli society is, and how little they actually know about it. Things that they had thought were clear to them suddenly do not seem that clear any more.

Confrontation with a different historical Perspective
The Israeli participants usually assume that the history of the Palestinians is just a branch of the Israeli's own narrative, and are therefore surprised to find

---

4   The dialog is taken from a discussion which took place in the Israeli group regarding their own historical narrative.

out that the Palestinians have their own history. I too before I met Palestinians did not know their perspectives, Palestinians were the "others", I knew only very little about their society and culture. While listening to the historical narrative of the Palestinians, the Israelis continue to realize that the history that they have been taught is actually only a part of the picture.

The historical narrative that the Palestinian participants present in front of the Jewish participants is usually assembled out of eight main elements[5]: First the Balfour Declaration which symbolizes the intention of the Jewish people and the Zionist movement to take their land. Second is 1948 – the 'Nakba' (the Palestinian catastrophe of 1948) – as a key point from which the Palestinians started their lives as refugees in their own country. Third, the foundation of the PLO (the Palestinian Liberation Organization) is mentioned as a symbol of the beginning of the organized resistance. Fourth, the occupation of 1967 is presented as the organized military rule of the Israeli army over the West Bank and Gaza. Fifth, the "Land Day" which symbols the evacuation of Palestinian lands by the Israeli state is mentioned. Sixth, the first Intifada is presented. It is described as resistance to the Israeli occupation. Seventh, they describe the building of the separation wall which separates the Palestinians who live in the West Bank and Gaza and heightens their inability to go and see the land from which they were deported in 1948. Last, the second intifada is mentioned. The second intifada is presented on the one hand as a resistance to the Israeli occupation, and on the other as another attack by the Israelis on the Palestinian people, started with the entering of Ariel Sharon to Al Aksa and continued with human rights violations.

Historical Narratives
During those encounters, many of the Israeli participants hear for the first time the term 'Nakba'. It is the first time for most of them to realize that there were Palestinians in 'Palestine' before the Jewish settlers came. Also it is the first time for them to realize that many Palestinians were expelled from their houses and that – in their eyes – 1948 is actually the beginning of the Palestinian catastrophe.

A 22 years old Israeli woman told me that when she heard the stories of the Palestinian participants regarding 1948, it was her first time to hear that they were expelled from their houses. She phoned her mother and tried to ask her what she can tell the Palestinians. Her mother replied that the Palestinians were actually telling the truth.

---

5   Those were presented by the participants in the meeting in which I carried out my interviews for my thesis.

"Now, I saw that they (the Jewish militias) had taken them (the Palestinians) with force from their houses, and I didn't know this point. I didn't know it. When I told this to my mother on the phone, I asked her: what excuse can I give when they said that the Jewish forces took them from their houses by force? What excuse can I give to them when they say this to me? She told me, 'We did force them'."

Hearing the Palestinian participants' historical perspective, the Israeli participants understand that the Palestinians are people that used to live in Palestine before it became the State of Israel. Through that acknowledgement, in the eyes of the Jewish participants the Palestinians turn from "enemies that just want to kill the Jews" into "refugees that are trying to survive". Moreover, they realize that the historical narrative that they were taught in school is not simply a fact, but rather one possible way to look at the past reality, and that their way hitherto to look at the past has a lot to do with legitimising the present.

Coming to terms with that is not easy since it raises a lot of anger among the participants against their own society and their own education. As a 30-year-old woman emphasized:

"...we were talking to the Palestinians and they were talking about the Nakba and their expulsion in 1948 and I am thinking to myself no one had ever, ever taught me this. And I have learned history from the first grade till I graduated, and none of the teachers, not even in the university..."

This new understanding is full of frustration. Many of them do not understand how come they did not know about it before. They start questioning the information which is transformed to them not only in the educational system but also in the Israeli media. As a 30year-old participant emphasized:

"... The media, once again, I think I have mainly seen during all years, now that I think about it, all the suicide bombers and all the pictures of people that died in the buses. It's something that affects me a lot..."

A new Understanding: History as a subjective Perspective
The difficult reality experienced in conflict situations usually leads the two sides to remove the other from the collective awareness. Once applied, a certain historical narrative turns into the negation of others. However, those encounters, most of them between the second and third generations after 1948, lead to a new understanding. The power of direct meetings lies in providing a safe place for the Israeli Jewish participants to meet the Palestinians and to hear their own and their families' experiences.

That new understanding creates profound implications for the Israeli Jewish participants as they start to question the information which is being transferred to them. Whereas the historical narrative taught in Israel is used to justify the military force that was and still is being used by the Israeli state towards the Palestinians, acknowledging the legitimacy of the Palestinians' historical narratives and the increased awareness about their daily life experiences raises major doubts among the Israeli participants regarding the basic justification for the necessity and implications of the conflict and of the occupation.

So far, in its nascent stages, the Palestinian-Israeli exchanges have not solved the conflict. The occupation, the war in Gaza shows increasingly worrying forms of inabilities to face the narrative of the other. Moreover, the encounters cannot bring about a direct improvement of the Palestinians daily life under the occupation.

However, I believe that one of the necessary stages in order to change the reality is to recognize the history of the place we all live in. It is a history with many narratives that seemingly excluding the other. But just as I, an Israeli Ashkenazi Jewess learned to accept the narrative of the Arab Jews or Palestinians, many others in the meetings did too. It is a first step to endure the ambivalences of our region and the entanglement of our identities with one-sided narratives.

Danna Bader, born 1981 in Tel Aviv, currently lives in Berlin. She is a facilitator of women, multicultural, and conflict groups. In Israel, she has been producing and coordinating the Israeli Activism Festival and worked in different organizations, among them the Van Leer Research Institute in Jerusalem. She wrote her thesis on Gender Relations in Asymmetric Conflict Zones, reflecting upon the life experiences of women on both sides of the Israeli-Palestinian conflict.

Addressing the Ruins*
(A Postcard)

HAGIT KEYSAR

In the summer of 2005, I was standing in a small second-hand bookshop in Jerusalem browsing through many old and used postcards which had been sorted in drawers with generic titles such as 'nature', 'art', 'cities' etc. In the 'nature' drawer I suddenly came across a photographed postcard showing people sun-bathing and camping on a beach. Behind them, on a hill, there was an archaeological site flooded with visitors. I glanced at the photograph for a moment and then turned it over to read the Hebrew inscription (written also in English and French) on its back: *Achziv – Ruins of an abandoned Arab village in Western Galilee, used to be an important town in biblical times. At the beach are remains of an ancient harbour. Today the place serves as a holiday village of the Mediterranean club.* Beside it there was a message, hand written with a blue ballpoint pen, by a woman who had sent this postcard to her family while spending her holiday during the summer of 1977 at the coastal city Nahariya.

A Ticket to Ride
Like most people I do not throw away postcards. It is a bit strange to think how emotional one can get with postcards despite it being a mass-produced image, made to fit and disseminate popular aesthetics and ideologies. A postcard is an amalgam of messages: some are inscribed – image and printed text; some are unpredictable – personal text added by the user; and some become transparent within the mechanism: stamps, address, producer, and photographer (in the many cases of photographed postcards). This variety of messages interwoven and experienced as part of everyday life makes visible

---

* Special thanks to Anat Rotem-Braun and Werner Braun who kindly met with me and generously granted permission to reprint the photograph.

the strong links between emotional life, social and political mechanisms and the ways by which these interlace and craft our lives and identities.

Achziv, photographer: Werner Braun

Foto 2 Hagit Keysar

Postcards become a relic by virtue of their materiality, use and collection; they store particular sentiments, moments, experiences which create a tension between the mental image of memory and the material photographic one, between the former's fleeting interiority and the latter's surfaced exteriority. It is raw material for memory and imagination to perform an experiment and create an experience in mind, stitching material and mental fragments into knowledge that is personal and idiosyncratic.

Second-hand bookshops and flea markets are unusual "archives" for endless "dead" postcards that were sent, read and thrown away or got lost, carrying personal fragments of other people's lives at home and away, handwritten in emotional yet concise text and phrased while conscious of its exposure. These archives are a celebration of contingencies, antithetical to official archives that were born to classify and generalize. Although they were originally reproduced commodities, each postcard found in such an archive is a unique object, a storage case for past memories awaiting to be picked from the unsorted piles and loaded back into the present. I bought the old and used postcard of Achziv for 10 shekels, which is more or less three times the value of a standard postcard. I assume that the additional sum is the cost of the "ride" I take travelling through someone else's intentions and memories.

This postcard is now part of my belongings and memories, and I am its contemporary end-user redefining the use for this "outdated" object. Thinking and writing through this postcard I am not only looking to uncover its hidden political messages, I am rather more curious to find traces of a "structure of feeling" which is long gone and forgotten and might tell me a bit more of this place and my place within it. Yet the ideological messages seem to be an essential part of every move I had to make while thinking and writing about it. I had to point to some and ignore others in order to allow a flow in writing my own personal observations. It is like what I have to do in order to live in such a place which is so deeply rooted in ideology which I resent and against which I resist; there are so many ways I could resist but just by having my life here I inevitably accept some of it.

Achziv, lit. Hebrew: Falsehood

This photograph is iconic and at the same time ordinary, not only by means of being a postcard rather by the moment which it captures. It seems casual, unorchestrated, it could have been easily exchanged with any other moment at that time and place. Standing with his back to the sea, the photographer took an antithetical marine portrait. Rather than looking at the great unknown of the open sea the photograph is showing a restricted human activity inside a national park and archaeological site. Whether consciously or not, the photographer was fulfilling a social mission by depicting, through an idyllic view, a fixed and condensed idea of the Jewish nation-state, and later also by selling it for reproduction and consumption.

The photograph was taken during the early 1970's. At that time Achziv's recent history was already washed from Israeli national consciousness, it was made an archaeological site connecting the traces of life, the ruins, to an ancient Hebrew history of 3,000 years ago. But only 30 years had passed since *Achziv* (Hebrew: Falsehood), or *Al-Zeeb* (Arabic: Trickster) as it was called before 1948, was inhabited by 2,000 Palestinian villagers. On May 14th, 1948, concurrently with the day of the founding of the State of Israel, Al-Zeeb was conquered by the Haganah.[1] The inhabitants fled and were forced to leave; later the village was destroyed in order to prevent them from coming back with the exception of a single house and the village's mosque that are now integrated in the so called archaeological exhibition.[2] Today the population of refugees originating from the village is estimated to be almost 14,000.

However, the inscription on the back of the postcard tells us nothing about the people who were forced to leave their homes. It says the village was "abandoned" but does not mention when or why. Rather it suggests or stages a contemporary view of the Jewish people in the "promised land", the abandoned and uninhabited land of Palestine, a "return" to the legitimate ancient homeland. The traces of pre-1948 Arab omnipresence in Israel are *there* and at the same time no longer there. The colloquial term "Arab House" invented for speaking about houses owned by Arabs before 1948 is a trivial example but expresses clearly this simultaneity. Although it simply says what-it-is, the meaning of the term is rather to typify a way of building and architecture while erasing its meanings relating to property and ownership, turning it into an idea that lacks the particularity and singularity of someone's home.

At places like Achziv, archaeology settled in place of the previous residents and turned their traces into "findings". One is invited to visit and see the remnants of the port, the grindstone and the houses and imagine ancient, biblical times. The ways of life, the agricultural and architectural knowledge which were passed through hundreds of years by the residents of Al-Zeeb, are made an object, a docile existence. A while after the 1948 war many Arab villages were kept as closed military zones preventing the previous residents from getting back to their lands and preparing it for resettlement by Jews.

---

1 Hebrew: "The Defense", a Jewish paramilitary organization that operated during the British Mandate of Palestine from 1920 to 1948. After the foundation of the state of Israel, the Haganah was transformed into the Israeli army.
2 Information extracted from an online archive dedicated to the memory of the 1948 destroyed villages: www. plestineremebered.com.

Achziv was not resettled[3] but was later made a part of a national park, a closed discourse zone, performing surveillance over the hollowed houses, and asserting dominance and presence over not only land but also the telling of the past. The gaze upon the empty houses is made scientific while being consciously neutralized from its connection to recent history of war and conflict. Like Baudrillard's simulacrum, the postcard pretends not to have what it in fact actually does have, that is, a political message.

Science allows scientists to make forecasts of future occurrences, observe natural processes and use their conclusions in order to anticipate future changes. The scientific, archaeological gaze enables the anticipation of a forthcoming collective memory and feelings in which places like Achziv become a "natural geography" for a holiday in Israel: "A myriad of options awaits visitors to the Achziv National Park [...]: a rocky embayed coast; lagoons; deep natural seawater pools; [...] the remnants of an ancient settlement; and large, grassy lawns. In short, Achziv offers everything required for an enjoyable and relaxing summer's day."[4]

A Command to remember

In today's terms buying the postcard is the equivalent of the instantaneous act of taking snapshots using a digital camera, and choosing the right frame out of many others kept in the memory-stick / postcard-stand. And so the woman who bought this postcard chooses a photograph that visually and literally depicts the feelings she would and should have in this place. She writes to her loved ones on its back, remarkably making the postcard's image and text an illustration to her own personal story. *I enjoy very much the wide sea, I swim and the waves carry me...* it seems like she is dubbing the women seen sunbathing in the foreground of the photograph. *...the rest of the arrangements are fine as well,* she writes, *and I hope to enjoy myself and relax...* A trace of distress is revealed within the words she is choosing, pointing at a barrier in the unknown future, but if any distress existed, she marks it with no more than a faint shadow, her story is in turn incorporated into the whole social mission the postcard stands for.

Her written words stand as a testimony – evidence to the authenticity of the postcard – that it is neither a battlefield nor is it pillage and destruction of civilian property; it is indeed a beautiful beach with ancient scenery, a *holiday village of the Mediterranean club,* made for a vacation. The body of her

---

3   In 1952 the Israeli sailor Eli Avivi established in Achziv a micronation, an enclave that was tolerated by the authorities. The enclave includes his house and a museum that he founded in the house of al-Zeeb's Mukhtar (Mahmoud Hasan Ataya), exhibiting artifacts and remnants of previous and ancient life in the area.

4   www.parks.org.il/ParksENG/company_card.php3?CNumber=335287#data, 13,2,09

message starts at the upper edge of the postcard and ends just where the printed, official text starts, it envelops the inscription and enshrines its authority. She signs her farewell on both sides of the printed text, protecting it from being covered by her words, fulfilling and delivering the command concealed in the historical description.

It is a command to remember, a *'Yizkor'*,[5] commemorating a celebrated military history of conquering and domination. As if by a transparent jigsaw ornamentation of everyday practices the command is implemented not only in the postcard's image and text but also in the stamps – miniature icons depicting a flock of sheep grazing on the southern slopes of Mount Hermon (Jabal el-Shaiykh) that were occupied during the 1967 war, and the former Arab city of Beit-She'an (Bisan) where the destruction of Arab houses was stopped in order to settle European immigrants there, many of them Holocaust-survivors. It randomly incarnates with the address to which it was sent – Etzel[6] Street 11/b in north-east Jerusalem – and as if to celebrate a decade of occupation, the date stamped on postcard marks exactly ten years since the first day of the Six-Day War, June 5, 1977.

There seems to be no one person nor institution, who can be pointed to as the author of this detailed network of correlating messages. Yet it originated with the photograph, taken by a specific person at that time and place. The photographer chose to fix this particular point of view that was later reproduced and distributed by Palphot a publicity company that had been producing postcards in Palestine since the 1930's and operates till this very day. For some reason, the name of the photographer was not credited on the postcard, which was only signed by its distributors, Palphot (Palestinian Photo). The company was founded by Tova and Yehuda Dorfzaun, a German couple who immigrated to Palestine in the early 1930's, and began with the production and marketing of postcards made from photographs the Dorfzauns themselves took, depicting Palestinian landscape as the Jewish homeland. The photograph of Achziv was not taken by the Dorfzauns, as I was told by Palphot, but instead by Werner Braun, considered to be one of a group of important photographers that documented life in Israel through the early years of the state. Braun, alongside other photographers, started to work with the Dorfzauns after the 1967 war, as the influx of tourists that followed it made

---

5 Literally: he will remember; term for a Jewish memorial service.
6 Etzel is an acronym for "National Military Organization in the Land of Israel", a militant Zionist underground organization that had split from the Haganah in 1931. It fought the British Mandate and was violently anti-Arab. It accounted for the bombing of the King David Hotel in Jerusalem in 1946 as well as the massacre in the Palestinian village Deir Yassin in April 1947.

the company's sales increase dramatically and contributed to Palphot when it emerged as one of Israel's leading publishers[7].

Braun was one of the central co-authors of this postcard yet his name was omitted from it. The act of omitting, whether done consciously or not, means disconnecting the postcard from the collections of events, people, and subjectivities that brought it into being. As the corporeal dimensions of its production become transparent, non-existent, the particular moment seen in the photograph is free-floating, ready to be recruited into an all-encompassing representation of this landscape and its meanings.

I met with Braun as I sought to reconstruct that particular moment in Achziv, when he had stood with his back to the sea looking at the people and the ruins. Was he sent by Palphot to create an idyllic view of Achziv, or did he take it while enjoying a vacation amongst the people he photographed? What did he see as he photographed the ruins of the village? Was there a conscious decision to document Israeli life in place of Palestinian villages? Were there other photographs he took at the same time? Why was this particular one chosen for a postcard?

A Tribute to the Real
I was sitting with Werner Braun and Anat Rotem in the living room of their house situated in Mevaseret Zion (lit. Hebrew, Messenger of Zion) on the outskirts of Jerusalem. Braun is 90-years-old, he smiles gently and talks but rarely. Rotem is 30 years younger, also a photographer, used to be his student and later became his wife. She was doing much of the talking, she seemed to remember everything for and of Braun whose memory was affected by age. I was not about to interview Braun about his life and work; I was interested instead in his personal memory of that time and place, captured in the photograph. We sat and looked at the postcard, Braun's eyes are covered by his falling eyelids, he looked at it closely, touching it with his fingers. No, he doesn't remember himself taking it.

Looking at the photograph, he was trying to reconstruct his own lost memory: *It was the contrast between the present and the past,* he told me, *a sight of life beside the ancient ruins...–* "This used to be a village, right?" I asked. *– No, not exactly the same place, the village was near by, very near but not exactly here.* "This is not the place that people used to live in?" *– No, what you see here are ancient ruins* – "From when?" – I asked, but neither knew and they suggested I should look it up. I was not sure whether Braun was remembering or forgetting. Did he imagine the ruins to be ancient traces already at the time in which he took the photograph, or was it his current reconfiguration of present mingled with past consciousness?

---

7   www.palphot.co.il

Braun was born in Nuremberg, Germany. He fled Germany in 1937 and arrived in Palestine in 1946. From 1947 till 2000 he photographed life in Israel through a vertical line: on the ground, under water and in a flight. The couple's house is densely decorated with art which includes a few of their own aerial photographs. I looked at one black and white aerial photograph that shows fragmented bodies of people floating, legs, heads, shoulders, knees, faces. *It was taken above the Dead Sea,* Rotem tells me: *Werner used to 'steal' moments while in the plane doing some other job that was ordered, and photograph instead what he wanted...* Braun explained to me that although most of his work was done in the field of reportage and journalism, he doesn't consider his photography as such. Until old age made it difficult for him to continue, taking photographs was his art, the force that moved his life, took him from one place to another, made him stay, move, or suddenly leave. He couldn't remember what brought him to Achziv, and whether it was his first time there or not. However, Rotem recalled, the photograph wasn't ordered from him, but was taken during a journey they made to the north.

Memory was turning liquid, it was flowing somewhere between Werner's withdrawn behaviour and Anat's plain directness, I was hoping to get some "concrete" information that was not affected by time, to learn about that visit to Achziv through Werner Braun's lens. We went up the stairs to the archive containing Braun's colour photography, there, under a divider named 'Achziv', I found maybe 15 or 20 photographs that seemed to have been taken on the same day, but I could not be sure. They were all variations of the "contrast between the present and the past" Braun had spoken about before. I could only guess why that particular photograph was chosen for a postcard: none of the others seemed to capture both a close portrait of individuals and at the same time a wide angle of the landscape and the crowded "archaeological" site. It was also the unusual angle from which Braun took this particular photograph, like the turning of one's head to observe the audience while watching a performance, Braun was looking from the sea towards the beach, he found his own getaway from the general public's view and positioned himself as an outsider. In turn, Palphot's omission of his name from the postcard seems to correlate in thematic terms with his composition.

Braun took the photograph which was later dubbed by Palphot with a caption and turned into a symbol, an icon. His personal memory did not animate the ruins that were to some extent dressed with a new interpretation of some undetermined ancient times. Braun could not dub his own photograph for me in any different way than what had been inscribed on the postcard and in Israeli consciousness, and it is hard to determine whether that was caused by old age or by pre-existing false perception.

Caught in Complicity

The past is irretrievable, it tells nothing leaving only traces; and emotional registers hardly leave even a trace. Yet this postcard is a trace. It is a perfect postcard idealising the sight of a place and fixing an everyday moment for a sensation of sweet nostalgia. Now I am delivering this postcard, with my personal message which is more of an inquiry, addressing my own relations and interactions with this history, looking at ways of recognizing, retelling and contesting it. When I bought it, it had already completed its "original" purpose; for unknown reasons it was thrown from its secured status as private property into the sea of consumerism and there it became a "floating" public resource. Free from possession by official state archives, newspapers, museums or other institutions, it can be curated in various ways into various stories and collections in tracing memory and identity in the present. I use this postcard as a lens through which I can zoom-in through someone else's memory and focus on contradictory threads in my Israeli identity and lived experience in this place. At the same time it allows me to observe from afar, finding an angle from which I can inquire how things work; like Braun, I am looking back at the audience, from the viewpoint of an outsider. The postcard's material affects, its uses over time and the exchanged emotional values seem to acquire a much deeper role in life than simply concealing or exposing certain mechanisms that produce identities and subjectivities. It is "raw material", no longer an object or a passive agent of global consumeris m, and it becomes a vessel that not only transfers but also transforms personal emotions.

I showed this postcard to friends of mine when we were studying together at a British University, removed from the material reality of the Occupation. They are from the West Bank, descendants of Palestinians dispossessed in 1948 from their villages which are now inside Israel. Looking together at the postcard deeply exposed an unmediated gap between us which had not been revealed as sharply through words. In the simplest sense, I wanted to share with them my thoughts in regard to this image but we could not really talk about it, especially not to share intellectual criticism. At a first glance it seemed like a resort in Greece or maybe Turkey, but once put in context by reading the caption, the opening of associations narrowed into a stare. Of course, we were all critically observing the photograph and the narrative inscribed on the back of the postcard, yet in our joint reading it evoked an emotional distress, almost horror, that was hard to reconcile with the photograph's irrevocable naivety. It revealed the corporeal imprints of the ongoing catastrophe it shadows. Suddenly there was not much to say, and I remember those few seconds of silence filling the air between us making me feel I am caught in complicity.

Hagit Keysar, born in Jerusalem 1976, currently lives in Jaffa. She studied Fine Arts in Jerusalem, during the last four years she has been politically active, employing art practices and academic research. She took part in developing a community art gallery in Jerusalem named Barbur (www.barbur.org) that promotes critical debate in issues relating to art, society and politics. She completed her MA in Visual Anthropology with a photo-essay documenting visual mechanisms in the enforcement of the Planning and Building Law in the Palestinian populated areas of East Jerusalem.

Wanderings

Alexander Brungs and David König

We are both a little over forty, both German citizens, both employed, and above all we both attended the same prestigious high school in Nuremberg. It was there that at some point an interest in art brought us together, although we neither attended the same classes nor studied in the same year. Since then, to the extent that the circumstances of our respective lives allow, we have regularly spent time together. In addition to what we share in common, there is of course also a great deal that separates us; for example, the distance between our homes and the fact that only one of us is married. In addition to these things, we are separated by our differing family backgrounds: David is the son of a Jew who survived Auschwitz, and Alexander, on the other hand, is the grandson of a Gestapo-man.

For a long time neither of us was aware of that fact, and more time would pass from its gradual realization to actual conversation about our family histories. As we discussed this, it became clear that these backgrounds which had so radically separated our forefathers were at once something that bound us together in a special way. Since then we have often travelled together through Germany and other European lands, visiting memorials and museums dedicated to the Holocaust and reign of terror, as well as monuments and other remains from the years 1933 to 1945.

Now and then we visit the greater, which is to say, the more internationally-significant, concentration-camp memorials, largely out of interest in the nature of such memorials and their participants (as in ourselves as visitors). Rarely do we find enlightening historical information at these places, and only seldom feel moved by something we discover about the past during a visit. One experiences this loss when one begins to comprehend the events a little more precisely, as opposed to allowing oneself to be led through the history in a didactic and ritual manner. Exactly what, however, have we actually lost? Did we gain anything from our school-trip to Dachau? Have we learnt anything since then? At any rate, many others seem to have learnt a great deal, and seem still to know it well today – so well that they always have apt judgments at hand regarding issues in the overlapping areas of history and morality.

However certain facts can render these insights uncertain. When one realizes, for example, that one's own father would not have survived without some active assistance from a criminal, the framework of simple certainties regarding what is good and what is bad can be shaken. It is relatively easy to regard the victim as victim and wrongdoer as wrongdoer; however, reduced to this, one remains within the limits only beyond which lie many of the genuinely meaningful questions that can be posed about human behaviour.

Because everyday life was completely and utterly steeped in the concentration-camp system and, consequently, the concentration-camp system became completely everyday, so was the plight of its prisoners also steeped in uncertainty and confusion. Accepted paradigms of order and relation suddenly no longer applied. Because a mass-murderer gave him a little more bread than expected, Wilhelm König said, "He saved my life". In this way he, unlike millions of others who were directly and unceremoniously killed, was on a whim left to hang onto his life's thread. Even a friendly smile from a capital-criminal came to be regarded as an act of humanity. On the one hand, an accused criminal by the name of Josef Klehr killed thousands of people through poison injections in the context of his work at the "Medical-services" division at Auschwitz, frequently on his own initiative and without orders. König called him "the greatest mass murderer of all time" likely because Klehr did not have them injected with cyanide *en masse* in a closed room, or direct the killings to be carried out in some otherwise depersonalized manner, but on the contrary killed each one of his victims face to face. On the other hand, the same Klehr provided higher bread rations and heated workspaces because he required William König for the composition of his correspondence.

The interactions are therefore much more complicated than a brief and schematic view of the historical situation would allow, and the relationships between the respective parties can in no way be understood simply as a victim-perpetrator relationship. In conversation and through the study of documents and books, we seek again and again to do justice to this complexity; however to some extent we also try to shake off the past of our fathers or grandfathers by rendering its details comprehensible. In solitary moments, when we are alone with our thoughts, we sense a weight whose burden can always be felt anew. For David's now-deceased father, suffering was a permanent condition, even though he never directly addressed it. The fact that he took early retirement at fifty-eight, only to lie on the couch rather than taking part in any kind of active life, was for David normal. Stories of life in the camps – from the humiliation and repression of the prisoners, to events such as the suicide of an aunt – were recounted incidentally, while the sportscast ran on television, in much the same way as König would occasionally exclaim, "Just let me die, already". The madness lay in these conversations' appearance of unspectacular "normality". The possibility of any therapy was never discussed, because officially and on the surface everything seemed to be in satisfactory condition. Hitler, Klehr and Mengele were not the names of people who operated on the so-called "dark side" of German history; they came up in conversation as though members of the family. Time and again, one talked about these figures, or sometimes more generally about "the Germans", but mostly as though they were a people who had lived far, far away, and whom one viewed as though a distant observer. In a certain sense, David's parents hated Germany; on the other hand, there were also people like Willy Brandt, who in Wilhelm König's view merited the highest respect.

For Alexander were some things, which in another environment would perhaps be striking, just as normal as the apathy of David's father was for him – things which only revealed their significance after many years. As a pre-schooler, he would hear his grandfather whistling or singing in the small bathroom of his grandparents' apartment. Only much later did he realize why and whence the Horst-Wessel song was so well known to him. Or the playing of the violinist Pinchas Zukermann on the Sunday concert on television: they could play music really well, those Jews, he said. To the question of who these "Jews" were, there had been no response. Better to change the subject.

Completely different backgrounds – and yet each produced in some respects similar patterns. These patterns manifest themselves in a special way, which we will call "small thinking". Some people come to it through the experience of humiliation and violence. Others enjoy the feeling of being subjects, like tiny limbs of a large body. It's about an unquestioned disposition, deeply rooted in family structures and grounded in a secret longing for unshakeable certainty, to see the world in a way that is reflected in such expressions as "that's just the way it was" or "what could anyone have done?". In both families, when the "war" is spoken of, the monstrosity of the situation is veiled and the actors rendered anonymous, even when incidents are discussed that were in no way due to the war. As with the order of threads in a knitting pattern, possible positions in society and options for action are fixed through this world-view. It's not so much that no one wishes to break free from these patterns, as that the possibility of such a breaking away does not even occur to thought.

David had always been artistically active. In a small studio space he had rented, he worked at times as intensely as though he were painting for his life. After graduation, however, he agreed with his family that he should learn "something reasonable", namely, a predictable profession which would offer security, and began an apprenticeship as a dental technician. This, even though it was clear to all that David would never actually lead the life of a dental technician. In an act of liberation only possible through physical separation, he left one day with his paintings for Salzburg, where he was accepted into a set-design class at the local art school.

As with countless grandparents everywhere who happily concern themselves with the development of their grandchildren, Alexander was regularly asked what – according to his wishes – he would someday make of himself. From Alexander's memory of his regular visits to the grandparents, one particular scene stands out, namely, when he came home from theatre-school one day as an adolescent to answer the question of what he wanted to be when he grew up. Having responded that he would like to be either a director or a writer, there was a short pause. Then the grandmother responded: "Oh, but you need skill for that! You'll have to become a bank clerk instead." Notable is not only how the people behind the counters were to some extent ennobled by their status as clerks, but above all that it in no way seemed relevant which of those things required of a writer the grandson could or could not do. Neither was the possibility of acquiring the relevant skills given any consideration. Today, Alexander's profession at least involves some writing.

Of course, our family backgrounds and respective starting and reference points in many – even essential – respects, remain unequal. It is one thing to be a descendant of the persecuted, another to be a descendant of the persecutor. Interaction with one's own parents has a different effect on one's character than confrontation with the history of one's grandparents – quite apart from the fact that, for David, grandparents were something entirely abstract, since he had never known his grandmothers and grandfathers. His father's mother was murdered in a gas wagon in the forest near Chelmno, his grandfather in the Lodz ghetto. His mother's parents died behind the Iron Curtain before he could make contact with them. Knowledge of the former existence of this once large family is something that he has only from stories; the family ties themselves are long gone.

Perhaps precisely because of these differences, however, we are especially interested in the eventual emergence of this "small-thinking". Against the background of a suffocating atmosphere of fear of the unknown and apathy towards the living, it was a form of liberation and an important manifestation of life-energy for us during high school to spend hours wandering through industrial areas, or to go to the Nuremberg Nazi party rally grounds at night, or to discuss art during nature excursions. When we added the past as a theme to our discussions, the idea began to germinate within us, that everything belongs to the heritage of one's ancestors.

It would be much too easy to say that they had left us only ruins, fear, and vacillation – certainly there was also the availability of a little money, which allowed us to grasp the good things in life. Nothing forced us to delve into the family histories, just as nothing is necessary about the journeys we undertake together. These trips, which are perhaps more like wanderings, are not least of all attempts to dissolve the clouds which obscure clear vision in our families.

We have often spent time at memorials, although we did not grieve there, nor did we think of any specific individual or particular event, at most going about with a greater stillness than usual. We drove more aimlessly than with conscious intent to these places, which, having been disguised as warehouses in their new function as memorials, are almost unrecognizable as the sites of industrialized barbarism that they once were. It is thus not at all the case that we feel ourselves able to imagine the dead in these places. Perhaps we hope for a levelling and orientation of previously aimless thoughts, or a recovery of intuitions residing in the dimness of the subconscious. Perhaps we observe the other visitors instead of paying attention to the site we are visiting. Perhaps we simply do what we would have done elsewhere at any rate. Indeed, it may be the latter. As in other places, we allow ourselves to be captivated by the peculiar nature of the site, to explore its properties and moods, to test its mass and weight. In contrast to other places, we seek always anew to understand why this place is like it is, how it came to be so, and whether that means anything. However, we do not reach the truth behind the memorial, and drive on having achieved no deeper understanding of the events which inspired it. Perhaps it is not the memorial at all that we visit, which is a mere placeholder for what once existed at these sites. We seek what *was* there, but find always unequal and inadequate substitutes. They form their own world, one which knows no beyond, neither past nor future.

Nevertheless, these memorials are landmarks on the mental maps of our travels which we seek to describe in our diaries. These accounts of journeys into the past have ultimately proven to be the most adequate means for recording our preoccupation with persons no longer amongst the living.

But what are we actually doing, in writing about the history of our fathers, or grandfathers? What is it to wish to understand the life of another, who died some years hence? Would it not have been better to try to understand him while he was still alive? Towards the end of his life, Mr. Geissler hinted to his grandson, Alexander, of his desire to tell the story of his life. However the then freshly-graduated student was far too caught up in his own, seemingly so important life, to make time for his grandfather.

When one wishes to understand the living, it is usually because one wants have an influence on their shared surroundings. However we have no such practical intent. Nor will it alter our character to uncover something about our ancestors that was long unknown *to us*, although it may have had great significance for *their* lives. Situations shared, as well as affections and antipathies felt, remain unchanged by any attempt to control memory; only the memory itself is falsified by such attempts to correct it. Unreflected memory, which has not yet been passed through the filter of valuation, remains awkward, incomplete, and morally open. Do we become more moral people simply through remembering more morally? Many seem to think that memory and thought must appear in a clear and unambiguous moral light, and have an accordingly strong will to remember only in an unambiguous manner, even at the expense of the facts. One seems, in retrospection, to wish to tap into the quintessence, in a sense the whole meaning, of one's being, whether in good or evil. Needless to say, one prefers to stand nearer to the side of the good. If, despite all efforts that is not possible, then appropriate outrage about events and "learning from the past" may permit a degree of self-orientation. Finally, as a last anchor, there is always the broader frame of value itself, which allows for a positioning within unambiguously demarcated fields.

However, these fields of good and evil, and people's orientation within them, based as it is on an imagined external perspective, reveal nothing more than our own wishes about how the world should be and especially about where we would like to find ourselves in it. Unfortunately, the world itself is not divided into moral fields, and therefore we gain no better understanding from our efforts to determine who stands on which field, who belongs to the good and who to the evil.

It depends much more on individual steps, on small movements along the path of life, which are the less visible the more generously we regard a person's life as a whole, and the more we remove the observer's perspective from the details of the action. For then we no longer perceive the individual steps from which a life is formed, and all appears straightforward, as in a film the projection of successive moments upon the screen creates the appearance of continuous motion.

One can quickly arrive at this sort of straightforward historical consciousness and moral self-certainty if one does not think from the perspective of one's small, personal view, but looks instead for the broad strokes. The broad strokes are, however, usually straight lines, which seldom if ever occur in the real world. We decided, therefore, to follow the curves. We wanted to look closely and try to grasp what had happened at the individual stations along the way. Who survived, who died, and who and where were the perpetrators? Not the abstract Jews and Nazis, but concrete participants. Where are the locations of the events, and how does it look there today?

The need for this was awakened in David when he was told the story of his father, and for Alexander a little later, when he became aware that something was not right in the dry stories told to him by his family members. His grandfather's membership in the SS had never been a secret – during his life he had regarded himself as having been part of an "elite squad" – although one certainly could not peddle this view openly. According to the official representation, he had participated in the war in various European countries as a member of the Waffen-SS. However, the places where he claimed to have served did not fit with the profile of any Waffen-SS unit. With the aid of documents from his estate, something completely different was able to be reconstructed. The youngest of five children of a "war-widow", Georg Geissler had, like his mother, become a supporter of National Socialism long before 1933. From the SS and auxiliary police he made his way to the Gestapo, where he was just about to be promoted from Lieutenant to Captain, when the Allied victory over Nazi Germany and the National Socialist system shattered his career plans.

Wilhelm König, on the other hand, had already begun to recount a very detailed history to his son David, when the latter was still relatively young. For a written version to be tackled, a reader on the other side end of the world was required – a professor of German studies in Japan. Might it have brought us something, if Wilhelm König had guided us on one of our journeys? We do not know, but it is not so important either. Perhaps if he had not so much explained – we had already heard much of what there was to know – as listened to us, watched us. When Alexander told Wilhelm König about his grandfather, it was a somewhat oppressive moment for the latter. However Mr. König had listened with the greatest attentiveness.

There is something liberating about the idea of Mr. König and Mr. Geissler undertaking a journey together, just as we sometimes travel together. One can imagine how well everything would have been planned, in contrast to our trips, how disciplined the schedule would have been, how intensively they would have devoted themselves to the details of the events and the technical developments of the last fifty years. They would probably not have spoken about personal matters at all. Perhaps they would have immediately hated each other, who knows? Nothing of the sort happened, however; they never knew each other, indeed, had not met even once. Only in our minds do they meet each other. At least in this world.

The questions, where one comes from, where life can go from there, and where one belongs, cannot be posed without looking into the past. These are important questions, and our journeys certainly have something to do with them. Ultimately, however, our own personal stories are so deeply intertwined with these questions that it can never be a simple matter of journeys into the past. They are much more (and how could it be otherwise?) journeys into the present: into the present of Germany, of Eastern and Northern Europe, as well as into their murderous histories. Sometimes on our paths we reach places where we feel as though we are gazing into the depths of the earth. From there too we drive on.

Alexander Brungs, born 1966 in Erlangen, is the grandson of a Gestapo-officer. He is a research fellow in philosophy at the universities of Zurich and Freiburg/Breisgau. Besides his job he writes about the impressions he gleans while travelling with his friend David König.

David König, born 1968 in Prague, is the son of an Auschwitz survivor. He is currently living in Berlin, working as an artist and set-designer. Besides his job he writes about the impressions he gleans while travelling with his friend Alexander Brungs.

"The Kashuas".
A Palestinian Family Memory in Israel

SAYED KASHUA

I used the format of a very well-known format called *Mazav Mishpachti* (family situation), published weekly in *Haaretz*, one of the main Israelis newspapers,* to transform it into a parody about myself as a *wannabe* Ashkenazi, a Jew with European origins, married to a Palestinian Arab woman... A Palestinian living in denial of his roots by adopting a typical Israeli discourse.

Twenty percent of the Israeli population are Palestinians, however, the only path available for them to be welcomed in this society seems to be assimilation beyond recognition. Hence, I invented a socialist grandfather who founded the village of *Kfar Tira* (translating the Arabic name of the village where my parents still live into Hebrew). For a proper Israeli identity I also need a grandmother who is a Holocaust survivor. And, of course, my bookshelf is full of Zionist writers (which is partially true). Consequently, I deny my wife's story about the Nakba: The flight and expulsion of about 700 000 Palestinians during and after the 1948-war, which in Israel is called the "War of Independence". The details about my wife's family, by the way, are true. At least the part about the destroyed village of her parents which was called Miske. After 1948 they became refugees and ended up living in the same village where I was born.

Regarding national memory, this column is a parody about two conditions, a Palestinian and a Zionist one. It is about the denial of the Palestinian story by most Israelis, their lack of respect for Palestinian memory. But above all it is about the impact of the Israeli national narrative on the Palestinians living in Israel. Hence, I present myself as a Zionist

---

*   The text first appeared in Haaretz, 20.11.2008; here it is slightly shortened.

Palestinian, married to a Palestinian refugee, living in the Jewish part of Israel's contested capital, Jerusalem...

The Kashuas

The cast: Sayed (33), his wife (33), their daughter (8) and son (3)

The house:
A seven-story, 28-unit apartment building. There is an elevator but they don't use it.
Sayed: It gets stuck sometimes.
His wife: He's just claustrophobic.
On the front door is a square sign decorated with a floral design: "Home of the Kashtan family."
Sayed: That's the original family name.
His wife: He's living in denial.

Denial:
Sayed: There is no such thing as a 'Palestinian people'.

Real estate history:
The wife comes from a village that was destroyed in 1947. Its residents were expelled and her family members scattered; many arrived in the village of Tira as refugees, others found refuge in the cities of the West Bank, Jordan and Denmark. Before then, the family had a lot of fertile land, orange groves, wheat fields, cattle, goats and sheep; after the expulsion they had nothing left.
The wife: We lost everything because of Zionism.

Zionism:
Sayed: I don't buy her whole story about her village. They weren't expelled, they fled. And besides, who was it that didn't agree to the Partition Plan? They forget to ask that. And I really don't want to get into 2000 years of history right now - It's not a topic I want to discuss with the kids in the living room.

The living room:
Two brown leatherette couches; in the summer they get heat burn sitting on them and cold burn in the winter ("Now we're sorry we bought them"). A rectangular white table and a matching buffet from ID Design.
Sayed: Thieves and sons of thieves.
His wife: The same quality as IKEA at double the price, and all because Sayed is incapable of turning a screw.

Turning a screw:
In the bedroom. Once a month on average.
His wife: Lately, not as often.
Sayed: Because of the financial situation.

The financial situation:
Excellent.

Sayed's bio (his version):
His grandfather was born in Pereyaslav in Ukraine. His father, who was a socialist and an activist in the youth movement in Odessa, did *aliyah*[1] in the 1920s and was one of the founders of *Kfar Tira*. In 1943, his mother (born in Krakow) did *aliyah* after a brief stay in Cyprus. "A very tough story." His father, an activist like the grandfather, was there to greet the *ma'apilim* (illegal immigrants to Palestine before and after World War II), and took his future wife with him to Tira.

Tira:
The idealism is dead. Nothing is like it was during his childhood.

Childhood:
Okay, overall. Even though it wasn't always comfortable for a half-Polish boy to grow up in Tira ("Coping was very hard for me").

Coping:
Alcohol.

The wife's bio:
Like everyone at the time, she too, was born in Tira. Tira Elementary School, Tira Middle School, Tira High School. Then three years earning a bachelor's degree, and two more for a master's degree. Now, at least three more years for another degree.

Sayed's education:
Like his wife's except that after high school he served in the *Nahal*[2] ("parachuted"). Oh, and there's no degree ("I was very busy at university").
His wife: He slept most of the time.

---

1 *Aliyah*, lit. Ascent, is the Hebrew term for Jewish immigration to Israel.
2 An elite unit of the Israeli Army.

The meeting:
Sayed had just returned to the dorms on Mount Scopus[3], drunk. "I actually remember it. I got back around eight, totally sloshed." His wife was just on her way out for her first class. She had long hair that fluttered in the breeze, and a leatherette bag slung over her shoulder; Sayed fell in love immediately. She didn't think anything of him, though noticed him when he collapsed right in front of the entrance to the dorms. His wife says that he had a very bad reputation as a lazy do-nothing who was always drunk. No one paid him any attention; she and her friends disdained students like him. But everything changed when he started sending her letters.

Letters:
His wife: I just felt really sorry for him. Every day, I got three or four letters that contained just one sentence - 'If you don't go out with me, I'll kill myself'.

Routine:
The wife gets up first, at six. She makes herself an instant coffee and drinks it while preparing breakfast for the children, and reads the newspaper while making sandwiches for the kids to take to school. When everything is ready, she goes into the bathroom. Then, when she's all ready, at around quarter to seven, she wakes up the children and gets them ready for school. At seven-thirty, she drives them there. Sayed is still sleeping ("I'm never up at that hour").

School:
Mixed. With Arabs who want their kids to grow up without an accent and leftists who are using their kids to ease their conscience. The kids really like it there; the girl is in third grade ("It's fun") and the boy is in pre-pre-school. The girl already speaks fluent Hebrew and this week the boy said his first full sentence in Hebrew: "Don't scatter the Lego all around, Ahmed."

Rest of the day:
The wife finishes work at three, and rushes to school to pick up the kids. By four, they're back home. Their mother plunks them in front of the television while she finishes making them something to eat. Then they do homework. Twice a week, she takes them to after-school activities. They come home and shower and then by seven or eight, if all goes well and the boy's pacifier can be found, the kids are asleep.

---

3   The Hebrew University of Jerusalem is located on Mount Scopus.

Sayed's schedule:
He doesn't have a regular schedule. He says he's an artist and refuses to have anyone dictate his work time. But he works hard ("I bust my butt").
His wife: I don't know about that. Basically, he sleeps just about all the time. On Tuesdays, he gets up, tosses off a column in half an hour and goes back to sleep.

Sleeping:
Sayed: "Sleep gives me a lot of inspiration. In fact, all of my thinking processes and work happen during sleep. I sleep, therefore I am."

Livelihood:
Sayed hastens to answer: It's all on me.
His wife: Unfortunately, he's right. There are elements that encourage his behavior and are ready to pay him for his actions and his books.

Books:
The wife: Ghassan Kanafani, Mahmoud Darwish, Emile Habibi, Emile Toma, Jibrin Ibrahim, Gibran Khalil Gibran, Salim Barakat and so on[4] ...
Sayed: The Bible, Bialik, Alterman, A. D. Gordon, Ahad Ha'am, Jabotinsky, Haim Gouri, Ben-Gurion, Jacob Perry and so on ... [5]

Happiness quotient (scale of 1-10):
Wife: 3 ("I still enjoy school, at least");
Sayed: 9 ("I need new pillows");
Girl: 6 ("I just found out my parents are Arabs");
Boy: 5 ("He only knows how to count to 5 and he got a soccer ball as a present two days ago").

Sayed Kashua, born 1975 in Tira, lives with his wife and two kids in a Jewish neighbourhood in Jerusalem. He writes satirical columns mainly in the weekly magazine of the newspaper Haaretz, addressing the situation of Arabs in Israel. Furthermore, he has published two novels in Hebrew that have been translated in several languages: Dancing Arabs (2002) and Let it be Morning (2004).

---

4   All names of famous Palestinian writers.
5   All famous Zionist writers.

No more Fascism – No more War! East German Reflections on Political Remembrance in Unified Germany

PAUL GRASSE

No more Fascism!
Born in 1975 in East Berlin, then capital of the former German Democratic Republic (GDR), I was named after my great-grandfather Paul Grasse. A steelworker born in 1883, he had fought and got wounded in the first World War, and – probably also because of this experience – joined the newly founded *Kommunistische Partei Deutschlands* (KPD) afterwards, after having been a social democrat for many years. After the National Socialists had come to power in 1933, he emigrated to France in order to continue organizing anti-fascist activities there. After he was arrested in 1943, he was imprisoned in Buchenwald concentration camp. In April 19, 1945, roughly one week after their liberation, 21.000 freed prisoners, among them him, held a memorial ceremony for the dead and took the famous "Oath of Buchenwald": "… The destruction of Nazism at its roots is our rallying cry. The creation of a new world of peace and liberty is our destination. This is what we owe to our murdered comrades and their relatives."

Paul Grasse would only survive for one more year, but his anti-fascist legacy has remained vivid in my family until today. He came to be somewhat of our family hero, even though no one alive today ever met him. I only got to know his widow, my great grandmother who lived with us until her death at the age of 99. But she would never talk much about him. However, my mother confronted us with the German Nazi past and the Holocaust quite early. She took us to see the remnants of concentration camps. I still vividly remember the documentary film shown at Sachsenhausen, a concentration camps near Berlin. Even as a child, I understood that the pictures I saw were not fiction. Confronted with black-and-white images of huge shoe piles, of heaps of human hair, of containers filled with the spectacles that had been worn by murdered people, I was deeply shocked and moved by how human beings were used as just another "resource". First they were worked to death, or killed, and before they were cremated, the SS took everything from them that could still be "useful". Because of such experiences and through discussions in my family, a strong consciousness of his struggle and suffering for his ideals as well as the decisive rejection of fascism became an integral part of my political consciousness very early on.

This family background is of course not typically German. But growing up in the GDR, we were also officially socialised in a strongly anti-fascist manner also in school. Demarcating itself from the other German state, the GDR claimed to be the new and per definition anti-Fascist German state, and to have fulfilled the "Oath of Buchenwald". Accordingly, we were taught the GDR's self-conception as being the "good" Germany – rooted exclusively in the leftist, revolutionary and progressive tendencies of German history – also in school. Hence, a visit to one of the big concentration camp memorials of the GDR[1] was an obligatory part of the curriculum. In what was shown to us there at the age of 13, all the horrors millions of people went through in the 1930s/1940s became graspable for me. But I remember even more vividly the conversations with veterans of anti-fascist resistance who were invited to our school on a regular basis to discuss with the students. Their stories left a deep impression on me. So one could say that in my case, my family background and the anti-fascist agenda of the state partly overlapped: I learnt to decipher "No more Fascism – No more war", a slogan that was omnipresent in our education, alongside studying the alphabet. For me, all this was not just something I had to learn in school, but was closely connected to the real figure of my grand-grandfather.

No more War!
I enthusiastically participated in the frequent solidarity campaigns that were run at school, be it for Cuba or Nicaragua. A call for eyeglasses for the Sandinistas got me turning the locker of my parents upside down. However, there were other political battles that I refused to take part in: in the GDR one had paramilitary manoeuvres at school – from fifth grade on we were throwing fake hand grenades instead of balls. I felt that obviously this contradicted the idea of "No more War!", so I insisted on throwing an

---

1   As opposed to West Germany, the GDR government installed memorial sites in the three big former concentration camps Sachsenhausen, Buchenwald and Ravensbrück already in the late 1950s and early 1960s. In Germany, the first memorial was installed in Dachau in the middle of the 1960s, however, it took until the 1980s until public remembrance of the Nazi period became something "normal".

alternative block of steel, which I had made for me. Anti-militarism had also been another crucial issue in my education at home. My mother was a rather critical citizen of the GDR already since the end of the 1960s: confronted with the brutal suppression of the Prague Spring in 1968, like many other intellectuals in the Eastern Block she had lost all hope that a "socialism with a human face" could ever be brought about in the prevailing framework of the Warsaw Pact.

In the early 1980s, when I started to consciously take notice of what was happening around me, my mother was integrated in a dissident group meeting under the umbrella of the protestant church, one of the so called "peace circles" that had by then evolved all over the GDR and its capital East Berlin. In these circles, discussions could take place on subjects which were not necessarily part of mainstream public consciousness, let alone the strictly regulated and censored public discourse. We criticized the stationing of new nuclear missiles in both parts of Germany, dealt with the grave ecological problems in the GDR, and, of course, with all kinds of human rights issues in the GDR. Thereby, solidarity with the oppressed and anti-racism emerged as living issues, complemented by strict pacifism and non-violence in all political actions. My mother and most of the other dissidents understood themselves as leftists or even Marxists, so partly this can be interpreted as a genuine socialist opposition against a ruling political elite that on ly claimed to be "socialist".

Maybe this combative yet antimilitarist ethos that I grew up with has informed my understanding of remembrance: remembrance is not only something to be *preserved* in museums and sermons on humanism or non-committal responsibility: instead it should be practically turned into an active and consistent, political assignment and struggle in the present.

Impressions of Israel and Palestine

By the time I had turned 14, the GDR had become history. Yet I kept my ideals and five years later became a conscientious objector, also declining to do alternative service. I was always politically engaged as a youngster, but not specifically in the Israeli-Palestinian conflict. Back in the early 1990s, when everyone on the left was sporting their *keffiye*[2] on all occasions, I didn't even have one. I decided not to wear the Palestinian national scarf because I did not have the slightest idea of what the conflict was about. Later, I was told that I was not the only one without a clue – the *keffiye* had also at this time become merely fashionable, without always displaying a clear message relating to

---

2   The *keffieh* ist the well known Arab headdress, that meanwhile has become a symbol of solidarity with the Palestinians. In Germany, it is also called *Palituch* (abbr. 'Palestinian scarf'), sometimes even *Arafattuch* (Arafat scarf), which does not always mean that people wearing it know anything about Palestine or Arafat.

Israel/Palestine. The people I knew then who had been to the region left the impression with me that there was no way of going there without becoming either racist against Arabs or anti-Semitic against everything Jewish. Those who had witnessed the Palestinian situation blamed it on "the Jews" as such. Those who had been to the Kibbutzim tended to see a terrorist in every Arab.

But in the late 1990s, my thinking changed. I became aware that to me as a political person it was no longer possible to engage myself against only some injustices, and refrain from touching others, only because of the strange tilt of the often irrational and guilt-ridden German debate on Israel/Palestine. In Germany, at the time I committed myself to the struggle against nationalism, fascism and social injustice. Now I developed a rather internationalist approach, based on the assumption that the structures of injustice and oppression are global, and that global and local structures are closely connected. Studying the history of the Israeli-Palestinian conflict thoroughly, I came to the conclusion that the Israeli-Palestinian conflict is – very similar to classic colonialism – a conflict about usurpation of land, and racism against the oppressed articulating itself in nationalist terms. And while nationalist oppression may justify a national liberation struggle on the other hand, nationalism not arising as a reaction to oppression is very likely to turn into chauvinism. In my analysis, this balance or non-balance is very visible in Palestine and Israel.

When I went to Israel for the first time, I visited my then girlfriend who was working in a kibbutz at the time. Living in mainstream Jewish society and with a rather limited scope, I had not become aware of the deep social rifts within the Israeli society, nor of the realities of occupation. I noticed the militarization of Israeli society, all those young soldiers with their guns in public, and also the strongly militarist ethos prevailing in mainstream Israeli society. But I had not seen the targets of this militarization until I went there at a later date.

That second time was in 2001 in the middle of my studies of political science. I came back to take part in a three-week project concerning minority rights in Israel as evidenced in the city of Haifa. The project was supported by the Heinrich Böll Foundation of the German party *Die Grünen* (Green party). It focussed on the violations of human rights in Israel: Arab citizens of Israel are discriminated against by more than 2,000 special laws, including marriage regulations or building permits, illegalized villages and house destructions. After coming back, I focussed on international politics and the Middle East in my further studies. I soon realized that it does not make much sense to isolate the Israeli-Palestinian-Conflict from what is going on in the rest of the region and the world. One example is the refugee-problem which is drawing all neighbours of Palestine into the conflict; another the Arab dictators who in the past always voiced their support for the Palestinians but who at the same time cut deals with Israel moving not one finger to support the besieged Palestinians. Moreover, I started studying Arabic. I planned to study in the region for a trimester in 2003/4. Birzeit, set in the Palestinian West Bank north of Ramallah was my university of choice. Bir Zeit is the oldest and best known university in Palestine and offers a special program for foreign students called 'Palestine and Arabic Studies'.

During my stay in Bir Zeit, I lived in the village and shared a house with four young guys from Gaza who also went to the university. I got to know well the daily routines of a life under occupation, even though as a European I was extremely privileged as soon as I pulled out my passport. The people I lived with, however, were virtually without any rights. They might have their house raided by the IDF and be sent back to Gaza any minute, something which actually happened in another house in the village. Even though it was fairly quiet while I was there, one could permanently sense the tension among the people, their fear – and their anger. Most of my fellow students had to live within a radius of two or three miles from the university, because there were checkpoints everywhere. I saw the Israeli army routinely take cars from Palestinians to then drive through the village and arrest people without being recognised as soldiers before. We had curfews every week. We also had power failures and broken water pipes all the time.

Hence I learned what it is like to sit in an unlit house, hungry, without water for drinking or washing, not being allowed to go out. The young men I lived with had not seen their families for years. When my room-mates father died, whom he had not seen for five years, he could not get a permit to go to Gaza even to attend his funeral. His family had been living in a refugee camp for three generations. When he was a child, they had played with the sewage. Quite a few of them had suffered from malnutrition: When they were kids there were periods with nothing to eat except for tomatoes and onions. So even in calm periods the effects of occupation were quite visible, and they left a deep impression on me: This is what war is like. Even though it is most of the time only "occupation", or rather a so called "low intensity war", it seriously degrades the quality of life of an entire population.

"No more Auschwitz" –
Unified Germany's discourse of political remembrance
The slogan I grew up with in the GDR was "No more fascism, no more war!". The same system, however, that taught us this slogan, betrayed it in practice: in school we were also told that "peace had to be armed", particularly since in "the West" fascism was allegedly "preparing its comeback" and hence we had to be ready to defend ourselves, which consequently justified "our" militarization. But that the actual meaning of the slogan "No more fascism, no more war" has been somewhat blurred in the GDR need not necessarily imply

that there is something wrong with the slogan itself. Moreover, I am sure that my great-grandfather Paul Grasse would have believed in this genuinely anti-fascist and anti-militarist command as much as I still believe in it today.

In unified Germany, however, the paradigm of "No more war!" has been inconspicuously skipped. Instead, the motto of the day is a mere "No more Auschwitz!" – as if "Auschwitz" could be separated from war and fascism. In any case, it has become possible to run a war in the name of the Holocaust. In 1999, Joschka Fischer, then foreign minister and head of *Die Grünen* – which had originally been strictly pacifist – justified a German involvement in the war in ex-Yugoslavia claiming that there "another Auschwitz" had to be prevented. So whereas before, "Never again!" had actually been the ultimate foundation for German pacifism, suddenly it turned into a legitimation for war. Since this first deployment of the German *Bundeswehr* abroad, German involvement in world-wide military operations has become completely normal – and at least this is how the discourse goes – these wars are never the result of power interests or economic motives, but always led by Germany's "historic responsibility" and the resulting commitment to "human rights".

And what about Palestine? A highly symbolic, all-party resolution against anti-Semitism[3] in the German parliament on the occasion of the 70th anniversary of the *"Reichskristallnacht"* in November 2008 states that "solidarity with Israel is an irrevocable part of Germany's state policy". Even though something like an – albeit nondescript – "permissible criticism of Israeli politics" is mentioned as well, the necessity to fight anti-Semitism is normatively entangled with an obligation to show solidarity with a somewhat unspecified Israel. In reverse, this implies that those who do *not* show this solidarity are highly likely to be defined as anti-Semitic. At the same time, it remains absolutely unclear what "Israel" is supposed to signify in this context: The Israeli state? The Israeli government and its politics? The people living there? To feel solidarity with the latter, however, does not necessarily mean to support the Israeli status quo.

Moreover, in the resolution, and against the normative backdrop of the *"Reichskristallnacht"* 70 years ago, anti-Semitism is simplistically paralleled to Anti-Zionism (and "Anti-Americanism"). The resolution refers back to the Iranian president's alleged call to "eliminate Israel from the map"[4] and

---

3 "Den Kampf gegen Antisemitismus verstärken, jüdisches Leben in Deutschland weiter fördern" [Strengthening the fight against anti-semitism, continuing to foster Jewish life in Germany] – for the text of the resolution (in German) see: http://dip21.bundestag.de/dip21/btd/16/107/1610775.pdf, 29.4.09.

4 In the meantime it has been proven that this was a wrong – and propagandistic – translation of Ahmadinejad's speak, see Jonathan Steele: If Iran is ready to talk, the US must do so unconditionally, in: The Guardian, 2.6.2006; Katajun Amirpur: Der Schlüsselsatz, in: Süddeutsche Zeitung, 26.3.2008.

defines "Arabic and Islamic Anti-Semitism" as a "global threat". Hence it claims, "that anyone taking part in rallies in which Israeli flags are torched or anti-Semitic slogans are shouted, cannot be a partner in the struggle against anti-Semitism. To show solidarity with terrorist or anti-Semitic groups such as Hezbollah and Hamas is going way past any admissible criticism of Israeli politics." Since it is hardly possible to avoid such phenomena when taking part in a demonstration against Israeli politics in Germany,[5] the resolution puts a taboo on practically *any* participation in public manifestations against the Israeli occupation regime.

However, the main question actually is: what does the "Reichskristallnacht" of 1938, in which fanaticized Germans attacked their fellow citizens and their property, have to do with present conflict constellations in the Middle East, that are also being reflected in present demonstrations against Israeli politics? Today's anti-Zionism and anti-Semitism in the Arab world originate in real political conflicts, while the "Reichskristallnacht" and the Holocaust have their historical roots in nothing but racial fanaticism. By comparing German eliminatory anti-Semitism with present-day resistance against Israeli politics in the Middle East – which sometimes unfortunately incorporates European racist anti-Semitic patterns – the German resolution in fact belittles the Holocaust:[6] "Those who still cannot differentiate between Jewry, Zionism and Israel, hence between anti-Semitism, Anti-Zionism and criticizing Israel will inevitably mix up what has to be kept apart."[7]

Before this all-party resolution passed through the German parliament, a remarkable political constellation had evolved. The Christian Democrat (CDU) members of parliament (MPs) suddenly refused to adopt the resolution together with the party *Die Linke* (The Left), which partly originates in the ruling "socialist unity" party, the SED, of the GDR.[8] Claiming that the official policy of the GDR had been genuinely anti-Semitic and anti-Israeli, the CDU MPs concluded there could not be a common base with the successor party to the SED in order to adopt a resolution against anti-Semitism. They even unsuccessfully tried to add a paragraph to the resolution, saying that anti-Semitism and anti-Zionism in the GDR had been part of the ruling discourse. This, of course, was meant to once more delegitimize *Die Linke* in the German political arena in a Cold War manner, which is, however, a typical

---

5   However, usually on those demonstrations the participants are asked to refrain from such actions.
6   For a similar analysis see also: Moshe Zuckermann: Verdinglichte Sühne [Reified Atonement], in: Junge Welt, 29.11.2008.
7   Ibd.
8   *Die Linke* originates in the former West German party WASG – consisting of trade union activists and former Social Democrats – and the Party for Democratic Socialism (PDS), which evolved from the former ruling state socialist party, the SED, in the GDR.

phenomenon in right-wing political discourse of the unified Germany i.e. equating the GDR with the Third Reich. In the end, *Die Linke* and the Christian Democrats passed the same resolution against anti-Semitism, albeit separately from each other. Eleven members of the fraction *Die Linke* abstained from voting, claiming that the resolution was implicitly directed against any leftist discourse and the anti-war movement. Predictably, they were immediately accused by the right and by the mainstream media of not sharing the consensus that fighting anti-Semitism in Germany was a political duty.

In the context of the resolution against anti-Semitism, not only any political opposition towards Israeli politics has been morally discredited, but the political right has also massively abused the issue in order to exclude the party *Die Linke* as well as a whole political tradition from the fight against anti-Semitism. What was even worse is that they implicitly equated the GDR with Germany during the National Socialist era by saying that anti-Semitism was a crucial element of the GDR's political discourse. The right-wing's propaganda message is not very subtle: anti-Semitism was an ideology that had been adopted by the radical left as well as by the radical right, hence both were equally dangerous even today. Most of the politicians enforcing that exclusion of the left from the political discourse on anti-Semitism even stand in a direct tradition to those who profited from military aggression and genocide. They or their ancestors did not fight against fascism unlike my great grandfather, the communist.

No more Fascism, no more War!
Historically – and as opposed to nationalist and rightist political ideologies of the 19th and early 20th century – in leftist socialist ideology and tradition, anti-Semitism was not an intrinsic element. If at all, one can accuse the left of having adopted mainstream, anti-Semitic stereotypes in their own anti-capitalist and anti-Zionist discourses; and for sure in hindsight one has to acknowledge that at the time of National Socialism they underestimated the murderous dynamics of anti-Semitism – like most contemporaries. Despite that, not only did my great-grandfather fight against fascism, but so did many other communists, trade unionists, socialists and social democrats. This struggle against fascism included fighting against the oppression of the political opposition, against racism, anti-Semitism and the persecution of the Jews – and against the looming Second World War. A great many of them were killed in this struggle, others had to go through Nazi prisons and concentration camps, and not all of them survived. The lesson that these survivors had drawn from their experience and wanted to tell the world was clear: "No more fascism, no more war!"

In unified Germany, the anti-fascism of the GDR – that also drew on this slogan – has often been called "prescribed" anti-fascism. Of course the official state anti-fascism did often result in empty sermons and rituals. But we also met former anti-fascist resistance fighters and listened to their very real stories. And last but not least, my great-grandfather left a legacy to our family that is still valid for me today. In the meantime, "No more Auschwitz" can obviously mean anything ranging all the way from ousting the political left, or supporting Israel in its politics whatever it actually does to maybe as the next step launching a war against Iran. Nevertheless the legacy of my grandfather seems quite explicit and unambiguous to me: "No more fascism, no more war". Which in this moment to me not only implies struggling against any form of racism or anti-Semitism, but also opposing any form of militarism and war. In the context of Israel/Palestine, this means to not believe in that the only solution to this conflict is radical segregation. To be with the people on both sides, against the occupation and in favour of a democratization of Israeli society. Both will not only free the Palestinians, but also the Israelis from a nightmare of war and militarism.

Paul Grasse, born 1975 in East-Berlin, two daughters, is earning his living as an academic assistant for a member of parliament of DIE LINKE. He wrote his final thesis on the role of women in the Intifada and has been and still is politically active since his early youth. He has been to Israel several times and studied in the West Bank in 2003/2004.

A Historical Narrative as the Basis for Current Political Consciousness: The Mizrachi Alternative

GALIA AVIANI

On my first trip to Berlin as part of a German-Israeli exchange project, walking through the historical streets, I could not help but relive the stories about Jewish life in Europe, before and during the Holocaust. They were stories I had been told all my life in Israel. I felt as helpless, anxious and rootless as I knew they felt at the time. Even if they had little to do with my family origin. Coming from the Arab world, the Holocaust had little to do with my personal background. But it was a story I had internalized to the bone.

Wherever one looks in Israel, there are fascinating personal stories. As a State that was built, among other things, on a revolutionary vision, conquest, immigration, expulsion, and pioneering, there is an uncountable number of stories in Israel. Some fit in well with the national historical narrative, yet the majority find themselves in the margins, or beyond them. The many stories that are not part of the national historical narrative – the core narrative – manage to create narratives that challenge the national one, through their interest groups or sectors. For instance, in the society of Palestinians citizens of Israel this was the case. The historical narrative of that society evolved through the stages of personal stories, a coherent structure, and then assimilation within the collective memory of this minority group.

This, however, is not the case with the stories of Jews from Arab countries. Today, some people are writing "Mizrahi History" and trying to present a challenge to the national narrative; however, this challenge has remained an internal discourse among intellectuals and activists, leaving a coherent narrative which Arab-Jews (Jews in Israel who emigrated from Arab countries) will be able to call their own, still way off in the distance. One of the main reasons for the lack of such a narrative is, in my opinion, the lack of political meaning for all the stories in this group. Generally, the power of any national narrative lies in its ability to produce a political consciousness that will explain the group's path from the past to the present, and most importantly, will outline its future. In this way, any narrative that challenges the national one has to bring with it a rival political consciousness. It is not enough to set one story in front of another, even if the other story is more "correct." The rival narrative cannot exist without it being politically challenging to the national one. Obviously, the Palestinian narrative does this; it presents a political challenge, but the Arab-Jewish one does not, and remains within general Israeli society, and within the Arab-Jewish sector, as a collection of more interesting or less interesting private stories.

I was born in Israel. My parents immigrated as young children to the country from Aden in South Yemen. My father's family came when he was a baby; and when my mother's family came, she was twelve. My mother's family reached Israel in 1949, just after the State was established. When they arrived, my mother's father realized that he would not be able to pass on a traditional education from their home country, and decided his daughters should behave in a way that was accepted in their new home, meaning they become integrated into the conventions and culture of the new, modern State. The education, food, music, language, and culture were in the spirit of the Israeli melting pot, but were without any traces of my parents' Arabic culture.

Since the various socialization systems used in Israel were modeled on the Western cultural model, the schools hardly taught the history of the Arab countries and their Jewish communities. This meant that the history of European Jewry became my history. As a child, the core of my identify was with the fate of the European Diaspora - which on the one hand comprised pogroms, persecutions, and Anti-Semitism, and on the other, the Enlightenment, modernity, and renewal. During those years I was especially influenced by the Shoah ethos as a defining element in my understanding of the Jewish People's relationship with the outside world.

However, the Jewish-Israeli establishment has never allowed an official space for Arab-Jewish cultures. If in fact they were manifested, it was behind closed doors, within private homes of Jews from Arab countries who had immigrated to Israel. In recent decades – it was in spontaneous actions, by grassroots, using music, food, and other popular cultural characteristics.

In his book, *The Mizrahi Struggle in Israel*[1] Sami Shalom Shitrit states that the Arab-Jews were refugees twice over, when they reached Israel. First, they were physically exiled from their native homes, and second, a cultural exile was forced on them. I understood this statement intellectually,

---

1   *Sami Shalom Shitrit*, The *Mizrahi* Struggle in Israel (Hebrew), Tel-Aviv, 2004.

emotionally and physically when I visited an Arab country – Egypt – for the first time in my life. There, I felt a strange sensation – it was as if I had returned home to a home I never knew I had. The language, scents, music, and human tapestry, were all so familiar and intimate. I felt a longing for a place I had never known. For the first time in a public space without any restraints, I experienced authentic Arabism- and this was a profound revelation.

I discovered that a large part of the "national memory" molded within me was not really mine, when I decided to study the political and historical background of the Israeli-Palestinian conflict. The discovery that the memory of the *Nakba* and the story of the Palestinian narrative were erased from the Israeli official history was the catalyst for beginning a search for other "lost histories" that were not discussed in the public arena.

The search for the "true story" demanded a critical learning process, unrestrained by the Israeli discourse. As a result of this search, I underwent an inner change when I acquired new knowledge, forcing me to reexamine the whole gamut of my previous understandings and beliefs. This journey initiated a difficult, even painful, process, because of the difficulty in giving up on the core foundation of the collective Israeli identity, which I too am part of. The fact that the Palestinian narrative is not only outside the Israeli dominant narrative, and that it even confronts it on many issues, in a kind of zero-sum game, forced me to rethink all those truths that I had unquestioningly grown up with. The importance of telling the narratives of minority or marginalized groups in the public eye, and accepting them as part of the majority culture has many cultural, emotional, and social implications. However, the aspect I chose to emphasize here is the primary importance of an alternative political consciousness which can be reached when these narratives are included in Israel's formal, canonical story.

I started to look at the collective Israeli experience as an incurable and anxiety-induced post-traumatic experience which is constantly nourished by the events of the Shoah. The threatening Other exists in every conflictual encounter with the outside world. The Jewish-Israeli concept of security has always been influenced by the personal sense of security carried by Eastern European Jewry, who lived with racial conflict for many years, and violently climaxed with the Shoah. The Sisyphean attempts of Jews to avoid the acts of hate in Europe, whether through avoidance and seclusion or through assimilation to the local culture, constantly failed. The plague of anti-Semitism lay in wait at their doorstep and they were defenceless.

Jewry from Arab countries brought with them a different knowledge regarding relations with non-Jews in their countries of origin. These experiences can contribute to this additional historical narrative and bring alternative information about ways in which Jews can live among non-Jews. I heard stories from *chutzla'aretz*[2] as my parents called their home in Aden. Aden had been a British colony at the time when my parents were born. My mother and aunt told tales of a childhood in an innocent world, a spacious house, and sleeping on the roof during hot summer nights. There were only a hundred Jews in my mother's town; they had Moslem neighbours and the relationships spanned religions. Aden was a colony with a central port for the Arabian Peninsula; it was a cosmopolitan state. My mother recalls the visual and cultural wealth – English, Indians, African tribes, Arabs from various principalities – it sounded as a pleasant, tranquil life. A longing to be "there" came up in family conversations; a longing that would never be fulfilled since there was no way to return.

These stories are not only typical for my family and our heritage. Good neighbours and close daily relations were part of the normative social fabric for Jews and Moslems for hundreds of years, in other Arab countries too. Minority groups who belonged to monotheistic religions had the special status of being protected in *Dar al-Islam,* an Islamic land. Although life under the patronage of the regime was only a tolerable status, since it lacked political and civil rights, at least the regime guaranteed their lives, property, and freedom of worship. In exchange for this, they had to pay a per capita tax, with a rate determined by the subject's income and assets. They organized themselves into communities with broad internal autonomy, and suffered almost no abuse due to their religion. If and when there was an occurrence, the regime intervened to protect them. Providing the Jews with protective status was an inseparable part of the Prophet Mohammed's edicts, "anyone who wishes to remain a Jew or a Christian must not be converted, but he must pay the per capita tax imposed upon every adult… and when he gives this to God's messenger, the protection of God, and the protection of His messenger, will be for them as a portion." (From Mohammed's letter to the rulers in South Arabia.)[3] Islam had no theological clash with Judaism, as opposed to Christianity and its long conflict with Judaism.

The twentieth century brought with it conflicts in some places where Jews lived: the closing years of the colonial period; the crisis regarding the rise of Arab nationalism; the spread of Nazism into North Africa and Iraq; the emergence of Zionism in Palestine, and the arrival of Zionist emissaries to Jewish communities in Arab countries. The tension that began in Jewish-Moslem relationships was a direct result of this new political situation. However, political conflicts, unlike theological or anti-Semitic/racial ones, are solvable, since politics is a dynamic of ongoing crises, litigation, and

---

2   A familiar, nostalgic term meaning outside Israel.
3   *Sami Shalom Shitrit*: The *Mizrahi* Struggle in Israel (Hebrew), Tel-Aviv, 2004, p.51.

solutions. Similarly, political clashes, unlike racial ones, are subject to rules of a universal nature, through which a solution based on compromise may be reached. Politics itself is characterized by the work of negotiations, allowing those involved to overcome the impulses and urges common to all human conflicts. This is the essential difference between politically-based struggles and racial or religiously-based ones – the latter can never be resolved rationally, since one's colour, religion, ethnic origin, or gender, are non-negotiable.

Structuring a national memory is first and foremost a political matter that has political impact. To choose one narrative and reject another is a political decision. In the educational system there is no Arab-Jewish narrative because it is perceived as inferior and incomplete compared to the European Jewish history, and for reasons linked to the Israeli-Palestinian conflict. European history is highly valued, and presented as significant to our lives today. When Middle East history and the history of its Jews are taught, it takes less space in textbooks, and taught as not being relevant to our world.

Any affinity to Arabism is devalued in Israeli society, which lives in the shadow of the conflict and Arab-Jews who immigrated became players in the conflict, were not only pitted against the countries where they had lived, but also against their own long-held culture. Some succeeded in removing all cultural characteristics from themselves and their children, some did not, but many showed their disassociation with the past by joining anti-Arab political movements. This need to be recognized by the hegemonic Ashkenazi society prevented the coherent Arab-Jewish narrative from being formed.

When I studied the history of the establishment of the State of Israel it was a thrilling tale, with a beginning, middle and a dramatic end. From the Shoah to Rebirth; the few against the many; the whole world stood against us – but "if you will it, it is no dream."[4] This history catalyzed and motivated me to want to continue to defend and struggle for my right to be here, live here.

I found that the Shoah ethos created a tangible historical-ethical yardstick, by which other events in our lives that refer to our relations with the outside world can be measured. The Shoah stories are embedded in the history curriculum, leaving one with a feeling that the entire Jewish history revolves around that central trauma. The Shoah is the cause and the effect. Everything that happened before is seen as prophesizing the coming calamity, and everything after is the result of that formative event. The end result is that the components of personal and national security in Israeli identity have been primarily defined by a traumatic event that occurred to a part of its

---

4 Theodor Herzl.

population. In the words of Hanna Yablonka[5], the "unhealthy" segment of the nation is the one defining the emotional, physical, and political security, both for itself as well as for the "healthy" one, both on a personal and national level.

In comparison to this, Mizrahi stories lack the dramatic components within European anti-Semitism. At the same time, they have relevance on many levels, beginning with the fact that they happened here, in the region where we live. To be able to use my parents' history, and through this knowledge attain political significance relevant to my life today, I had to learn to value a new set of human relations, between Jews and Moslems, constructed on a rationale which is different, and not part of the common knowledge held by, and accessible to the Israeli public. The high regard for the law as a restraining force is one example here. Jews living in Arab countries experienced the law differently since their survival in Arab countries relied on the law, custom, and regime that guaranteed their safety. Feeling threatened was not part of their existence since, unlike Jews who lived in Europe, the law was always on the side of the Jews in Arab countries, and despite discriminating against them during some periods, their lives as a whole were assured and protected.

Despite the key role European history plays in world history, it cannot overrule the history of the region where we live. From the many stories told by Arab-Jews, though not yet complied into a clear picture, we can begin to construct an alternative history that challenges and questions the existing national narrative. This effort will allow us to think creatively, and bring new tools and strategies into Israeli politics on many levels, particularly when addressing the geopolitical region. This is an expansion that may allow us to build new bridges to the outside world, to become optimistic and to have faith in the other's rationale and in its willingness to live together. Indeed, articulating an alternative, non Eurocentric story may allow us to accept the proposition that the other is not so much an Other.

Galia Aviani, born 1961 in Jaffa, has lived most of her adult life in Haifa, working in marketing management in a publishing house. By training, she is a social worker and also studied international relations. She is engaged in Isha LeIsha, a feminist centre in Haifa, and an initiative for Economic Empowerment for Women. She is involved in activities promoting civil rights in Israel and against the Israeli occupation in the Palestinian territories.

---

5 Hanna Yablonka: Off the Beaten Track - The Mizrahim and the Shoah (Hebrew), Holon, 2008.

Colonialism and Holocaust Remembrance. Disguising the Continuity of European History

MARC BELLINGHAUSEN

When on January 7, 2005, Oury Jalloh burned to death in a police detention cell in the small German City of Dessau, it was first claimed that he had set himself on fire. Only as a result of the unstinting commitment by Mouctar Bah and a circle of Oury Jalloh's friends did the details of the incident finally come to light: Oury Jalloh had been taken into custody to check his identity. His feet and hands were chained and he had been lying on an inflammable mattress.

It took the public prosecutor's office five months to press charges against two police officers for failing to assist a person in danger and only after continuous media attention, numerous demonstrations and public events did the case finally come to trial two years later[1]. The police version of how and why the fire started was never questioned, either by the prosecutor's office or in court. After one and a half years, the trial came to an end and a verdict of not guilty delivered due to lack of evidence. "The Germans have killed millions of people but who are we – the blacks" said a resigned participant from the demonstration held outside the court building. Even though colonialism, the Holocaust and everyday racism are connected, the implications of colonialism and racism are dulled in German "remembrance" of the Holocaust. Within the German *Vergangenheitsbewältigung* (the "struggle" of coming to terms with the past) the perception of the Holocaust as "a break in civilization", an incident positioned outside the continuity of German and European history, makes present and historical forms of colonialism and racism appear normal and further cultivates this perception of normality.

---

1   See initiativeouryjalloh.wordpress.com (initiative in memory of Oury Jalloh).

The National Socialist Past and the Holocaust as the absolute "Other"?

Oury Jalloh's story is one of many, and just making it public took an immense amount of effort. Demands calling for justice, compensation and finding out what really happened were never met. Nor were they for Dominique Koumadio, who was shot by a police officer – who was never even charged – or Laye Kondé, who died on the same day as Oury Jalloh, drowned by a doctor – now acquitted – who had administered an emetic and water "to preserve the evidence of possession of drugs"[2].

In these years and the ones before, I had began to get an idea of what it meant to be a "foreigner" in Germany and to be turned into the "Other" because of origin, passport or skin color; to be subject to special laws, ostracized and deported. To be expected to be the one to fulfill the demands of "integration", to be seen as a problem, an enemy, a multi-cultural challenge or a refugee who needs to be looked after. Just as I, a person of German descent, raised for the most part in Germany, know the "normality" of the image of humans derived from Western classifications, I am also familiar with Holocaust discourses that see it as a part of German history that has nothing to do with existing Western racism, and cannot be compared with it.

Ever since my school days, the years 1933 to 1945 of the National Socialist government's reign have been an omnipresent monolithic era – as if they had no connection to what happened in those before or after. Images of the period directly after World War II the era known as *'Stunde Null'* (zero hour) in 1945 just like those of the *'Wirtschaftswunder'* (economic miracle) are based on denial of all political and economic continuity. The Holocaust is seen as a "break in civilization" and the epitome of evil whose basis is no longer or almost no longer virulent in German society. Even in my own family, all I found out from the only living witness was that she had had no idea what was happening and that at some point neighbors or people she knew just suddenly vanished. It was obvious that she was reacting on reflex to the anticipated accusation that she must have known something and should have attempted to do something. Also in discussions about the "Third Reich" in left-wing political contexts, the main topics were guilt, the special responsibility of the Germans and the uniqueness of the crime, a "relapse into barbarism" remote from Western civilization.

Such demonizing of the Holocaust makes it difficult to analyze the normality in which it developed and took place. Even though survivors' stories and reports, for example about "Aryanization", give us an idea of the malice and confidence the participating Germans displayed in their racism against "the Jews", the prevailing discourse, within which most metanarratives are positioned, obscures the everyday occurrences of social

---

2 See: thecaravan.org (Caravan for the rights of refugees and migrants)

exclusion and extermination of those who were defined as Jews. The more the Holocaust is dissociated from historical discourses, the less focus there will be in Western societies on the normality of racism and its connection to the West's imperial power.

Resisting de-humanizing Practices in the Present
Usually, the only way to enter Germany without a visa, money or a passport from an industrialized Western country is to seek asylum – so avoiding being designated "illegal" and being forced into permanent hiding. Most applications for asylum are refused. Sometimes an exceptional leave to remain in Germany (*Duldung*) is granted but there is always a threat of deportation. Aside from many special provisions for asylum-seekers like accommodation in camps – often called homes – or reduced welfare payments and work bans, Germany has a unique decree, which is one of a kind in Europe, called *Residenzpflicht* (obligatory residency), where asylum-seekers are under obligation not to leave the administrative district of their assigned *Ausländeramt* (aliens' registration office). In Germany, there are comparatively few, self-organized political groups of refugees or migrants without documents.

In autumn 2004 an initiative called "*plataforma der Flüchtlinge und MigrantInnen*" (Platform of Refugees and Migrants) was founded during the 10th anniversary meeting of '*The Voice*', an organization of asylum-seekers predominantly from Africa. In the following years, most of the members who participated only had temporary or revocable residence permits, or some other problematic status e.g. no documents or visa, their stay dependent on marriage. A goal of "*Plataforma*" was to create a space where refugees and migrants could exchange experiences and generate a common voice against the conditions they faced. The challenges they encounter in the West correspond to the historical and present day conditions in their home countries, be it Columbia, Chile, Palestine, Cameroon, Togo, Argentina, Brazil or Mauritania. The violence and exploitation in these countries that was introduced and institutionalized by the Western system is resumed through discrimination, exclusion and the deprivation of rights within the Western countries themselves. Policies on foreigners and refugees along with the Western image of the "Other" are only different aspects of world-wide practices that have prevailed for hundreds of years, and in turn have been called colonialism, imperialism, globalization or development.

So it was important to have a space in which experiences could be exchanged and not ignored, distorted or erased by Germans but which are instead heard, complement each other and lead to collective strategies. This space was important for me, to learn to understand these experiences and their contexts, to see what they mean for my criticism of Western self-images and viewpoints and to develop a common mode of resistance.

In the following years, we organized different events with movies, food, discussions and music to exchange ideas and information about international affairs and create a common meeting place. These activities included information events with lawyers, sometimes held directly in the asylum-seekers' housing facilities, to report on new restrictions like the immigration laws, and all of the numerous obscure details with which migrants are harassed by authorities and police. In court, on the street or with the other limited resources at our disposal, we supported friends in their fight for their right to stay or against the *Residenzpflicht,* for their right of free movement. "*Plataforma*" organized and participated in countless protest actions against the second Lebanon War, the Western financed terror in Columbia, the war against the Mapuche in Chile, or refugees in Ceuta and Melilla as well as the murder of Oury Jalloh.

Over the years, various events were held with Rosa Amelia Plumelle-Uribe, the author of "*Weiße Barbarei – vom Kolonialrassismus zur Rassenpolitik der Nazis*" (White Savagery – from Colonial Racism to Nazi Race Policy, Zürich 2004). In her book she writes about repression of colonial genocide in the Western perception of history, which is crowded out by the way the West deals with the Holocaust. She also analyses how the two are connected and their historical continuity. In these discussions it became clear to me how the relationship of the Holocaust and NS to colonial history is conceived in Western metanarratives, as well as to the West's definition of itself as civilization. This image of civilization that is only perceived as a way to solve problems obscures that fact that it also causes them. Because the victims of the Shoah are perceived as "White" (often excluding Sinti and Romanies) and seen as part of the Western world, the violent creation of borders between the West and the rest of the world is not part of the *Vergangenheitsbewältigung*, the process of coming to terms with the past.

European and German Colonial Traditions
Declaring the Holocaust to be a benchmark in human history is accompanied by the fact that it is given far more attention than the history of colonialism, which is perceived as a kind of nebulous prehistoric era. Be it the conquest of the Americas, the 19th century Belgium atrocities under King Leopold in the Congo or the colonial war in Algeria. When Cristóbal Colón "discovered" - as is still often taught in european and Latin American schoolbooks - Latin America in 1492, a historical period emerged that has been dissected, obscured and trivialized in the Western narrative. Colón's first act on October 12, 1492 when he landed at Guanahani with a notary was to declare the island property of the Spanish crone and to give it the new name, San Salvador (the

holy deliverer). This set an example for the further course of events. By 1519 Hernán Cortés had in two years conquered Mexico, and 50 years later of the original 20-25 million inhabitants only 2.5 million people were still left alive; and so it continued throughout the entire continent. According to present-day estimates, about 80 million people were living in America in the 1500s but by the middle of the 16th century only 10 million remained.

In Tzvetan Todorov's book *The Conquest of America: The Question of the Other* (University of Oklahoma Press, 1999) there are numerous sources documenting the genocide of the Latin American inhabitants and the ensuing debates about their "value". In his 1552 "*Short Account*", the Dominican theologian Bartolomé de Las Casas, writes about children being thrown to the animals, the repeated rape of women by European mine owners or about the hundreds of people who were thrown overboard from the slave ships. Or about the massacre in Caoanao in Cuba, where the Spanish used animals and people to test their swords – leaving no survivors. The bishop from Yucatan, Diego de Lunda, wrote about how children were stabbed to death because they did not walk fast enough and how, when members of a group of people chained together by the neck were not as fast as the others, their tormentors cut off their heads so that they would not have to stop to unchain them.

In 1550, the great debate in Valladolid, Spain on the "nature of Indians" was staged between Las Casas and the scholar Ginés de Sepúlveda. Sepúlveda declared: "The Spanish are superior to these savages like grown ups are superior to children and men to women." Las Casas responded that the Christian religion, the only true way, shows Godly compassion for all people. And that at least it should be possible to have compassion for the "Indians" unlike for the Turks and Moors who really stood for the genuine chaos of savagery. The societal dialogue conveyed the idea that Western identity should still be accessible to inferior peoples, and yet called for the handling of slaves and Indios for profit. In the next 350 years the deplenished manpower in America was compensated for by shipping 15 to 20 million black African slaves, a large number of whom died during the sea passage.

In the 17th century, England and France became the leading powers in the division of the world. With the establishment of its national state in 1871, the German Empire began military assertion of its colonial interests in Africa and the South Pacific. In 1884, Southwest Africa, present day Namibia, became the first German "protectorate" for its capitalists, settlers and missionaries. The war against the Herero and Namaqua resistance (1904-08) was coupled with an explicit order for their extermination: only about 15 to 20 percent survived. After which, their complete submission began with the introduction of the *Eingeborenenverordnungen* (Native Ordinances): All Africans had to wear a *Passmarke* (registration tag) and were only allowed to leave their place of residence if they had a passport, which in most cases was held by their "masters".³ After World War I, Germany had to abort its "brief adventure", as it is called today.

In the middle of the 20th century, wars of liberation converted most colonies into self-regulating states. Due to the era of colonization, most of their people were cut off from production, the concept of private property was established everywhere and land, people and natural resources were open to Western access. Anyone who took independence from the West seriously and wanted to escape its grasp was confronted by the powerful mixture of business and violence. Furthermore, there was not just a geographical resemblance between the new nations and the structures that were created and marked off by the colonizers. Prices for their agricultural products and natural resources are and were treated as a form of political credit for those countries offering the products, and are determined by the supply and demand of Western capital and on the stock markets in New York or Frankfurt.

As in the times of the triangular trade, raw material is carted off and cheap goods are delivered, bringing ruinous consequences for local farmers and manufacturers. To create profitable locations for Western capital, easy terms are set regarding environmental restrictions, tax payments and transfer of profits. Generally, the only option left for these countries to procure resources and foreign currency is to remain in a permanent state of indebtedness, with conditions dictated by the creditors, or to directly couple their monetary system to a "strong currency". Today, the term for the central African currency, CFA-Franc, no longer stands for *'Colonies françaises d'Afrique'* but for the 'Financial Community of Africa', *'Communauté Financière de l'Afrique'*.

'Ausländerpolitik' in Germany

From the beginning, colonization was not only characterized by appropriation but also by exclusion of the Other. At the same time, as the German nation came into being *(Reichsgründung)* in 1871, there was a workforce shortage which was offset by bringing in foreign workers. At this time, political means of control called *Ausländerpolitik* (Policy on Aliens) was developed, which to a great extent is still implemented today. It included the regulation of compulsory and forced return, seasonal resident permits and work permits (*Arbeiter-Legitimationskarten*), which were restricted to a specific employer.⁴

---

3   For more information see Jürgen Zimmerer/Joachim Zeller (Eds.): Der Völkermord in Deutsch-Südwestafrika [Genocide in German Southwest Africa], Berlin 2004.
4   For further accounts on the history of Germany's migration policy: See Ulrich Herbert: Geschichte der Auländerpolitik in Deutschland, Bonn 2003; Kien Nghi Ha: Ethnizität und Migration reloaded, Berlin 2004.

After World War I the policy of *Inländerprimat* (Priority of Nationals), which is still in force today, was introduced that determined that aliens can only fill a job if there are no German applicants. In 1936, the National Socialist regime signed quota agreements with Poland, Italy, Spain, and Yugoslavia to guarantee its supply of workers. After ethnic-German refugees from Central and Eastern Europe were integrated into the German labor market in the 1950s and the erection of the Berlin Wall in 1961, the huge need for workers in the "new" West German industry was met by recruiting *"Gastarbeiter"* (guest workers) who were first called *"Fremdarbeiter"* (foreign workers) – a term soon considered not acceptable in new language usage. Repeatedly, politicians and the media enumerated how low the costs were to utilize "guest workers" – in regard to education, health care, pensions and unemployment benefits – compared to the profits they turned out.

The 1965 comprehensive *Ausländergesetz* (Alien Act) was largely adopted from the 1936 *Ausländerpolizeiverordnung* (Immigration-Police Decree) and the 1933 decree concerning "foreign workers"; its further amendments treat and regulate foreigners in respect to their intended function: As a mobile and flexible reserve army for the German economic market, who have no further needs, are invisible and disappear on command. Despite all attempts at control, there were four million "foreigners" living in West Germany by 1973 when the ban on recruiting foreign labor was put into force. People had come to Germany with their own goals and purposes and independently transformed their situations, for example by leaving the camp barracks and finding their own place to live.

In the meantime, the German public has declared them an "integration problem" and has expressed demands of subordination to German expectations and to this definition of problem, which do not entail merely assimilating but instead permanently taking on the role of the deficient and inferior "Other". After the establishment of the ban on recruiting foreign labor, further restrictions were introduced on refugees, whose reason to immigrate was not to fill the needs of the regular workforce. In the early 1980s the Asylum Procedure Act was stiffened and after the end of the Eastern Bloc, the right of asylum – which in general was only applicable to refugees coming from "The East" – was put to rest. Refugees who enter Germany through a safe "third country" – which in this case means all of Germany's neighboring countries – do not have a "right" to asylum. Ever since, continuous work is being done to limit the legal means of immigration, be it family reunification or the granting of visas. Germany is the leading EU force in the coordination of migration polices when it comes to introducing restrictive measures. Nevertheless, people will find a way to get where they want or have to go – even if the West stubbornly pursues the strengthening of the borders between itself and the "Others".

Colonialism and Remembrance of the Holocaust

In the Western world view, colonialism is, thanks to sovereign states, a thing of the past, racism is a rightist phenomena and xenophobia is something found in every society. The real story behind this is something known to most people from the colonized parts of the world, in one way or another. It is a different story in the West and its dialogue on the Holocaust and NS has not affected a change. Ever since Germany initiated and lost the war against the Allies, the Holocaust has in the Western view of history been seen as a kind of "industrial accident", which should never be repeated (symbolized by the much-invoked phrase "Never again").

After the "*Judenfrage*" (Jewish Question) in Europe was basically resolved by expulsion, genocide and Zionism, Germany has further attempted to banish it from its borders by paying "*Wiedergutmachung*" (reparations) to the state of Israel and by legitimatizing Israeli state politics. The real or alleged anti-Semitism of Arabs and Turks in Palestine or Berlin has now become a German problem that at times has displaced European anti-Semitism as a topic of German debate. Also on other occasions, references to remembering the Holocaust are drawn on in Germany to reprimand others to reflect on the state of their country and as a demonstration of Germany's integrity.

"Now they are demonstrating at our expense again. We give them everything and they want more. And even my grandmother wasn't responsible for the colonies in Africa." These are statements I heard from a Dessau resident at a demonstration held in remembrance of Oury Jalloh. They tell us a great deal about his outlook on the Holocaust and it is not difficult to guess what his political views were 70 years ago. In Germany, the desire to finally draw a line under the past is all-pervading: It's time to close this troubled chapter; others have had bad times, too. Today, the way to get there no longer involves denial and relativization but is accomplished by the discursive distance between the Holocaust and the continuity of European history. Reference to uniqueness obscures the Holocaust's connection to the history of European racism and global power structures, which for example are signalized in the slogan from *Plataforma*, "*Karawane für die Rechte der Flüchtlinge und MigrantInnen*", and '*The Voice*': "We are here because you destroy our countries".

The numerous demonstrations against Neo-Nazis are part of the self-image that we Germans from the third generation have of having come to terms with the Holocaust and having learned from our past. Meanwhile, life against the colonized world continues.

Marc Bellinghausen, born 1968 in Aachen, has gone through many diverse political groups before and during Plataforma, and is still searching for further means to understand what makes my generation tick and what else is happening in this strange universe.

Travelogues

Plan B for Zionism "Medinat Weimar"

RONEN EIDELMAN

"Have you ever killed anyone?"
Boy, I hate it when people ask me that question. Especially, when it comes from someone that I barely even know. Like once that Irish guy with the rotten teeth in the bar in Prague: "You people in Israel have to serve in the army, no? Have you also served in the army? Did you see action? Did you kill anyone?" – "Yes, I killed hundreds and ate their children. Who's buying the next round?"

It's amazing. For three years I lived with a girl I loved and she never asked me if I killed anyone. None of my childhood friends have ever asked me if I killed anyone, nor my older sisters, my younger brother or my mother. But that photographer from Philadelphia, or the Korean couple I met in Amsterdam and all those Spanish guys I met had no problem asking me, and don't get me started on all those nice young Germans that I meet in Israel who also ask but with a compassionate voice. The logic is simple: I was a soldier; my profession was to kill, so I surely killed someone.

But this time her big brown eyes made it clear that I can't avoid the question with a joke or a cynical answer. She just stood there in the middle of the street, her hands all tensed and her little body did not move.

We were actually on our way to drink and dance at one of the bars next to the port in Barcelona. Talya wanted to go to the "Palestinian" bar that offered contemporary Lebanese and Egyptian pop, a lot of young Moroccan boys and even more not so young German tourists who like young Moroccan boys. The only thing that was Palestinian in the Palestinian bar were old PLO posters in fancy wooden frames and a huge picture of Al-aksa mosque hung in the middle of the hall, just behind the bar. It was essentially a nice experience, drinking overpriced beer listening to Egyptian pop star Hakim while strange men stroke your ass. But I wanted to go to the "Moroccan" Bar across the street. Also there they sold overpriced beer, played Arab pop and Moroccan boys and northern European men did business or maybe even love, but here instead of a picture of Al-aksa hung a huge painting of Laila Morad, the most elegant, beautiful and classical of Egyptian movie stars.

I tried to explain to Talya and Ranya why I wished to go to the "Moroccan" bar. I described the differences in the décor and the photos behind the bar counter, and then I asked Ranya if she knew that Laila Morad was Jewish, and that she had converted to Islam in order to succeed as an actress. Ranya laughed and asked if that is also one of the Zionist lies that we are fed, just like I claim that Um Kultum is a lesbian. So we continued walking and laughing, then Ranya told us proudly that when she volunteers to teach at the Shatila refugee camp next to Beirut, and when the children say that all the Jews should be killed, she corrects them and teaches them that not all Jews are bad and are responsible for killing Palestinians. She tells them they should instead say Israelis should be killed, not the Jews. Then she looked at us. "I can't stand you guys, you are so confusing me, it was so much simpler before I met you."

We had met Ranya only a few days earlier on our first day in Barcelona. We were sleeping on the roof of an old factory where an anarchist theater group was squatting, and had made it both their home and rehearsal hall. She sat in the entrance hall wearing a tank top and shorts. And with short hair and darkish skin, I thought she might even be Israeli. When I got closer I noticed she had a necklace with a silver olive tree, the stylish symbol of secular Palestinian struggle, hanging from her neck, but I still thought that she was one of the European Palestinian solidarity enthusiasts. She immediately told me that she is a Palestinian refugee living in Lebanon. I answered that, "I'm Israeli, I'm against the occupation and I did not vote Sharon," and immediately felt really stupid for saying that.

She said that it was very nice to meet someone who is living in her grandmother's home. I corrected her and said that I certainly know that I live in a house of a family that now lives in Jordan but if she would like to meet some Jews from Haifa, I would gladly introduce them to her. She told me and Talya about her family's home in Haifa, how it is still standing empty, and we considered how we could take it over like the squatters in Barcelona. We would receive permission from Ranya's family to "hold" the house for them, and the police will have no legal way to kick us out. We will have a home, yet also turn the house into a cultural center. Further, we will even make a political statement about the Palestinian catastrophe and the refugee problems that are so often forgotten.

We strolled down La Rambla, laughing and trying to decide at which gay bar we would like to spend our beer money and, without thinking I said to Ranya, "You know, I visited Lebanon." She looked at me strangely, "When? How?", "When I was a soldier, I served in south Lebanon". I said it just like that, with a stupid smile on my face, without fully understanding what I did or why I said what I said. Ranya completely froze. She then walked away, returned and walked away again. After about five minutes she stood right in front of me, looked me in the eyes and asked, "Have you ever kill anyone?"

I wanted to say that it was not my fault, the stupid sergeant wrongly-estimated the amount of explosives needed, that he was kicked out of the unit and even was sent to two weeks in military prison, that I was under a lot of pressure, the soldiers from the Golani brigade were yelling on the radio that rockets were falling on them, I had no choice. At that moment when I located the source of the rockets on the radar, what could I have done? Not send the information to the command post? Not prepare the artillery battery? My measurements were correct, the little girl and her mother were not my fault. It was that idiot sergeant who made the mistake, he was punished, I did not shoot, I just gave the order, I did not know that they were there, and anyway they were shooting rockets at us. But I just looked down at my sandals and said to Ranya, "My job did not involve shooting." Ranya turned round and just walked away.

"You just don't know when to shut up," Talya yelled at me and ran after Ranya. So I turned the other way, I went to a bar called 'Kentucky' where they play Aerosmith, and behind the bar counter there is a head of a bull with a cowboy hat, and the beer only costs one and a half Euros.

"How could you live in Germany?"
Boy, I hate it when people ask me that question, and especially how it always comes from someone that I barely even know. It's not that people are badly intentioned they just don't understand how I could live in the country that is responsible for the murder of at least six million of "my people" and maybe even some of my family members. When asked by older people in Israel, I still hate the question, but I kind of understand. Many of them lived through the war and it is clear why some of them would want absolutely no contact to Germany. Also when young Israelis or American Jews ask, it's upsetting but still relatively understandable because of our upbringing.

For many years many Jews boycotted Germany. When I was growing up, my parents refused to buy a German car or washing machine and anyone in the neighborhood who drove a Volkswagen was frowned upon. All the kids agreed that German was an ugly sounding language, and the only German words we knew were "schnell" and "raus". In American movies, all the bad guys spoke with German accents and German movies were almost never screened in the cinema even though French, Italian, Yugoslavia, Czech and movies from many other countries were screened on a regular basis. I don't think I ever heard a German song on the radio except '99 Luftballons', but even a proud and strong country like Israel was not immune to Nena's pop-ish power.

But what really upsets me is when I'm asked that question by Germans. By this, I don't mean fascist Germans whose desire is that no Jews or any non-German live in their Deutschland. With those people I don't have much dialogue that does not involve the riot police. I'm referring to the good-hearted, caring German. The kind that if they were alive during the war would probably have been a tank commander in north Africa or maybe a Luftwaffe fighter pilot, definitely not the type that would hand you a bar of soap and tell you to "take a shower". So I have to ask myself what they really mean by posing me this question. Is it not reasonable that I live in Germany? Should I feel uncomfortable? Is there something they know that I'm missing? Are they feeling weird in my presence?

When I'm in a humorous mood I just say that I came to get what is mine, and they should not worry, because after I finish I will go home. But when I'm in a more serious mood, I try to understand where they are coming from. I think many who ask sincerely mean well and are genuinely concerned. But I'm still not really sure what are they actually asking? And why does this question upset me so much when it comes from Germans?

A couple of years ago, a few days after Christmas, in a club in Hamburg located in a bankrupt department store I got a small answer to my dilemma. The club was not unusual for the German alternative scene with its regular mix of artists, students, media people, musicians and sadly-dressed fashion victims but what caught my attention was a large number of young, scruffy-looking, Antifa punks wearing hoodies with political badges and clothes in all shades of black. This was an unusual sight at a club with a cover charge and where beer costs more the two and half Euros.

The first band that played was an electro cabaret duo that was pretty pretentious and boring but not something you wouldn't expect from a town whose biggest claim to fame is that the Beatles played covers of Chuck Berry in their clubs before most people had even heard of them.

But when the second band started to play then something happened. The Antifa kids got off their asses and joined the hipster crowd. Everyone was dancing. The band, Egotronic, an electropunk duo was shouting over the cheesy sound of Commodore 64 rave tunes very political, but also very funny lyrics. We were dancing like crazy but also laughing hysterically while the crowd joined the band yelling "Raven Gegen Deutschland (Raving against Germany)," "Die Partei hat immer rechts (The party is always right/ rightwing)," or, "Diese bekackten Deutschen, nichts hat sich geändert, bekackte Nazis! (These shitty Germans, nothing has changed, shit Nazis)." A big crowd was getting their thrills and laughs by being anti-German and saying that Germany is still Nazi. The highlight of the concert is when they sang a song thanking Sir Arthur "Bomber" Harris (the head of the British bomber command during the Second World War) for bombing Dresden. The crowd thought it was brilliant.

This was not the first time I had come into contact with Germans who call themselves "anti-Germans". I had heard of their ideas and thought most of them were ridiculous, felt close to a few of them, and completely disagreed with their extreme "solidarizing" stand on Israel and Zionism, but that's another story. This time I was not having a theoretical debate but experiencing a mass orgy of "self-hatred", a very funny one, with a cool soundtrack but still pretty disturbing. So this made me wonder if what I'm hearing from Germans who ask how I could live in Germany, is their own distrust of their own people, and that they think deep inside that a Nazi in every German is just waiting to burst out.

The first time I came to Germany I also felt that way. My Zionist education with its emphasis on studies of the Holocaust made my encounter with the country extremely difficult. I was eighteen and backpacking with a friend through Europe, our big trip of fun before we went back to do our mandatory military service. We were in Switzerland and decided to go to Munich, and from there we would travel to what was then West Berlin (we had no possibility to go to East Berlin and the former GDR with our Israeli passports). In Munich we had a hard time enjoying ourselves. People speaking German brought back memories of all the holocaust movies we had to watch as children. I couldn't help wondering about every old man I saw on the trains and about what he had done during the war.

The train to the hostel where we slept was en route to Dachau, so at every station we heard the announcement that we are going in the direction and we only knew the name of this town as the name of a concentration camp. Touring the city we joined a tour group, and the guide was telling of all the beautiful buildings that were destroyed by the Allied bombings and what I pity it was. I just could not care less about the buildings and the only thing going through my mind was that Munich deserved all the bombing it had got. I probably would also have thanked "bomber Harris" if I had known who he was at the time. So after a few days in Munich we decided that we were not yet ready to deal with Germany, and decided to continue our travels in Italy.

"Will there ever be a peaceful Israel?"
This question really hurts. I really don't know what to say when asked this question. I really wanted to believe that there is a chance, but looking at the reality I lose hope. The future I see is that Israel is becoming more and more an apartheid state, A Jewish theocracy, a country in a constant state of war, choosing apartments to live in by the thickness of their cement walls that can withhold rocket attacks, choosing not to have children so they won't learn

racism at school, and then be drafted to the army and become traumatized killers like their parents. This pessimism that I feel about the future of Israel drove me into an art project when I studied in Germany one year ago.

Living in the Diaspora, ten minutes by bus from Buchenwald, strengthened my belief in the need for a Jewish homeland, and understanding the desire of not wanting to be a minority in the place you live in. But I also had to admit to myself that the Zionist dream of a Jewish homeland in Palestine, a place aspiring to live up to the vision of being a "light to the nations", generating a cultural and spiritual renaissance as well as "normalize" the Jewish people and establish a safe haven, has failed. I had to admit that the whole place is rotten and alternatives have to be suggested. That we need a Plan B.

In December 2005, Iranian President Ahmadinejad, while talking about the Palestinian–Israeli conflict on Iranian TV suggested that: "The Europeans can give parts of their territories to Israel. We are in favor of this idea. They can give them as much aid as they want so they can found their state, both in terms of money and in terms of weapons. Germany and Austria in particular could place some of their provinces at Israel's disposal in order to solve its problem at its root." First of all, one must admit this idea was quite amusing. I recall telling a German journalist friend who was covering the story, that she should write, "Israeli youth are really excited. They are already checking out places in the Internet." Secondly, even if Ahmadinejad's suggestion should be considered as pure propaganda embedded in a common anti-Semitic discourse, it inspired me. If one takes the statement literally and extract the words from their original (anti-Semitic) context, one could hijack his message in a very mind-provoking and non-conformist way.

So I created a movement whose goal is to convince the German people to call the Jews (and anyone else who wants to be one) to gather in Thuringia, a post-industrial German state losing more of its population every year, in order to found another Jewish state. I claimed that this state would not only satisfy the need for a secure Jewish home, appease the Israeli-Palestinian conflict, and help German people to come to terms with the past, but also save Thuringia from its own bleak future.

On the 6th of May 2008, "Medinat Weimar" went public on the website (www.medinatweimar.org) declaring the movements manifesto as well as thirteen principles in English and German. Immediately, blog entries from around the world and Germany appeared, long discussions took place, journalists worldwide contacted me, and dozens of articles about the movement followed.

The debate raised by Medinat Weimar wanted to disengage from this kind of blood-based definition of a *Volk*, or "people", and build an identity based on an affiliation of ideas. To become an "aware pariah" (Bernard Lazare,

1894): an outcast by choice, yet not a passive withdrawer from society, but a critical thorn in its ass, using the outsider position as a power.

But to adopt a pariah position means also to be equally critical of one's own minority group. The creation of the state of Israel resulted in the Palestinian Nakba (catastrophe) and in the immigration of hundreds of thousands of Jewish refugees from Europe, the Moslem countries, as well as the thousands who came from all over the world over the last sixty years, who together built a group of people bound in common fate. So these people bound in common fate, immigrating together to Germany to establish a Jewish state in Thuringia, can become the "aware pariah" for Europe.

In addition, Medinat Weimar provides an opportunity for the Germans to really come to terms with their past, by inviting Jews to live with and thrive with them. Jews should not only be supported when they are far away in Israel, in the Middle East. This is nothing but outsourcing the "Jewish question", which was what anti-Semites have always wanted. Shouldn't the German people instead support the expression of Jewish nationalism in Europe? The place of origin of so many Jews. Would that not give the German people a reason to be proud German again?

"So do you really want to live in Thuringia?"
I get asked whenever I tell people about Medinat Weimar. The honest answer is no. No way. This was an art project by which I wanted to irritate German and Israeli mainstream discourses. I myself want to live in the Jewish state on the Mediterranean with its thriving Hebrew culture, and amazing energy. It is the only place I really feel at home. However, sadly there is no evidence in the political sphere or in the public discourse in Israeli that there is hope for a peaceful future. And any suggestion for a Plan B for Zionism seems to become indeed realistic.

One must look hard for hope. In the cracks, in unseen corners, in gaps between the words, in gestures of lovers and strangers that have lost all words. In Abirs, Ranyas, Talyas, Ronens who can get drunk together on the streets of Berlin and Barcelona, and get homesick together in the classrooms and studios of Amsterdam and New York. Or in the few thousand Jews and Arabs who marched together under threat of violence and shouted in the streets of Tel Aviv, Haifa and Jerusalem that "we refuse to be enemies" as during this last war in Gaza. The hundreds of poets, artists and musicians who came with their scribbled notes, guitars and laptops and yelled from their heart against the killings and destruction. All those, who unswervingly try to build not a Jewish state or a Palestinian state but a state of mind of living together.

Ronen Eidelman, born 1971 in New York City, grew up in Jerusalem and today is based in Tel Aviv. He is an artist, writer, activist and cultural producer; engaged with linking art, culture and grassroots politics. He is founder and editor in Maarav (www.maarav.org.il), the leading Israeli online art and culture magazine, and a graduate of the MFA program for Public Art and New Artistic Strategies at Bauhaus university in Weimar, Germany.

Meet the Migrants.
A Migrant Policy of Remembrace as Political Intervention

MASSIMO PERINELLI

2001: Kanak History Revue

Easter 2001, the Volksbühne theatre in Berlin gathered spectators, half of them migrants, to watch the 'Kanak History Revue'. On stage, a powerful tour through Germany's history of migration since WWII. The performance featured sound files of news broadcasts, video streams showed a host of campaigns initiated by migrants over the past fifty years, while young people staged stories about living in Germany from their own or their parents' perspective – sad stories as well as stories that could blow you away. Even though no-one referred to the concept of 'migrant policy of remembrance', everyone was well aware that the people on stage were 'writing' a history which hitherto had not been accounted for.

It was not the individual stories or well-known historical events which touched the audience but the fact that for a glimpse of time their own lives were connected to the past, which was however not a past in the sense of myth, genealogy, or national identity. What was most moving was the fact that the history of migration has always been a fight for rights, for a good life, whether for the student from Belarus, the Turkish production line worker, or the African refugee. What was new here was that no one was appealing to the German public to show a 'compassionate understanding for migrational history'. There was only a simple implicit invitation to look at history from the perspective of migrants themselves. For a brief moment, a collective knowledge emerged and could be shared: The history of migration reveals the striving of its subjects to create a better future than the one in the midst of whose miserable past we currently live.

Departing from this paradigm, the aim of my article is to sketch a different perspective to look on the history of migration to Germany during and after WWII. Migrants do not appear here as mere 'victims' or 'suppliants', but as historical actors on their own behalf. I write this from the perspective of a third generation migrant, whose own political engagement against racism emerged in the aftermath of German 'reunification' and the resulting neo-fascist pogroms during the early 1990s.Ultimately, I want to try and take stock – of course in an abridged form – of the present status of what I call 'migrant politics' in Germany: where are we heading to?

1939: Rome-Berlin Express

My grandfather Salvatore left Naples – which was extremely poor at that time – as early as the year 1939 to avoid military service and find work in Germany. In the 1930s, many Italian factory workers had come to National Socialist Germany to allay its thirst for workers for the German war industry. They were Italy's biggest exports in exchange for resources and industrial goods from Germany. Then however, in 1943 Italy sheered out of the Axis alliance Berlin-Rome and capitulated. Thus, those workers all of a sudden were turned into enemy foreign workers who then suffered German hatred and were deported to corresponding camps as Italian Military Internees. After this experience, most of them returned to their home country in early 1945.

For my grandfather, however, the story went a little bit differently. He helped out as a waiter on the Rome-Berlin Express – the high speed train that commuted between Rome and Berlin – where he fell in love with a German lady, and went with her to Kassel, Germany. There he waited on table in the dance hall 'Hotel Reiss'. In its time, the Reiss was highly popular, also amongst influential National Socialists, who protected my grandfather and hence enabled him to continue working unmolested in the restaurant – even after 'Badoglio's treason' as the Germans called Italy's capitulation September 1943. Hence, he was not interned and remained in Germany after the war, working as a cook in the US Army's night clubs. In the late 1950s, when the buying power of the dollar decreased and with it that of the American occupying soldiers, he opened up his own ice-cream parlor in Frankfurt which in the winter season became a pizzeria – the first pizzeria in Germany.

1969: Fremdarbeiter, Gastarbeiter, Spaghettifresser

As early as in 1943, the Reich Ministry of Labour had suggested the continuation of the recruitment of foreign workers after the war, who they suggested should then, however, not be called Fremdarbeiter (foreign workers) anymore, but more euphonically Gastarbeiter (guest workers). In 1955, the West German Federal Department of Labor adopted this suggestion and concluded the first so-called Anwerbevertrag (recruitment contract) with

Italy. Thereby, the uninterrupted importation of foreign workers for the German industry was to be guaranteed – and more importantly – be regulated. The National Socialist infra-structure was partly retained: Many Italian migrants arrived on platform 11 of Munich's main station, where during the National Socialist period foreign workers and forced laborers had arrived. Often the Gastarbeiter were brazenly accommodated in factory-owned camps which during the war had served as sub-camps of concentration camps that rented out their prisoners to German industry.

Under these conditions, Italian Gastarbeiter slowly but surely arrived in Germany: in order to rebuild the country, and level the German class structure by enabling the native population's upgrade to universities and white collar jobs. My grandfather, however, had already established himself by then, and my father was in his late teenage years. In the late 1950s, the Germans began to shape their first post-war wanderlust, tasted pizza for the first time, acquired the cultural technique of eating spaghetti, came to know that there were actually plenty of spices for cooking with, and that every night the red sun set in the sea at Capri. With their growing wealth, German mass tourism southwards began. At home however, despite all the love for pizza and ice cream, a veritable racism against the so-called Spaghettifresser (spaghetti devourer) prevailed.

When I was born in 1969, the second generation of post-war Gastarbeiter went to kindergarten or was not even born yet. In my teenage years, Turkish working migrants – who as a result of a Turkish-German recruitment agreement in 1965 became the principal group of migrants to Germany – had replaced the Italians as the main target of German racism. However, in a highly selective German educational system, a friendly elementary school teacher does not mind whom she sends to the lowest type of secondary school – little Paola from Italy or little Imran from Turkey. Even as the only Italian high-school graduate of my year, I was subjected to a particular Southern German discourse on Spaghettifresser. Ultimately, it was my move up north to Hamburg – where traditionally there are but few Italians – which brought about genuine changes to my situation as an Italian in Germany. There, positively racist connotations about Italians, as for example the Latin lover phantasm, substituted for the less romantic picture of the dirty Italian industrial worker prevailing in the south. However, events such as the racist attacks on Italian and other foreign adolescents by Sieg-Heil roaring soldiers of the German Bundeswehr in the city of Detmold in 1996, reminded me never to feeling too cozy and safe also in the North.

1989: Antifascism, Antiracism, Anti-German
On October 3, 1990, one year after the fall of the Berlin Wall, a news channel broadcast the end of the German Democratic Republic (GDR) and the so-

called "Re-unification". At that time I had already been living in Hamburg for one year and was busy participating in the squatting of the abandoned theatre Rote Flora in order to turn it into a leftist community center. Apart from a feeling of tragedy regarding the arrogant West-German annexation of GDR and some cynicism about the naivety of the hopes of many GDR citizens to get as rich as their fellow citizens in the West, I and my friends were but little interested in the whole topic of Re-unification. We were content with the often chanted leftist slogan "Nie wieder Deutschland!" (Germany – never again!), fooling ourselves by thinking we could blank out what had happened.

However, this changed instantly when racist assaults on former foreign contract workers of the GDR exploded, especially on those from Africa and Vietnam. In 1991 for example, African working migrants in mortal danger had to be evacuated in the course of a severe pogrom in the East German town of Hoyerswerda. Every day, there were assaults on foreigners and arson attacks on their houses and shops. Ultimately, in summer 1992, for several days hundreds of adolescent Germans attacked a big apartment block inhabited by Vietnamese families in Rostock- Lichtenhagen, while thousands of residents watched and applauded. While in Lichtenhagen the situation was allowed free play to continue, the police were busy preventing anti-fascist leftists from West Germany and Berlin from entering the scene, It was only the embittered resistance of the tenants and some luck which prevented the deaths of more than one hundred people unable to escape from the apartment block. In West Germany too, there were nocturnal arson homicides on Turkish families in the cities of Mölln (1992) and Solingen (1993).

Instead of taking a solidaristic or even protective stand concerning the desperate situation of refugees and immigrants, both the mainstream media and the government reversed responsibilities for these racist assaults, declared that what had actually triggered the neo-fascist riots was the unbearably high number of foreigners in the country and coined the slogan: "Das Boot ist voll" (The boat is full). In 1993, the Christian Democrat-led government – supported by the Social Democrats – changed the German constitution, de facto abolishing the laws on political asylum instituted after WWII against the background of the fact that many refugees who had tried to escape National Socialist Germany hadn't found a country that would let them in.

Given this heated situation,[1] the new nation state together with notions of racism and neo-fascism became the focus of our political actions. Due to frequent Neo-Nazi attacks also on leftists, most people I knew amongst the

---

1   This situation is perfectly portrayed in Can Candan's documentary *Duvarlar - Mauern - Walls*. For this film, shot in 1991, Candan interviewed German Turks about their attitudes towards Germany – three decades after the first Turkish 'guest workers' arrived in Germany, and one year after the country's 'reunification'.

radical left went into the martial arts to gain some fighting skills, focussing, however, on physical defence strategies rather than on analytical weapons. Those times of fighting against racist mobs and organized Neo-Nazis, both in East and West Germany, in effect made the 1990s a decade of anti-racism: the left, parts of the liberal public, the Antifa (anti-fascists), and large groups of migrants met on this minimal common political ground – sometimes for the first time – without however sharing a mutual understanding of what racism actually was. Instead anti-racist activities, were divided pragmatically: Harassed asylum seekers and 'illegal' refugees were taken care of in an affectionate paternalistic manner by liberal citizens and engaged priests. Hundreds of thousands of concerned citizens formed candle-lit demonstrations to prove their disgust with regard to the many racist killings,[2] and to manifest to the alarmed world that there also was a 'good Germany'. The Antifa on the other hand fought against Neo-Nazis on the streets, while Antiras (anti-racists) practiced political lobby work. Second generation migrants organized themselves militantly, forming a strong movement of resistance against racist attacks. This genuine division of the anti-racist movement, however, turned out to be a political cul-de-sac. In the course of the 1990s, internal fights broke out: organized migrants accused German Antiras' 'paternalism' towards migrants as an especially perfidious form of racism, young and martial Antifas had to face the reproach of 'blind actionism' without real social relevance. Meanwhile, the migrants who had engaged in the political concept of migrant-self-organisation got stuck in an identity-trap. Being completely at odds with themselves, they nevertheless could not leave their position of being essentially foreign nationalities and hence excluded victims. In such way they unwillingly affirmed the very strategies of exclusion imposed on them by society's majority.

The anti-racist coalition between very distinct political actors eventually collapsed when in 1998 the Social Democrats and the Green Party formed a new government. The state now involved many of the rather leftist liberal actors in its own – rather rhetoric – proceedings against Neo-Nazis and racism, and in the debate on the design of a first German 'immigration act'.[3] At the same time, beyond mainstream politics, this new situation gave way to some analytical re-orientation. Groups like Kanak Attak, Respect, Society for Legalisation, no one is illegal and others developed a new and more complex

---

2   For a list of 136 people killed in Germany by neo-fascist attacks since 1990, see www.opfer-rechter-gewalt.de/www/service/down/opfer-rechter-gewalt.pdf, 26.4.2009.
3   This was indeed the first time a German government acknowledged the fact that Germany was an 'immigration society'. Nonetheless, in the end the new law was titled "Gesetz zur Steuerung und Begrenzung der Zuwanderung" (Regulation and Limitation of Immigration Law).

analysis of racism without, however, conceptualizing migrants as a homogeneous group, let alone classifying them as victims by definition. And more important, these new movements were not aiming at a dialogue with society's majority or even the government, as large parts of the anti-racist movement in the 1990s did.

1999: Kanak Operaism and the End of the Culture of Dialogue

Frustrated with what I perceived as a deadlock in the predominantly German radical left, and intrigued by these new modes of thinking I joined Kanak Attak,[4] which had emerged as another by-product of the split that took place within the anti-racist field. The name of the group played with words and associations: on the one hand, Kanak is derived from Kanake, an extremely pejorative German slang word for 'foreigner', so that the name Kanak Attak precisely reflects the angst fantasies of German society, a frightening image of raging Turkish adolescents. On the other hand, Kanak Attak somewhat undermined this imagery in practice, since its political actions hardly corresponded to the imagery implied in its name. Furthermore, the group abstained from passport controls of its members which made participation by native Germans possible.

From a migrant and self-organizing, yet post-pogromist perspective, Kanak Attak rejected any unambiguous notion of 'collective identity'. While one could pursue an identitarian politics as a Turkish or African German, this was not possible from the position of what we conceptualized a Kanake: The identity of the Kanake can always only mean the shared experiences of exclusion as well as the common fight against it. Consequently, it is temporary and ambivalent. Moreover, Kanak Attak re-defined racism beyond the usual binarism of perpetrators and victims. It no longer appeared sustainable all the time to uncover and treat racism as a scandal in Germany. On the contrary, it seemed that the continuous (self-)positioning of migrants as victims of racism cemented their very status as powerless historical objects. Not only did Kanak Attak consider this victim-identity as boring but also as politically feeble.

Hence, we were interested in the actual counter-strategies of those being stratified by racism. We assumed that they were not at all powerless, but that their actions had already always shaped the specific historical and social conditions of racist discourse. For example, when the trade unions and the government under the social-democratic Willy Brandt wanted to end the era of "guest workers" during a recession at the beginning of the 1970s, trying to send them back to their original countries, the migrants on their part used existing legal loopholes in order to take their families to Germany in time. So

---

4   See www.kanak-attak.de.

contrary to the actual governmental plans, the number of immigrants suddenly doubled. We also learned that Germany's labour recruitment contracts with Italy, Turkey and other countries had not only been planned in order to recruit working forces, but that they were also an effort to channel an otherwise uncontrollable migration. However, in the end the phantasm of regimenting migration in terms of a tap that could be turned on or shut off proved unrealistic. In the long run, and even though the 'immigration act' passed by the German government in 2005 once more attempted to gain control on migration and therefore remained a racist discourse, it still represented a factual recognition of migration to Germany.

Thus, we learned that racism was not a monolithic structure of exclusion but that it transforms itself historically, first and foremost reacting to the implicit and explicit strategies directed against it. As a result we understood racism as a social condition that embraced both the successes and the defeats of the fights against it. The conclusion that first of all there was the constant struggle on the side of the migrants for a better life, and that racist efforts of regulation were only reactions, was our operaistic light-bulb-moment in Kanak Attack: If you want to learn something about how to fight racism, look at the marginalized, not at the majority.

Hence, Kanak Attak set itself the task of perceiving racism from the perspective of the struggles of migrants against it. This kanak-operaist policy of remembrance tried to explore and re-tell the history of migration to Germany after 1945. For almost two years we collected stories of our parents and grandparents; we searched archives, talked to former migrant activists and eventually translated our collected material into a presentable format.

The result was the event at the Volksbühne already mentioned above. For a whole week-end, we held workshops and discussions, there were film screenings, lectures and much more. At the core of the event was the aforesaid 'Kanak History Revue', in which we performed the history of migrant struggles in Germany. This was moving not only for the audience, but also for ourselves. It made us see that our parents' generation had not virtuously sacrificed itself and grafted for a better life for their children or even their homeland. Instead, their history emerged as a history of an uninterrupted fight against racist conditions in Germany. We learned that many modes of actions which later became renowned leftist practices, such as squats or self-governed community centers, were introduced to Germany by migrants.[5] But their struggle was not only expressed in terms of political activism, but especially in everyday situations, passionately and shrewdly

---

5   Examples are the squats of 1970/71 in Frankfurt's Westend area launched by Italians in the tradition of the Italian rent-strike movement, or the Circulo Cultural, a Spanish community center established in 1972 in the city of Essen.

forming mini-tactics for survival and the improvement of one's life conditions.

However, from the 1970s onwards, the state as well as large parts of society had responded to these claims for better living, housing and working conditions by posing a counter claim called integration. The attitude prevailed that claims by migrants, even if considered 'legitimate', could only be met if the latter fulfilled certain individual, additional requirements. Eventually, not only the government formulated various tasks for 'successful' integration such as an emphatic acknowledgment of some mysterious German 'Leitkultur' (dominant culture), official language tests or resolving a highly ideologized quiz about 'Germany'.[6] But also the individual German drafted all kinds of integrationist fantasies, whether on the political left or on the right: "If only the foreigners were cleaner, more hard-working and less sexist. If only they did not steal that much, were more fluent in German, had the right religion and did not smell so much of garlic; then, yes then they of course could easily live with and amongst us."

Parallel to this integration discourse, however, there has been a folkloristic multi-cultural attitude which positively formulated as an "enriching" societal endeavour what the neo-fascist German party NPD had always postulated, i.e. that every culture was worthy of being maintained (however, in the NPD's mindset, of course strictly separate from each other). Taken together, the dispositif of integration thus came to contain a paradox: "Assimilate! But stay different!" Our 'kanakish' response was a broad political campaign in 2001/2002: "No Integration!" Thereby we wanted to point at what has actually always been most important to migrants: neither culture, nor religion, neither assimilation, nor maintaining one's 'authentic' roots, but simply gaining the right to a good life. This right to a good life, on the other hand, does not only matter to migrants. It is what actually matters to everyone. The claim for the right for rights coming out of the long tradition of migration indeed was and is a revolutionary one.

2009: War, Frenzy, Hope

Today, there is no report on foreigners which does not assert the need for integration. Our call for "No Integration!" has been defeated. Not even the romanticising Multikulti imagery has remained official policy within German

---

6 Since 2008, there is an obligatory 'Naturalization Test' containing multiple choice questions about: "Living in a Democracy", "History and Responsibility" and "People and Society". For details see the website of the Federal Ministry for Migration and Refugees: www.integration-in-deutschland.de where one can also download a sample text (for integrational reasons of course only in German). Also see on this page the conceptualization of "particular challenges posed by the integration of Muslims" under "Integration and Islam".

society in the context of the new martial world order that has emerged since 9/11. Instead, the world is thought in terms of monolithic and genuinely incompatible cultures and identities, and strong notions of anti-Islamism as well as anti-Semitism re-entered the political scenery. The migrant community and the political left suffer severe fissures alongside the current, world-wide ideological and real war fronts, too, which many times prevent them from struggling together. Also Kanak Attak ultimately fell apart.

But the challenge still is to look for answers beyond the notion of God, party or fatherland in order to take up the migrant tradition of a multiple and rhizomatic struggle against any methodological nationalism, hence for a better life. Despite the grim ravages of the present era, our generation should start demand the unrestricted right to have rights for everyone – beyond binarisms and easy solutions, against an overwhelming reality of war and crisis.

Massimo Perinelli, born 1969 in Frankfurt am Main, works at the University of Cologne on the history of sexuality and on film-history. He wrote his PhD on body and gender in Italian Neo-Realist movies. He is member of the network Kanak Attak.

Tonguerilla

TOMER GARDI

> מוכר הספרים הושיט לי את 'מורה נבוכים' להרמב"ם והציע לי שאקנה אותו.
> הספר היה משומש והוא ביקש בעדו מחיר מועט. אבל אני העדפתי את 'ספר
> גורלות אחיתופל השלם'.
>
> יעקב שבתאי, *ביקור*

1.

I was holding the heavy chain controlling the small chains locked on to H, his ankles, his wrists and neck, chains which themselves attached us by communicating links. H and I were seeing visions, visions of our escape, visions we have slowly woven into the fabric of a plan. Our escape from commanders, old dead ones or new, our escape from the officer and his penal machinery; our escape from this dusty periphery, frequented by to-and-fro going travelers, explorers, researchers, goodwilling pilgrims; our escape from these chains tying us together; our escape from the already-written-through story of our lives, the completed narration of our destined fate, as was put so many years ago by the old master of minor mythologies, translated to us from his foreign tongue. But today, H and I knew, we will change the story. Today, we will break free.

The officer was getting ready to start. "Es izd en aigen tumlihe abarat"*, he said to the explorer and surveyed the machine. Yet another traveler landed our shores only this morning, and the officer was doing his usual act. Ach, how many times have I heard this sentence before! And how wasn't the officer bored of repeating that same explanation over and over again! But his boredom was of no interest to him, no concern; his life was a chant and this was its text, the only one he had ever known, numbly reciting it over and over, year after year, to generations after generations of explorers.

---

* Congruent with the title, the author forewent English proofreading and translation of Yiddish, Hebrew and German terms.

The one who has just arrived must have felt the mechanical fashion in which our officer spoke, the weariness of it all. "Aren't you hot in this uniform?" the explorer asked him. He was dressed lightly, in a costume he'd bought for his travel to the far south-eastern peripheries especially. Our officer wore his usual military outfit, worn down from time and from use and the hot sun and light, yet still too heavy, unfit for our climate. "But they mean home to us", the officer said, "we don't want to forget about home! Now Just have a look at this machine", he added at once. "The organization of the whole penal colony depends on it". This aroused the traveler's interest. Indifferent to H and I, he walked around the apparatus, examining its parts: the Bed, covered with cotton wool, the needled Harrow, the Designer, the gag of felt which was to silence the screams of the condemned man, the straps, used to tie the man down, straps for the feet, for the hands, and straps for the neck, to bind him fast.

Let not the reader be fooled by the cleanliness distant of my words! I am still caught in the immense narrative power of our previous storyteller. The man to be executed was not any man. It was H. And the one that was to bind him fast for the kill was I. H and I drew closer together. "Now," I told H, "the officer will explain to the traveler how the sentence is run. I have seen this so many times and can foresee all the steps. Then he will complain of the present commandant's new, liberal ways and show the explorer the previous commandant's own drawing. Then he will nostalgically tell of how great the executions used to be when the old commandant still was alive, and then complain of the new commandant some more. Then he will switch the machine on. This will be our cue." We waited. As always what always happened happened again. The officer explained and complained and explained and complained and then turned on the machine. This was our sign. From behind, H pushed the officer into the machine while I reached for his pocket and pulled out his keys. The Harrow went down, its thousand needles carving H's intended lesson on the officer's back: "HONOR THY SUPERIORS!" I unlocked our chains.

2.

The explorer was standing astound. He thought our colony's penal system wrong, that is true. A man of the West, he found our laws backward, unjust and unfit for any society guided by principals of human honor and dignity. Our colony's penal law was in need of a change, sure, but this has for him gone too far. The traveler now was afraid. He looked here and there, and seeing no possible help all around, started running towards our harbor, where the ship he arrived in was anchoring, waiting to take him away after his expedition was over. H and I too started to run, not after the traveler but with him, heading his ship.

How could have our previous narrator imagine a tired, heat stricken traveler, armed with nothing but rope, chasing away two men, determined with desperation and anger, this I cannot begin to imagine. Goodbye, old storyteller! Now, I am writing the story! From the ship the traveler waved his rope at H and I, trying to scare us away. We both looked him in the eye. We smiled and said nothing. With an easy jump we boarded the deck of the ship, and sailed away from this penal colony's shores.

3.
"So, how was your day?"

Any reader knows how challenging that question can be if taken seriously, which was what I decided to do.

"Well, you remember some days ago I got this email from this man who somehow heard of ILAF?" - I was back then involved with the Israeli Liberals Against Fences - "You know, the one who wants to nominate us for the Dortmund Peace Prize? Well, already a couple of days ago – can you pass the hummus?" We were sitting at home eating our dinner. She passed me the plastic box and I spread some industrial hummus on a slice of dense black rye bread I bought in the Russian shop on Allenby Street. Good black bread and inexpensive pork are two of many good things the Holy Land gained through the big post Soviet immigration waves of the 90s. I took a bite from my piece of culinary fusion and said, "Well, for the last couple of days I've been thinking. This prize thing doesn't make me happy but rather angry, and so I try to think why. You know how analytic I can sometimes be." – "Hhmm", said my love. I don't mean this cynically. She was concentrating on her beer, a fancy Pilsner Urquell that she so much adores. I myself am more for the inexpensive local beer that comes in these big returnable bottles. "So", I said, "I was thinking to myself: What is a prize? Which kind of prizes are there? And so I came up with this typology. There are the kind of prizes like those that are given for a film or a book, like the Oscar or Pulitzer. In this type of prizes, individuals are gathered, who are considered an authority on the field they are judging, and they decide who, according to their best judgment, mostly deserves the prize. Then there is the second type of prizes – are you all right?" Our cat just jumped her hand to snatch away what she had thought may be of interest to her. The olive rolled on the ground to gather some dust under the sofa. "Anyhow," I said, "the second kind of prizes is those that adults give to little children when they behave well, or people give to their pets." Our cat was looking straight at my pastrami. Looking her in the eye, I put it in my mouth. "And then", I continued, "there is the third type of prizes, those that depend on pure luck, like the lottery, or in a game of bingo."

"A peace prize, I would say", said she after opening another bottle of her imported Czech beers "has to do with the first two kinds of prizes."– "נכון", I said to her, which is Hebrew for "you're right". This whole dialogue, this is maybe the place to make clear, is a total make belief, purely fictional, and is conducted in our special version of English, the lingua franca of our partnership. "It is of the Pulitzer or Oscar prize type, since at its basis is the assumption that people who have experience in peace making and who are able to judge peace making efforts, give recognition and reward to those who are trying to achieve peace", I said. "And it is of the parent and child or human being and pet order", she said – getting warmed up after three Pilsners – "since it is always the rich and the powerful white side, that give rewards and peace prizes to those individuals or small outstanding groups, who have finally seen the light of peace, and now seek to further enlighten the rest of their backward, war driven societies. Have you ever heard of a London based project getting the Abuja peace prize? Or a New York based NGO receiving the City of Gaza Prize of Peace? Have you ever opened the radio and heard, 'This year's Algiers Peace Prize will be given to the Milan Woman for Peace'?" We were now both laughing. "And so," I told her, "I was thinking of this. I have a theory. Tell me what you think. Israel is like a penal colony. During the nineteenth and twentieth century, Jews almost all over Europe became outlawed, practically illegal, and long before the penal for the crime of being a Jew was the death sentence. Although not in a direct manner like for example those British outlaws shipped to Australia, European Jews were forced out overseas to a penal colony that was then called Palestine. And now, the same societies which deported my ancestors here only three generations ago, now they want to grant me a peace prize for the efforts I and others are making, to stop killing each other, the penal colonial deportees and the natives who lived here before! It's crazy!", I said, "Absurd!". I had by that time switched to my imported Polish Vodka and was going full speed. "Now look. What is the symbolic economy of a peace prize? Those who are getting it get recognition for their efforts for peace. This is the obvious side of the exchange. The other, rather unspoken side of this formula is, that those who accept the prize, give recognition to those who are granting it, that they have the authority, the status, the position, to rule, to judge, to decide who is worthy of peace prizes and who isn't. And so in short this is the deal: we will acknowledge in public the importance of your efforts for peace, and you will acknowledge in public that we have nothing to do with this war, that we are but distant, concerned observers. An economy of whitewashing colonial responsibility. The Dortmund peace prize?" I screamed, "Fuck the Dortmund Peace Prize!" Chewed pieces of humus and bread flew out of my mouth. "I need to piss," she said and got up, as I wondered how long already during my speech she was holding it back, waiting.

4.

When she returned I had already moved to the sofa. She sat on the couch in front of me. "After thinking all this," I continued from where I thought I had stopped, "I remembered the story by Kafka, In The Penal Colony, and I had this idea, to write my own version of Kafka's short story. But unlike in his story, I decided to make the Soldier and the Condemned Man in the colony not stupid and passive but strong and potent and sovereign, not to describe them from above, helplessly caught in their story, out of control, but rather have one of them tell it, invent it, create it. I wanted to retell a version of the story in first person and from the inside, when at the end of the story, contrary to the way Kafka's tale ends, he tries to chase them away but they mock him. They are two and he is one. They are used to the climate and he is exhausted from the heat. They are angry and desperate to leave. What can he do against them? Tschja, not much, נכון? And so the two board the ship and sail away from there. It didn't turn out too bad, but the style is not really mine and I feel there's a problem with the rhythm, the music. Nu," I said. "Maybe this is the problem of writing in what is not my mother tongue. I have only one, how do you say משלב? This word I have to look up in the dictionary. Wait." I went to the other room where my desk and books are and looked for משלב. "REGISTER", I shouted from the other room. "You see", I said as I sat in front of her again, "I only have one 'REGISTER' to use. Maybe this is why also Joseph Conrad had to invent his storyteller Marlow, to narrate through him and his speech. Needed spoken language to narrate. What? What you look at me like that? Ahh. I know," I said. "You think to yourself, 'this arrogant bastard is now comparing himself to Joseph Conrad! He must have had more of that Vodka then I have thought!'" – "No", she said, "It's not that. I know you are a genius." This now was her subtle irony at play. And she IS scared of being 'the woman behind the great writer'. "I was just thinking," she said, "quite a lot has been written about the Conrad-Marlow relations. You are suggesting some hasty literary conclusion here..." – "And what?" I was angry. "I can't say anything about Conrad before reading a whole library first?" Then her phone rang and she took it to the other room with her.

5.

With her in the other room, I went to the kitchen, to get me some water. The clock there as always said quarter passed four. This time it was wrong. I have this habit of buying cheap stuff that don't last for more then two weeks. I drank some of our filtered Tel-Avivian tap water and went back to the living room. Then I thought, perhaps what I first saw as the faults in my Penal Colony story are in fact its success. Maybe Kafka's machine is language itself, made of "STRAPS" and "HARROW" and "BED", of "COMMANDANT" and "SOLDIER" and "PENAL" and "COLONY", of "YES" and of "NO" and of

167

"NEW" and of "OLD". Maybe the lexicon is the sum of the parts of Kafka's machine, maybe syntax and grammar are its mechanism, its rules of operation. Maybe there's literature of officers and literature of soldiers and condemned men. Officer's literature which tries to gain perfect control of the machine, to know how to control every part of it, and condemned men and soldiers' literature, whose sovereignty is of sabotaging the machine from the inside, to misuse its parts, to puke on its shiny parts, to operate it in crooked order, to – "Hey, listen", I cried out as she entered the room, the phone in her hand. "Listen," I said. "Language is the machine and it's made out of words and its rules are grammar and syntax and the story is the world we are in and to change it," I said, and then ducked escape the phone she flung right at me. I bent forward and heard it crush on the wall behind me. "YOU!" she said. "YOU YOU YOU! What is the matter with you? Talking-Talking-Talking! Books and Languages, Narratives Grammars and Lexicons, Syntax and the Story and the World! YOU! YOU!" She said. "What do you know about the world?"

"What DON'T I know about the fucking world?"

"Well," she said, "for example, that two people today cut down the tree outside."

"Which tree?" I asked. But just to win time. I knew which tree she was talking about because in our dusty periphery, in our concrete jungle of a street, there is only one tree, and because I knew how much she loved it. It makes me sad even now when I write down these words. "Was sind das fuer Zeiten," I quoted, "wo ein Gespräch über Bäume fast ein Verbrechen ist, weil es ein Schweigen über so viele Untaten einschließt!" She grinned. She likes it when I speak German. And I AM quite a literary guy. "Klugscheißer", she murmured, →→→→→→→→→→→↓

↓←שבעברית זה משהו כמו חכם בלילה, אבל מילולית נשמע יותר כמו אחד שמחרבן חוכמולוגיות

I then smiled and said something else to try and amuse us. But what I really wanted to do was to kill the sadist assholes who cut down the only green thing on our street, which was exactly the first thing I did when I woke up the next morning.

Tomer Gardi is an ambitious young man. He was born 1974 in a rural hospital in mountainous Tsfat, from which he was brought down, to the Galilean Kibbutz Dan, to contribute his small share in the masterplan that was then called "Judaizing the Galilee". He is currently Tomerizing Tel-Aviv.

Between Individual Origin and Alien Territory: On being a non-Jew working for a Jewish newspaper

MORITZ REININGHAUS

> Not everyone is free to
> not belong to my
> Absence from the community.
> *Georges Bataille*

Having been an editor of the *Jüdische Zeitung*[1] for some years now, I'm used to being asked in a more or less roundabout way whether I'm Jewish whenever I do an Interview. I have developed a certain experience in informing my counterpart that I'm not, and I have learned to anticipate their reaction, which is normally oscillating between downright disappointment, curiosity and incomprehension – at the very least, I'm always in for a brief, awkward moment of irritation.

My interlocutor's response is easily accounted for. Their disappointment is obviously caused by the fact that they were assuming I actually *was* Jewish, and, hence, "one of them", only to find that this is not the case. Curiosity quickly changes into incomprehension, often followed by a sense of irritation about what they feel is an act of presumption: A non-Jew having an opinion on and a perception of Jewish life in Germany. Alternatively, I get the well-intended question why on earth I'm doing this to myself. The reactions of my non-Jewish dialogue partners, however, are just as interesting, since they are even more convinced of the fact that I must be of Jewish origin. Their

---

[1] The *Jüdische Zeitung* is a monthly founded by a Russian-Jewish publishing house in fall 2005 in order to create a German equivalent to the Russian *Evreyskaya Gazeta*. It is the attempt to establish a monthly operating independently from the Central Council of Jews in Germany, thus speaking more explicitly on behalf of Russian-speaking immigrants.

reactions upon discovering the truth are almost identical with the ones described above.

Nevertheless, it has not happened once during the two years I have been doing this that the question caused a rupture or even the cancellation of the dialogue. Quite often, the person I'm talking to reassures me promptly that the question of my origin actually "doesn't matter". While this may be true for them, it fails to convince me – especially since the frequency with which the question itself is asked obscures its alleged negligibility. And it is not necessarily any anti-Semitic, but rather the "philo-Semitic" positions which manifest themselves in "anti-German" attitudes[2], the desperate quest for "Jewish roots"[3] within one's own family or even the construction of Jewish origin[4], that are responsible for the larger part of the uneasiness I experience when it comes to the issue of my individual origin. There's a good reason why these positions are considered with suspicion: They are still suspected of blurring the line between Germans and Jews, and, hence, between perpetrators and victims, thus consisting a mere variation of the "Germans as victims" master narrative – a narrative that, when push comes to shove, is implemented at the cost of denying one's own German origin.

Running the Gauntlet: Between Germans and Jews

All the phenomena described so far are consequences and moments of German-Jewish coexistence. It is a relationship which would hardly make sense without the raised awareness caused by German-Jewish history, and, hence the Holocaust. So, what this is all about is a kind of "secondary discourse of memory", the question of what is appropriate in terms of referring to each other in face of an ever-present historical abyss which is not to be negated by any means. In spite of the hope for "normalization", Jewish

---

2   The "Antideutschen" (The Anti-Germans) are a group of people considering themselves "leftist", a claim which is substantiated by the fact that much of its member's argumentation is based on the Frankfurt School's Critical Theory. Unlike the traditional German left, which has been taking a critical or even dismissive stance towards Israel ever since the Six-Day war, the Anti-Germans maintain a distinctly pro-Israeli and pro-U.S. attitude, which is often accompanied by anti-Islamic resentment. The name refers to the fact that the group simultaneously developed anti-German resentment which goes as far as to "celebrate" the destruction of German cities during World War II, which reflects warmongering attitudes in present conflicts.
3   The last years saw a slew of "half-Jewish" family biographies published. The quest for the "good German" within one's own family, a person that, for instance, saved the life of Jews during the Third Reich, is a similar phenomenon.
4   The case of "Binjamin Wilkomirski" cannot go unmentioned in this context. Wilkomirski had entirely made up his Jewish biography, deceiving both the public and the Academic world with his experiences during the Holocaust in the mid-nineties.

and non-Jewish life in Germany can neither be described, nor comprehended without "Auschwitz" – this applies both to the Jewish and the non-Jewish communities. On one hand, I am confronting the suspicion of eschewing the historical responsibility I have as a German by seeking shelter with the Jewish community – whether it is uttered explicitly or whether it goes unsaid. On the other hand, the limitations and restrictions I encounter provide ample proof of the taboos and the multitude of limitations within the memory discourse in Germany. It's like running the gauntlet of Jewish-German demarcation lines.

One possibility to avoid the problem would be to retreat to the *professional distance* of the journalist. After all, a successful political editor is not required to have any political experience, and I sincerely doubt that sports journalists would make good soccer-players. The shortcomings of this comparison, however, are so obvious given the subject-matter in question, that they don't need any further explanation – nor do they provide an exit strategy for my aporetic situation. The problem, however, is not so much caused by the fact that the historical gap the genocide caused between non-Jews and Jews becomes visible here, but rather by the medium's claim to speak *for* someone as opposed to *about* someone. At least that's what the name "Jüdische Zeitung" suggests. And in my opinion, it is also what makes the whole matter particularly explosive with German history in mind.

Just Another Item on Display in "Jewrassic Park"?
One of the objections to be considered is that there is a certain danger in making a newspaper objectifying Jews and Jewish life, thus moving the whole enterprise in dangerous vicinity to either philo- or even anti-Semitic attitudes. Indeed, a problematic point is reached when it comes to non-Jews commenting or even criticizing Jews. If the Jewish community in Germany refuses to tolerate this, it's hardly possible to object – normality, so it seems, is obviously not conjured quite as easily, even if six decades and three generations separate us from the genocide.

It is by no means coincidental that Germany's mainstream society, with the exception of some anti-Semitic hostility and ethnological interest, has been considering the respective Jewish communities in both German post-war states an exotic and hermetic alien element with few points of contact with its surroundings. For a long time, this was mirrored by a more-than-comprehensible policy of isolation on part of the Jewish communities, a policy that featured a great deal of mistrust and an obvious need for self-protection. It was not until the mid-eighties, when a larger part of the perpetrators had already died and what can be considered a holocaust memorial boom began, that German mainstream society altered its relationship with the Jewish, which all of sudden was up-to-date. Since the Jewish community becomes increasingly visible again due to Jewish migration from the former Soviet Union, it is often instrumentalized as an evidence of innocence and historical rehabilitation of the "reunified" German republic.

According to its largely non-Jewish staff and the majority of its likewise non-Jewish readers, the *Jüdische Zeitung* is consequently in danger of becoming just another product of "Jewrassic Park" – which has been expanding ever since the 1980s - thus smoothly settling into a never ending line of phenomena such as "Jewish" culture festivals or "Jewish" museums. When venturing to describe "Jewish memory" and the more or less authentic Jewish presence in Berlin, Canadian-Jewish writer and historian Régine Robin wearily points out that there's not only Lea Rosh's[5] "Shoah business": "Most editors and publishers of Jewish newspapers and magazines are not Jewish […]"[6].

This, however, is contradicted by the very effort of the *Jüdische Zeitung* to discuss such phenomena, to scrutinize them and to actually address Jews living in Germany nowadays, or at least to make a commitment to them and their problems, which distinguishes it clearly from said museums and culture festivals.

Maintaining a balanced profile

The post-holocaust history of German Jews also has consequences for the media output of the (west-) German Jewish community – consequences that can still be felt today. A tendency to isolation is still prevalent, which turns out to be problematic whenever a high profile is maintained consciously while protests against anti-Semitic or even anti-Zionist manifestations are simultaneously directed towards the mainstream.

I experienced this in December 2006, when I congratulated the chairwoman of the Central Council of Jews in Germany, Charlotte Knobloch, on her re-election, while simultaneously criticizing the fact that the election had been held in-camera.[7] The Council's Secretary General Stephan J. Kramer stated in response to this criticism that, while the press's wish to attend the assembly meeting was legitimate, it was entirely up to the council to hold assemblies and elections behind closed doors: "The Central Council never adopted this kind of exhibitionism and has no intentions of doing so in

---

5 Lea Rosh, (full name: Edith Renate Ursula Rosh), is a non-Jewish German journalist and publicist, who has decisively contributed to the creation of the Memorial to the Murdered Jews of Europe in the centre of Berlin. She was born in 1936 in Berlin to a father who was a soldier in the German Wehrmacht.
6 Robin, Régine: Berlin. Gedächtnis einer Stadt, Berlin 2002, S. 267.
7 Moritz Reininghaus: Habemus mamam!, in: *Jüdische Zeitung* 12 (16), December 2006, 1.

the future."[8] Kramer continued: "The public's claim to information ends where the interests of the Jewish community are to be protected."

It is quite revealing that Kramer treats "transparency" and "exhibitionism" as synonyms, but it is even more striking that he distinguishes between "the public" and "the Jewish community", thus ruling out the mere possibility that something like a *Jewish public* even exists. His rhetoric simultaneously challenges elementary democratic rules within the Jewish community, and it makes it crystal clear that the media field I'm working in seems to be quite a special one, albeit no one outside the community seems to be seriously interested in it.

I'd like to further illustrate the thin line we're walking with our newspaper by referring to "Petition 5767", the so-called Berlin Declaration, an issue that was extensively debated in the *Jüdische Zeitung* in early 2007.[9] The declaration, penned by a group of Jewish intellectuals, asked the German government to fundamentally re-consider its political stance towards Israel in light of the Lebanon war. The larger part of the guilt for the escalation of violence in the Middle East is blamed on Israeli politics: "Israeli occupation of Palestinian territory, which has been going on since 1967, is the root of all evil.".[10] What made "Schalom 5767" so special was that the declaration had been signed by altogether 71 persons, some of them German-, some Israeli Jews, which made it interesting for me as an inner-Jewish debate.

A deeply felt bond with the state of Israel as well as an enormous amount of loyalty with Israeli politics was and is crucial to the self-conception of West German Jews, which rendered the petition a considerably higher degree of explosive force than similar movements emerging simultaneously in other countries: It broke a taboo. Although German national dailies *Süddeutsche Zeitung* and *Frankfurter Allgemeine Zeitung* had published the petition as a paid ad, there was almost no coverage of the subject matter. Neither seemed the Jewish media interested in breaking the silence: The *Jüdische Allgemeine Zeitung*, a competitor three times our size published by the Central Council of Jews in Germany,[11] elided publication or discussion.

For us, things got off the ground when I asked Kurt Julius Godstein, Honorary President of the International Auschwitz Committee, to write a text for the *Jüdische Zeitung's* January 2007 issue. Goldstein was supposed to

---

8   Stephan J. Kramer: Verschwörungstheorien helfen nicht!, in: *Jüdische Zeitung* 1 (17), January 2007, 1.
9   Cf. Verleger, Rolf: Israels Irrweg. Eine jüdische Sicht, Köln 2008, 94ff.
10 Ibid., 98.
11 The Central Council of Jews in Germany is the representation of Jews living in Germany towards the mainstream society.

explain how he, being a Jew, had been able to sign such a declaration.[12] After the text, in which Goldstein outlined his critical stance towards Israel – which is quite typical for a Jewish citizen of the former GDR – had been published, we received myriad protest letters. Both Jewish and non-Jewish "friends of Israel" abused the whole editorial staff as well as the author, who'd been a largely discredited figure even before the article due to his past as the director of GDR radio stations "Deutschlandsender" and "Stimme der DDR". The debate as such is not of particular interest here, one of the arguments uttered repeatedly as the onslaught unfolded, however, is: What Goldstein had written was not to be published in a *Jewish* newspaper. That the man expressing his concern was a Jewish-Communist Veteran from the Spanish civil war as well as a survivor of several concentration camps didn't mean a thing to the critics, as did the discussion that had been triggered, which at leas satisfied the less dogmatic minds.

The "Berlin declaration" was a downright paradigmatic case of active Jewish cosmopolitism: Jews as Jews advocated universal human rights. But even I, being non-Jewish, considered this inner-Jewish discussion by no means irrelevant for both the Jewish public and those interested in Jewish matters and was therefore happy to see a debate well under way.

Transformations of German Jewishness

I think my more or less "neutral position" as a non-Jewish journalist writing for a Jewish newspaper was quite an advantage when I made the decision to pick up the issue. Thus, an ongoing Jewish debate became public at least for a brief period of time. Moreover, this was the rare chance to observe how the gridlocked misunderstandings between Jews and non-Jews might be overcome, last not least because the history of segregation and separation of both groups reaches way back into the old Federal Republic of Germany.

Until the 1980s, a small and largely homogenous group perceived as "Jews" by the public had emerged. Its members were critical intellectuals and artists, who often avoided to speak as Jews in public and who didn't want to be associated with the "Congregation Jews" described above by any means. After the radical political change in 1989/1990, however, the Jewish community became more diverse. The religiously orthodox, conservative communities were supplemented with some liberal ones. Conservatism lost the predominance it had had for many years as the dominating socio-cultural structure of mostly Eastern European "displaced persons", who had stayed after the war more or less intentionally, dissolved. Russian-speaking

---

12 Kurt Julius Goldstein: "Ein Staat wie jeder andere. Israels Zukunft hängt von der Wahrung der Menschenrechte ab" [A state like any other state. Israel's future depends on the preservation of human rights", in: *Jüdische Zeitung* 1 (17), January 2007.

immigrants, who came in large numbers, accounted for most of the transformations occurring after 1990.

The German public, the media and German politics, however, are all perplexed about this religious, social and political diversification, or they try to ignore it. Since the 150 000 Jews living in Germany are nevertheless a quantitatively irrelevant group with reference to the country's total population, this is not too difficult, although at least some media have recently expressed a cautious open-mindedness of sorts towards the events. However, the still widespread, but in modern times genuinely anti-Semitic basic perception of "the Jews" can – at least as profoundly as it is necessary – only be overcome by specialized media, whose staff do not only represent the interests of the groups that emerged. Even the discussion surrounding the "Berlin declaration" was hardly reflected at all in general media. If at all, critical positions towards Israel were spread affirmatively unreflected by "leftist" media whose stance towards Israel is to be considered "critical" nevertheless.

Consequently, it was the very fact of being a non-Jew getting involved in the interests of the Jewish community via his occupation that enabled me to overcome polarization and to spark dialogue. The fact that the grandson of Nazi-party members gets himself in trouble six decades after the Holocaust because of the media public's black and white thinking is all the more disturbing because it took such a long time until this was possible. But there's also a positive aspect to it: At least our awareness of limiting German-Jewish demarcation lines in our allegedly tolerant present has been sharpened.

Moral Universalism?
"Among Europe's export goods, moral universalism is still one that is in high demand, although this does not take into account the fact that the particular experiences made during the war are the reason for the post-national constellation being communicable as a universal message to the world today."[13] Israeli sociologist Natan Sznaider introduces an argument to the discussion which is worth considering since it is particularly relevant for the coverage of and commenting upon the Middle East conflict, but which is, slightly varied, also valid for many parts of the German-Jewish discussion described here, especially when it comes to respecting the distinctiveness of the Jewish community while simultaneously applying universal standards to it. This is, last not least, a large part of what the *Jüdischen Zeitung* is endeavoring to achieve.

---

13 Szanider, Nathan: Gedächtnisraum Europa. Visionen des europäischen Kosmopolitismus. Eine jüdische Perspektive, Bielefeld 2008, 11.

My point is by no means to level the difference between German Jews and non-Jews. Neither do I want to construct a common master narrative of these two groups, the existence of which Sznaider has good reasons to deny.[14] And my work is definitely not about any kind of paternalism.

In fact, it is much more about the "post-national" thinking addressed by Sznaider. I do hope that I, being a member of the third post-Holocaust generation, will be able to address both the Jewish community and the German mainstream applying certain universal values independent of my own origin, while simultaneously respecting the distinctiveness of the Jewish community. Being a non-Jewish journalist using the media to communicate to both sides just how vivid, diverse and contradictory Jewishness can be, might be one step towards equality and the disbanding of unnecessary differentiations.

For me, this has also become a vital aspect of memory in Germany during the last couple of years. Even if – or maybe because – this causes irritation once in a while both among Jews and non-Jews. The state of insecurity described in the beginning of this text offers the chance to abandon established role models, or, at the very least, to reconsider them – last not least my own. No one ever said that such processes were going to be easy or painless.

And yet, the emergence of limitations of freedom of speech and polarization within the Jewish and non-Jewish public in Germany must not be the ultima ratio. The reasons why I've chosen the *Jüdische Zeitung* as my field of occupation include coincidental moments as well, such as my historical studies at Potsdam University's renowned faculty for Jewish studies. I can't even be entirely sure not to end up sailing the troubled waters of philo-Semitism or to venture into territory that's actually none of my business. Nevertheless, I hope the day will come when I won't be asked anymore why I'm doing what I do, but only how I'm doing it instead.

Moritz Reininghaus, born 1978 in Heilbronn, studied History, Philosophy and Literature in Potsdam and Berlin. After freelancing at the Moses Mendelssohn Zentrum for European Jewish Studies in Potsdam and as a freelance Journalist for several newspapers, in 2006 he became an editor at the Jüdische Zeitung. He lives with his family in Berlin.

---

14 Sznaider 2008, 106f.

The Bureaucracy of the Occupation:
A Love Letter to Hannah Arendt

YAEL BERDA

Dear Hannah,

I wish we could talk. Your insights have been powerful for me during these last few years. I wonder what you would have to say about the bureaucracy of the occupation in the Palestinian territories, a regime that on the basis of bureaucratic categories denies people their freedom of movement and the possibility to pursue the basic needs of life. I'm curious to know what you would think it says about the racial categories in which people think by in Israel and what are the possible categories we can think by, or imagine, in order to change the path of the administrative road taken in Israel.

I'm sure you will have some insight into how *We refugees*[1] create other refugees, even when they are living on their own territory. You may say that it is simply a form of the *end of the rights to the rights of man* because of the *decline of the nation state*, the thesis you lay out in the 'Origins of totalitarianism' over 50 years ago.[2] I'm not sure we can use that analysis in the Israeli case. And unlike you, I am not republican. I do not believe that human and political rights depend on the state for their existence. That view is too pessimistic.

I'm writing to you from Princeton, where you were the first woman to be admitted as a professor. Legend has it that you said when you were in the Institute for Advanced Study in 1959 that there is nothing more absurd than writing a book called 'On Revolution' in Princeton's quietude.

Anyhow, if you have a few moments, I wanted to tell you some of my thoughts and experiences in what I have come to call Planet Israel/Palestine. It is not organized as an academic argument but I thought you would not mind

---

1 Arendt, Hannah: We refugees, in: Menorah Journal, January 1943.
2 Arendt, Hannah: The origins of totalitarianism. New York 1958.

since it was a chance to convey some of the personal experiences I have had as a human rights lawyer amidst the crowded labyrinth of the bureaucracy of the occupation.

Documents

It was the strange wind that I felt when I first went to the military court on route 443; called "Ofer Camp" that was a first hint. A hint that when I stepped into the barbed wired military base, which encompassed a prison, a court (the Military Court of Judea and the Military Court of Appeals) and an interrogation center, that I had entered a different planet. This was an Israeli military court and prison designated to try and confine Palestinians who had violated military decree 378, the criminal code administered in the occupied territories. It was that feeling of difference, the difference of the way my body related to the space of the military court in Ofer, that compelled me to study what I came to call and know as the Bureaucracy of the Occupation.

A few years later, I began to think of that wind as a manifestation of what Walter Benjamin called "divine violence"[3], a violence which is outside the law, and of the difference as the difference of race, between myself, a Jewish Israeli with a passport, and my clients, Palestinians, residents of an occupied territory, who at best had a lese passé. I was governed by the Israeli criminal law; they were governed by a military decree.

Being Palestinian meant that one's movement was controlled by a permit system, checkpoints, border police and the general secret service which offers to give Palestinians a permit in exchange for working with them and betraying their people. I was free to leave the military court, get in my car and get to Jerusalem in twenty minutes. My client would remain detained in administrative detention without charge without ever having an idea what evidence the military prosecution had against him. His family could exit the military court through the Bitunia checkpoint, and it would take them between four to six hours to pass the checkpoints to get home. It was all about the documents people carried.

Something about that wind outside the military court drove home the realization that everything seemed to begin and end with the documents that one possesses: the passport, the visa, the permit, the papers, white papers with black letters and a signature that defined the boundaries of possibilities for a human being. This difference was not about what people believed, the music they liked, how many children they wanted to have, their passions. It was

---

3   Benjamin, Walter: Critique of Violence, in: Id.: Selected Writings, volume 1 1913-1926, ed. M. Bullock and M. W. Jennings, Cambridge et. al. 1996, pp. 236-53.

about the documents they carried. As Bertolt Brecht wrote, "The passport is the most precious part of a person."[4]

Race

"The conflict" had not been new to me. I made my first steps as a political activist at the age of 15, as part of the youth movement of the United Workers' Party (Mapam), when I was focused on issues of social equality within Israel. I had decided to become a lawyer so I would have power to advocate social rights, the right to education, housing, livelihood, the right to have a voice. At that time the organizing principle of my budding political agenda was one of class, of redistribution, of equality. That as it seemed to me was the basis for any left-wing agenda.

After serving in the Army, I went to volunteer at the Committee Against Torture, a small Israeli organization dedicated to raising awareness and advocacy against the use of torture in the interrogation of Palestinian detainees. It took months of recurring experiences for me to believe that my country was actively engaging in methods that were considered torture. It went against everything that the Israeli education system had continually instilled in us.

It was then that I began to understand that politics were not only about class they were about race. It was not enough to fight for equality; one had to make sure that equality was for all colors. All races. Politics were about race. They were about the category that the state decided one belonged too. And like Sociologist Collette Guillaumin said,"'Race does not exist. And yet it does." And: "Race does not exist. But it does kill people."[5]

Still in the last days of my army service, working for the Committee Against Torture raised new questions in my mind about the Israeli narrative, questions that have only grown since then.

Banality

I first learned about racism in elementary school, when we were taught about the Holocaust. I attended elementary school in the 1980's, at the neighborhood state school of Gilo Bet, on the outskirts of Jerusalem. It would take me another decade to find out that my school was partly built beyond the Green Line, the 1967 border, on the lands of occupied Beit Jala (near Bethlehem) in Palestine.

The main message that I got from the commemorative ceremonies, the books and the movies about the Holocaust in those first years of elementary

---

4   Brecht, Bertolt: Flüchtlingsgespräche [conversations in exile, 1940/41], Franfurt a.M. 2003, p.7, transl. C.S..
5   Guillaumin, Colette: Racism, Sexism, Power and Ideology. London/New York 1995, p. 13.

school was that something terrible had happened in Germany, something that made people silent, that enabled them to go about their daily life when the craziest things were happening. A huge force of evil had taken over in Germany, and had silenced everyone. How could it be that all these people engaged in evil? How could it be no one said anything? How could they believe that all Jews were not worthy of life? I had not known than that many other groups comprised the victims of the third Reich. It was not pointed out in state schools. Or that they were bad just because they were part of a religion, belonged to a group? It sounded crazy to me. How were they silent?

That was long before I read Hannah Arendt's 'Eichmann in Jerusalem: report on the banality of evil',[6] when I first began to see a glimmer of a possible answer to that question. Why were they silent? There was a system, it was about bureaucracy, it was about the categories of people the state decided to make and pursue, and then turn those categories into administration. White paper, black letters and a signature. Selections, statistics, operations, filing, processing. Papers moving from one desk to the other. There were no people there. Just papers that moved around. Categories of people became suspect populations, than they became objective enemies. That means that their identity made them dangerous. Consequently, they were turned into a demographic threat.

Obviously, this was not the reason the Holocaust happened, but it did shed light on the possibility of the instrumental management of the morally impossible, the administration of the unimaginable. Of the banality of evil.

You may be upset now, dear reader. In these few paragraphs I have crossed a line by writing about Israelis and Palestinians and Jews and Germans on the same page. You may be thinking: "How can she compare? How can she even form a link between the two subjects? They are totally different. Qualitatively and quantitatively!"

You are right.

The Israeli military occupation of the Palestinian territories and the series of events we call the Holocaust are incomparable, and I have no intention of comparing them. As a matter of fact I believe that using big words such as genocide and massacre too freely has a detrimental effect on the possibility of exposing and shifting forms of violence and racism deployed against people. Both the use of the Holocaust as political capital or a form of justification on the one hand, usually by persons who call themselves pro Israeli, and the melodramatic comparison with the Holocaust on the other, by those who call themselves pro Palestinian seems like a cheap and terrible political game to play, one that blinds and perpetuates violence to a great extent.

---

6 Arendt, Hannah: Eichmann in Jerusalem; a report on the banality of evil. New York 1963.

What I do find highly important is the role that bureaucracy and race play together when there is an asymmetric relationship between peoples, and what we can learn from the past in order to avoid the ubiquitous perils of a bureaucratic administration that differentiates its practices on the basis of race.

Hannah Arendt writes on race and bureaucracy in her 'The origins of totalitarianism'. In the section on imperialism, she perceives the racialized bureaucratic practices developed in the European colonies; she focuses on the writings of prominent colonial bureaucrats such as Lord Cromer in Egypt and Cecil Rhodes in Zimbabwe, as the laboratory, a general rehearsal for the bureaucratic practices deployed in the European totalitarian regimes. Practices of racialized bureaucracy developed in the colonies were subsequently shipped home to the metropole, where they ripened into administrative practices that enabled the holocaust structurally. They also enabled the silence. For the reason that if one got used to running a system based on racial hierarchy in which there were different laws for different types of people, those ideas and practices were transported back to Europe, where they made their way into dismembering the universal rule of law.

In Israel today, the bureaucracy of the occupation is a vast and complex set of decrees and practices that are used for the management of the Palestinian population. Many administrative bodies from the bureaucratic labyrinth, from the military civil administration, police and border police, the Ministry of Labor, the Defense Ministry to the general secret service, which together constitute the permit-based regime that categorizes and distributes permit or denies to Palestinians entry from the occupied territories into Israel, and within the West Bank itself. From 1972 to 1991, 30 to 85% of Palestinian workers worked in Israel. The Oslo process ended the open borders policy and bought into being a structure of military decrees designed to control the movement of the population, both within the West Bank and into Israel. The permit regime is based on the sovereign control of territory through checkpoints, road blocks and the Separation Wall, on the deployment of armed forces and on an administrative system that produces, checks and disallows movement by Palestinians, based on their categorization as "security threats".

Over 200 000 Palestinian residents of the West Bank are categorized as "denied entry" because they are security threats. The reasons for denial are unexplained yet from practice we know that it is enough to have had a family member in jail to be denied entry, and that the denial is used to recruit informants for the secret service. One who is denied entry never knows the reason for this denial, the identity of the official making the decision, or the law or regulation that gives the authority to do so. Out of the 90 cases I represented in the Supreme Court on this issue, over 40 were resolved before the hearing. The state attorneys had convinced the secret service that there was no need for the denial.

Disenchantment

When I began representing Palestinians who had been denied entry because the secret service had categorized them as security threats in the Israeli supreme court, I gradually began to understand the extent to which the elementary school education in the Israeli state school had made its mark on me, and how much it was precisely that education that compelled me to petition the Supreme Court against the secret service and the military commander of Judea and Samaria in their unexplained decisions to profile people as security threats.

What we had been taught about the Israeli democratic state, about the Israeli Declaration of Independence which guaranteed equality to all its residents, fell to pieces dramatically in the face of the anonymous document; a laconic decision by a faceless secret service officer, who denies without explanation a father's possibility to work and feed his children; a woman's ability to obtain medical care; a student's possibility to study at the university; and families who live five km from each other from visiting each other for years.

Hundreds of thousands of people who are denied the conditions for life. Because they are who they are. Because in the view of the bureaucrats of the occupation, inside every Palestinian body, the ghost of a terrorist may be lurking. Because in the face of security, the law crumbles, relinquishing the procedural monopoly of the state on violence to security experts, who ubiquitously perpetuate the Israeli public's fear of anyone who is Palestinian, because "you never know".

Standing in the empty Supreme Court room hearing after hearing, the questions that I had asked as a child grew in my mind. How were people silent in the face of such injustice? How could the Israeli public allow and support policies in which people were denied the conditions of life based on their belonging to a group? How could such power go unchecked, the Supreme Court bowing its head to three sentences written by a secret service officer? How could this entire bureaucratic, quasi–legal apparatus comprising the permit regime function without public outcry? How does fear of people boil down to shuffling of white papers, black letters and signature?

Imagining new categories

Hannah, you write of post-revolutionary France and America, that according to revolutionaries established the two republics, it was the only form of government that is not eternally at open or secret war with mankind. You write: "But in this republic, as it presently turned out, there was no space reserved, no room left for the exercise of precisely those qualities which had been instrumental to building it."[7]

Israel today is not at all what it was originally dreamed to be. Or what we were told as children that it was, or was supposed to be. Its neo-liberal economic policies are creating an experience of social atomization that is all the more acute because it is juxtaposed with the narrative of equality, of being the light of nations, of "the chosen people" that you have so deeply criticized in your 'Origins of totalitarianism', deeming the concept a possible root cause of anti-Semitism.

What happens to those great powers that form a nation, linking people's hearts to a territory, creating an imagined string of DNA that seems to bind bodies together, creating an imaginary border, turning people into a community that dreams of a new world, one of equality, of peace, of independence, of liberty of fraternity?

Where do those dreams disappear to when it becomes time to actually manage a nation, create an administration, run a bureaucracy?

Why is there "no space reserved, no room left" for the dreams that inspired people to partake in formidable, strange tales of belief and bravery, to make revolutionary changes once that dream realizes some material form?

I believe that the bureaucracy of the occupation and rule of racial difference it entails does not remain confined to the occupied territories. It seems to me that the banality of evil, the merciless shuffling of papers with moral disregard to what the documents say and the categories they define are a danger, not only to Palestinians, but to Israelis as well. Procedure and administration can never be divorced from the actions it wishes to manage. No-one has shown that better than you.

If you have any thoughts or ideas on how to understand this all, or how to imagine new categories we can all think by on Planet Israel/Palestine, email me at yberda@princeton.edu please.

Yours, Yael

Yael Berda, born 1976 in New York City, is an Israeli human rights lawyer and activist. Currently, she is completing her PhD in Sociology at Princeton University. She co-founded Mahapach, a student led movement for education, housing and livelihood, organizing empowerment of local leadership in disempowered neighbourhoods and villages. Her doctoral thesis on the bureaucracy of the occupation in the occupied Palestinian territories will be published winter 2010 (in Hebrew).

---

7 Arendt, Hannah: On revolution. New York 1963, p 29

On Filipina Caregivers and the Limits of Israeli Belonging, or: Sentimental Zionism and the Solace of Southern Tel Aviv

CLAUDIA LIEBELT

On sentimental Zionism and multiple returns

In 1996, only days after finishing high school in Germany, I left for Israel to "discover my Jewish roots," join my then boyfriend in discovering his Israeli roots and maybe – so I thought whenever I was in a melodramatic mood – never come back. As to my Jewish roots, these were an identification project very dear to me in my teenage years and the fact that this was so almost certainly had to do with my feelings of dislocation and a yearning of belonging as an adopted child. While I was raised by German protestant parents, I always knew about my (Jewish) biological family and became very attached to my biological mother after I met her again, shortly before turning eighteen.

Leaving towards Israel in 1996 as sentimental Zionists, we took a ship from Cyprus, arriving at the port in Haifa at the crack of dawn. One year later, however, I returned to Cologne, having become instead a disappointed post-Zionist, not travelling to Israel again for several years. The experiences I collected during that year nevertheless affected me deeply, and were of crucial importance to a political and academic project that led me to write on Filipina domestic workers in Israel.[1]

For one thing I attended a Hebrew language course in a state-sponsored school in Tel Aviv, a so-called ulpan, alongside dozens of *'olim chadashim*, that is (Jewish) immigrants from all over the world. During the course, we were taught not only the Hebrew language, but cultural stuff that the Ministry

---

1 While about ninety percent of Filipinos in Israel are female, in the following I will use the female form only when referring exclusively to women.

of Immigration and Absorption apparently thought proper citizens in the making should know. The language course was part of the Zionist encouragement of Jewish mass immigration to Israel.[2] Nevertheless, the state-centred "we Jews against the world" discourse I encountered in my ulpan was too much for me at the time. The contradiction of having been engaged in anti-fascist and anti-nationalist politics from early teenage years onwards while now actively becoming part of an ethnic entity, participating in national identity politics and rituals, was obvious. Nevertheless, it took some time for me to realise this, and when I did, I felt increasingly estranged from life in Israel rather than at "home".

Secondly, whereas throughout the mornings I lived the life of an ambivalent Jewish immigrant, a *'ola chadasha*,[3] in the afternoons I turned into an *'ovedet zara bilti chokit* (an illegalised foreign worker) in order to make a living. Alongside mainly Nigerian, Ghanaian, Latin American, Rumanian and Filipino migrant women whom I met on the buses and at the bus stops on the way to and from our workplaces in the affluent north of Tel Aviv, I cleaned apartments as a part-time domestic worker, which was – and most likely still is – the easiest way to earn a relatively large amount of money without a legal work permit in Israel. There was a huge contradiction between these mornings and afternoons: While on the one hand, I experienced Israel as a state that embraced me as a potential Jewish immigrant (a "returnee"), I also learned from my acquaintanceship with other illegalised domestic workers that it rigidly excluded non-Jewish immigrants from staying on – not to speak of citizenship and belonging – even while it desperately needed and actively recruited cheap labour migrants, and even more so since the ousting of Palestinian workers from the Israeli labour market after 1993.

During another visit to Israel in 2001, I met a number of sympathetic, young Israeli activists. Only recently had *Ta'ayush*[4] and other similar minded groups been formed. Suddenly, the idea of spending more time in Israel made

---

[2] The state encouragement of Jewish immigration to Israel was legally sanctioned in 1950 through the Law of Return (Hebrew *Hok HaShvut*). The Law of Return still forms the basis of Israeli immigration policy today, granting virtually unrestricted immigration rights and citizenship to Jews (as well as their children, grandchildren and spouses).

[3] I never actually applied for Israeli citizenship, and do not know whether I would be granted it in the current political climate within the Israeli Ministry of Interior, which has become much stricter since the mid-1990s. Explaining my situation to the Ministry during my first visit in 1996, I was granted temporary residency instead of a tourist visa, in order to have time to decide whether to apply for immigration.

[4] "Co-existence" in Arabic; an Arab-Jewish grassroots movement "working to break down the walls of racism and segregation by constructing a true Arab-Jewish partnership" (retrieved 7 January 2009 from www.taayush.org/new/we.html).

sense to me once more. In 2003 I returned in order to work in a south Tel Aviv workers' centre.[5] By then, I assume, most of my acquaintances from the mornings as a virtual immigrant seven years ago had settled in Israel, acquired houses, founded families, and obtained employment in relatively secure jobs. Those from the afternoons as illegalised "foreign worker" though, had most likely either been deported or were continuing to work in Tel Aviv as illegalised cleaners, spending their days commuting between the poor southern neighbourhoods where they lived and the affluent ones where they were employed.

Originally planned as a relatively short post-study stay, due to a large-scale deportation campaign of "illegals" by the Israeli government, which now violently drew attention to itself in Tel Aviv, I perceived a state of crisis and urgency that made me stay on. Hundreds of migrants threatened by deportation now streamed into the workers' centre to seek practical help and legal advice: because they had been fired by their employers (who feared being punished for employing an "illegal"); because family members or friends had been arrested and made subject to deportation orders; or because they themselves feared being forced to leave, and did not know how to protect themselves. In this desperate situation, people started telling me about their lives in Israel and I decided to record their stories, feeling the urge to document them.[6]

Against the background of my political engagement in Cologne, where the anti-deportation group No One is Illegal had been very active and a no-border camp[7] had just taken place, I was interested in the Tel Aviv situation from the viewpoint of a "European" activist. How was Tel Aviv, as a gateway city towards "Schengenland"[8] affected by EU migration policies? What kind of struggles took place in this relatively wealthy part of the "other side" of the Mediterranean, crossing which every year dozens of people lose their lives on their way into the EU? Were there social movements in Israel, which like those in Europe made demands such as "No One Is Illegal", "Freedom of Movement", or even "No Borders, No Nations, Stop Deportations"? In the following, I shall discuss my subsequent research in the light of personal experiences and observations.

---

5   Kav LaOved, see www.kavlaoved.org.il, retrieved 9 January 2009.
6   This eventually led to a doctorate in social anthropology.
7   See www.noborder.org/camps/03/ger/display.php?id=234, retrieved 9 January 2009
8   Named after a small town in Luxembourg where in 1985 29 states (25 European Union states as well as Iceland, Norway, Liechtenstein and Switzerland) signed an agreement in order to facilitate free movement of persons within the area and better control and "defend" the zone's external borders.

Research stories: on Filipinos' Care and Claims
Within Israel's ethnically segmented labour market, Filipino women have long since become the prototypical caregivers of the elderly in Israel. The image of an aged person resting on a Filipina's elbow, as well as Israeli parks where the elderly sit in one corner chatting and their Filipina caregivers in another, have become a recurrent motif not only of Israeli street life, but also in Israeli films and the arts. As described in much of the literature on Filipino domestic workers elsewhere, Filipinos in Israel are typically highly educated but suffer from low wages, unemployment and economic misery within their deeply indebted home country, where – some claim – colonialism never really ended. Typically they pay about (U.S.) $5,000 illegally demanded "placement fees" to Israeli recruitment agencies in order to obtain a job in Israel, where they earn wages of approximately (U.S.) $500-900. At least at the beginning of their stay, they often live in the private homes of their employers being available for work six days a week, 24 hours a day.

Domestic work involves great dangers, structural abuse and exploitation for those who engage in it. Filipino domestic workers in Israel have been found to suffer from underpayment, non-payment of social benefits, passport confiscation, sexual abuse, and frequently dehumanising discrimination. Even though, migrant women are not mere passive victims but have developed collective knowledge and strategies to fight abuses and exploitation. Moreover, in situations typified by spatial density and continuous presence, caring work is a deeply affective form of labour that to a great extent involves always complex affection and intimacy between employers and domestic workers. As caregivers for mainly elderly Jewish persons, many Filipino domestic workers in Israel were and are directly confronted with the ongoing sufferings and traumas of the Shoah, anti-Semitism and the Second World War.

Filipino caregivers employed by Shoah survivors often talk about how their employers' memories and trauma relating to anti-Semitism, racial persecution and the war and these have a deep emotional impact on the Filipinos' own everyday lives. For example, I was told how they would be woken up from their employer's nightmares, and often spent hours comforting them at night. On talking about their first encounter with the painful, violent and often traumatic past of their employers, Filipina interviewees typically speak of a shock, as well as something they felt completely unprepared for and initially helpless at dealing with. Filipinos recount that, upon their coming to Israel, their knowledge of the Second World War in Europe, the Shoah and anti-Semitism had been rather superficial. When confronted with employers' emotionally upsetting stories, many feel the urge to understand them better. One of my interview partners, Novelita, who for years took care of an Alzheimer patient, a survivor, began to read numerous books on Jewish history and the Shoah. Furthermore, she visited Yad Vashem, the Jerusalem Holocaust memorial site and museum, on several occasions. Apparently, the wish of Filipina caregivers to understand frequently matched their employers' willingness to share. For example, another interview partner, Rose, who also took care of a survivor, sometimes talked to her German-speaking employer Deborah for hours about the torture and sufferings she had endured in a concentration camp. Throughout these talks, Deborah had told her things (about being raped, for example) that Rose was sure Deborah had not even told her own children. "I might be the last to know her stories," Rose once told me and added: "And I know better German than her children do."

While I never met Deborah, I was introduced to many of the German-speaking employers of my interview partners. Some refused when their caregiver asked them whether they could bring me home. One woman, a survivor of Theresienstadt, who suffered badly from Alzheimer's disease, started to scream when her caregiver told her upon my arrival (although I did request to announce my visit beforehand) that I was from Germany. On the other hand, many of the elderly nevertheless seemed happy about having a visitor with whom they were able to communicate in German, and urged me to visit them regularly. Others preferred speaking Hebrew, and refrained from talking about anything that had to do with their lives prior to immigrating to Israel. Some of those who spoke Hebrew with me even apologised for (still) reading German books and watching German TV channels, assuming that I – like the Israeli mainstream, so they apparently felt – would judge their linguistic/cultural attachment as an inability or unwillingness to integrate into the national culture.

Their daily roles as the managers of households make Filipino domestic workers not simply the caregivers, but the symbolic—and in some cases even material—heiresses of Israel's elderly. From this typically affective, but also boring and difficult work, Filipinos derive a sense of belonging and claim the right of being part of Israeli society. Belonging to the large global diaspora of Filipino contract workers and familiar with Jewish history and Israeli discourses, Filipino activists and interviewees in Israel increasingly claim: "We are the Jews of Today!" Hereby, and also by simply staying on after their work permits expired, forming families and appropriating parts of Tel Aviv's urban space, migrants implicitly call into question the most fundamental aspects of the Israeli state: its definition of Jewishness and of being a Jewish state.

As in European labour-importing countries, it took Israeli state institutions some time to realise that contract migrant workers might "dare" to stay on and become an integral part of Israeli society. In 2002, the Israeli Central Bureau of Statistics announced that by the end of 2001 there were 240,000 overseas labour migrants in Israel, the majority of whom possessed no legal status.[9] Soon after, in alarmist manner the media compared the number of unemployed Israeli citizens with the number of non-Jewish labour migrants rounded up: 300,000! The stage was set for a huge deportation campaign of labour migrants. This campaign forms the background of the event described in the following.

Activist tales: on not shouting "No Border No Nation" in Israel

On 3 September 2003, the economically deprived, south Tel Aviv neighbourhood Neve Sha'anan received public attention of a kind which it had not received since at least the most recent, large suicide bombing in its streets, on 5 January 2003.[10] This September evening, the area saw one of the largest anti-deportation demonstrations that took place in Israel after the government had launched its large deportation campaign of "illegals" in September 2002. Several hundred demonstrators marched down the pedestrian Neve Sha'anan, the heart of the neighbourhood which like no other space has become associated with the presence of labour migrants in Israel. In Neve Sha'anan, Chinese, Rumanian, Filipino and African workers have shared rented apartments, created families, opened places of worship and shops to serve the needs of immigrants. It is here that they organised collectively so as to struggle for political, social and legal inclusion into the Israeli state and society.

The weeks prior to the demonstration saw the neighbourhood turned into the major battleground of a large deportation campaign, which – so the Police Chief Inspector General Shlomo Aharonishky had advised his officers – was to be tackled like a "military operation."[11] In the wake of this campaign, the urban neighbourhood, unhomely at the best of times turned into a space of unregulated violence, with teams of the newly formed Migration Police unit breaking down doors and windows of private apartments in search of "illegals", blocking streets, arresting and carrying people away to detention in waiting coaches, and more generally checking everyone who, to the officers, did not look Jewish and middle-class enough.

Most of the demonstrators that day were activists of leftist, Zionist youth movements or volunteers of the three NGOs that had organised the event, namely the KavLa Oved workers' centre, Physicians for Human Rights, and

---

9   See KLO and HMW 2003. *Immigration Administration or Expulsion Unit?* Joint report May 2003. Tel Aviv: Kav LaOved, Hotline for Migrant Workers, p. 6.
10 Neve Sha'anan has become one of the most seriously affected areas of suicide bombings in Israel. Among others, suicide bombings hit the neighbourhood on 6 January, 25 January and 17 July in 2002, as well as on 5 January 2003. Many of the victims were (illegalised) migrants.
11 Quoted from KLO and HMW, op.cit, p. 35

the Hotline for Migrant Workers. Furthermore, there were several prominent figures, such as singer Chava Alberstein, actress Gila Almagor and member of parliament Yossi Sarid.[12] As the demonstration was coming to an end, they made speeches: in his contribution Sarid demanded "a more dignified and intelligent way" of doing away with illegalised guest workers; after him, Gila Almagor spoke out against the deportation of children, who had been born in Israel to "illegal" parents. Neither speech questioned the illegalisation of people as such but appealed instead to the compassion of a Jewish audience, who had collectively experienced migration, persecution and deportation. Their speeches resonated well with many signs carried by demonstrators which read "Stop the Deportation of Children," "For More Humane Deportations," and "We Are All Migrants".

During this demonstration, I noted not only the absence of the Israeli radical left, but also the more radical slogans popular in European demonstrations and "No Border" camps at the time, such as "No Border, No Nation, Stop Deportation." One could argue that the more radical political activists were preoccupied with the struggle against the Israeli occupation of Palestinian territories and what is generally called Ha Matsav (Hebrew, "The Situation"). Moreover, within a situation of increasing militancy and the violent creation and demarcation of ever more physical, national, cultural and not least economic boundaries in Israel/Palestine, such a demand seemed to appear far too threatening to many.

My personal despair about the ordeals I witnessed in the wake of the deportation campaign, and my anger about the political weakness of the anti-deportation campaign were mixed with the feeling that I did not belong "enough" to Israeli society to be in a position to mobilise or criticise: for example the non-usage of slogans like "No Border, No Nation, Stop Deportations," which – so the Israeli activists I talked to had rightly concluded – implied the dissolution of a Jewish state. Accordingly, I felt increasingly uneasy about my political engagement in this field which in turn became more and more "academic" in style. Would this have been different, had I applied for Israeli citizenship or decided to stay on in Israel after my first "return", I wondered.

***

As so often, it was silent actions in everyday life rather than shouted slogans that changed reality. While neither the recruitment and illegalization nor the deportation of labour migrants have stopped, the de facto limits of Israeli

---

12 Co-founder and former chairman of the liberal left-wing Meretz-Yachad party and MP until he withdrew from party politics in 2006.

citizenship rights have been in a state of flux ever since. Even though civil marriage is still not available in Israel, many Filipino women have managed to marry Israeli citizens and be granted residency. A first generation of second generation, non-Jewish migrants, born to illegalised parents who managed to stay on, has grown up and claims equal rights in accent free Hebrew.

Indeed, in 2005 an inter-ministerial committee initially set up to tighten up Israel's immigration laws – based on the assumption that the demographic "balance" and thereby the Jewish character of the state were being acutely threatened by non-Jewish migration flows – ultimately recommended granting citizenship to a group of these youngsters. Filipinos and other so-called "New Israelis" are increasingly present in the Israeli public, starring in films, talk and talent shows as public figures. This changing face of Israeli society is to a large extent due to migrants' assertions that they belong to the country. The social, legal and political citizenship rights gained from this were negotiated by appeals to compassion, often by persons, who in the media were actually portrayed – in spite of their non-Jewishness – as ideal olim chadashim, that is hardworking, Hebrew-speaking residents knowledgeable about Jewish culture and religion.

It is important to note though, that these negotiated citizenship rights did not (yet) result in a transformation of the categories Jew / new immigrant / returnee versus non-Jew / foreign worker / temporary "guest" themselves. Otherwise, the many Palestinians who have lived in Israel without legal permits for many years or were born there, would have had to be included.

Memory threads: on the Solace of southern Tel Aviv
As I write this, I am sitting in my new home in Manchester, having left Tel Aviv once more, and happily enjoy the luxury of holding European Union citizenship and life in a place, where the so-called Middle-East conflict is far away indeed. A place, where locals would understand the notion of "The Situation" as something related to the weather, I assume. Over the course of the past year spent in Israel, I admit to having become fed up with the ethno-national, mainstream politics and aggressive rhetoric – not to speak of the actions – of a society at war. But as I obsessively read the latest news about the war in Gaza, the minimised icon of the website of the Israeli paper Ha'aretz constantly tempting me in my laptop's taskbar, writing up stories gathered in southern Tel Aviv and feeling rather detached from the rainy reality around me, the following situation comes to mind.

On a grey and windy afternoon in February 2008, my mother on her visit to Tel Aviv, and I sat in a Tel Aviv sherut (a share taxi) heading up Allenby Street towards southern Tel Aviv. This being my biological mother, as they say, from whom I was separated during childhood and whose absence made me construct my own "Jewish" childhood fantasy-world. She grew up in a small German town with Jewish parents who kept a distance from their Christian neighbours, sent their daughter to a boarding school, and never spoke about the past. Nevertheless, her parents regularly took her to spend the summer holidays in Israeli beach hotels in the late 1950s and 1960s.

Sitting in the sherut that day, she confided, "I feel at home here like I never felt anywhere else." At first I was angry, and thought how unfair it was that she could actually say that, and most Israelis would probably not think how bizarre it was, but understand. As a matter of fact, she could decide that this would be her home and be granted citizenship in no time, while thousands of those who had spent most of their lives in Israel, would remain excluded. But then, I became aware that she had not said this sentence during the previous days, when we had gone to see friends in a Kibbutz – a very Zionist space – or had visited Jerusalem (even more ideologically charged). In the sherut at this moment, apart from us there were two middle-aged women with their shopping bags debating in Russian, two young American students, a Filipina who looked tired after a day's work, and a young Tel Avivian shouting into her mobile phone in Hebrew. Outside, against the background of the colourful, slightly shabby shop windows of Allenby Street on the verge of becoming Ha'Aliyah Street, the streets were crowded with the residents of this poorer part of Tel Aviv.

And I had to admit that I too, wildly loved, and somehow felt at home in this part of the city, an oasis not of retreat from the violence and shabbiness and injustices of social reality, but a space of the often unspectacular, everyday struggles against them.

Claudia Liebelt, born 1976 in Cologne, has completed her Ph.D. in Social Anthropology on Filipina domestic workers in Israel. She is currently working as research assistant in a comparative project on diaspora and religion at the Institute of Law, Politics & Justice at Keele University, UK. She has published on gender, migration, domestic work, the Filipino diaspora and urban anthropology.

Radical Pedagogy under the Migration Regime

URI ELLIS

In the years 2003-2007 I was involved in an educational project in a public school in South Tel Aviv. Because of the poor neighborhood the school was in, it served a variety of underprivileged populations: children of poor "Mizrachi" families – a general name given to Jewish immigrants from Arabic countries - , new immigrants from the former USSR, Palestinian Arabs of Israeli citizenship, and a large group (about thirty percent), are children of migrant workers. Together with a group of young educators we tried to cut down the rate of students dropping out from school, and to give them a chance to pass the matriculation exams which provide a genuine opportunity for social mobility. It was because of the poor socio-economics of its students that we chose to work in that specific urban school. Informed by the tradition of Paulo Freire and other radical educators[1], we all moved to live in the neighborhood, and wanted to work with the local community in order to make a difference in political terms. In this essay I will describe our work with the children of migrant workers as a process of revealing and learning seemingly remote from the memory of the Holocaust: revealing the social-economic context of the lives of migrant workers in Israel and its relevance to the political order, as well as learning a lesson about education and humanism in this era of militant neo-liberalism and nationalism.

---

1 Radical pedagogy, also known as "critical pedagogy", "pedagogy for radical democracy", or "pedagogy of possibility". Paulo Freire was a Brazilian educator and the most influential theorist of radical pedagogy.

Migrant Workers in Israel – some Background[2]

The emergence of migrant workers in Israel is a fairly new phenomenon, although the conditions enabling it are deeply rooted in the Israeli political economic logic. Though neo-liberal ideology suggests seeing migrant workers as a temporary solution for a temporary economic need, the Israeli market has always been based on underpaid underprivileged workers filling the permanent void of what is known as the "triple D" jobs: jobs that are difficult, dirty and demanding.

This void was at first filled by Mizrachi Jews and Palestinian natives. After Israel's occupation of Gaza and the West Bank in 1967, they were replaced by Palestinians without Israeli citizenship. In the late 80's, when the first Intifada began, Israel exerted a foreclosure policy on Gaza and the West Bank, in which extreme restrictions were put on Gaza and West Bank Palestinians who wanted to work in Israel. Eliminating these workers from the Israeli market, together with an accelerated globalisation process that took place in the mid-eighties, made the import of workers from Third-World countries a "legitimate" solution to the shortage of easy-to-exploit workers. As a result intensive importation of migrant workers started in the early nineties, so that by the year 2000 there were already 240,000 legal and illegal foreign workers in Israel, comprising 8.7% of the Israeli labour market.

This major shift made possible by the depiction of the Gaza Strip and West Bank Palestinian workers as a "security threat", sheds light on the many ways in which the field of labour is used for political and economical manipulation by the State. In this case, it serves as a means of penalisation against Palestinians and of oppression of the Palestinian uprising; demonstrating as it does the extent of the Palestinian unilateral dependence on Israel; in turn rendering possible further oppression of the Palestinians, and thus further exploitation. Moreover, such an intervention in the so-called "free market" provide wealthy employers not only with cheap manpower, but also helps to keep working wages low in the entire Israeli labour market, making it more profitable for employers.

At its peak, the percentage of migrant workers in Tel-Aviv reached up to 16% of the city's population. Many of them were illegal under Israeli labour law. The migrant workers, especially those with children, have tended to cluster in south Tel-Aviv, in the neighborhood surrounding the central bus station. Children of both legal and illegal workers attended a school in the area, together with kids from other poor neighborhoods in the area. It was in this school that our encounter with those children began. Rents for property in

---

[2] For further reading on immigrant workers in Israel see the Adava Center's excellent report (2003) at http://www.adva.org/UserFiles/File/ovdim%20zarim%20kamp.pdf (Hebrew) which I have used in writing this section.

this area are the cheapest in Tel Aviv because it is a center of criminal activity, prostitution, and drug addicts, making apartments in this area the only affordable choice for the migrants. However, it is not a good place for children to grow up in, and providing those children with an alternative, after-school hang-out location was a top priority for us.

"Tel Aviv's Trash-Can for unwanted Children"

In 2003-2007 I directed the activities of an NGO in the Tel Aviv-Jaffa region. One of the projects we started involved a group of 18-year-olds, highly committed activists who volunteered to live in a commune in the neighbourhood and work with local children. The local school we started working with is often thought of – especially by the school's staff – as "Tel-Aviv's garbage-can for unwanted children". It gathers children from the poorest backgrounds: students from veteran Mizrachi families, newcomers from the former U.S.S.R, Palestinians from Jaffa and from the occupied territories[3], children of immigrant workers, and lately also children of African refugees. Tel Aviv's current mayor, a former air-force official, is also a former school headmaster in one of Tel Aviv's largest schools. As a headmaster, he became infamous for his school segregation policy, having separate classes for students from the southern and northern neighborhoods of the city. As mayor, he directs the municipal educational system in the same manner he used to direct his school. One of Tel-Aviv's high officials once told me "off the record", that even though the city was obliged by law to give all children education, the law still did not specify the quality of that education. And so, although in urgent need of extra resources, the school hardly received municipal support.

We decided to offer the school assistance teaching maths, as well as reading and writing skills. Working only with the students whose status was the worst in their class, we got to meet many of the migrant workers' children. Their future, regardless of their school achievements, was sealed: turning eighteen and becoming legally an adult, they would automatically become illegal dwellers facing deportation. Returning to the original country is hardly ever possible as a result of financial or health related constraints, civil war, or simply because the child that was born in Israel has already lost any link to their parents' original country/countries, including the language(s), and as a result deportation means losing his/her whole world. Consequently the only choice these children have is to become illegal workers like their parents. Naturally, the decision to teach them drew much criticism: why wouldn't we

---

3 Children whose parents had been pushed to collaborate with the Israeli security forces in the occupied Palestinian territories, and because their security had been compromised were afterwards relocated by the Israeli Government to neighbourhoods of this kind.

prefer working with Israeli students? And what use would preparing those students for the matriculation exams be?

I believe the decision to work with migrant workers' children is an ethical choice rather than a pragmatic one, and I will return to this point later on. At this stage, I would only like to stress that giving those kids an experience of success, even in maths, facilitated an initial connection to them and their community, which enabled further acquaintance with their world. And their world, as we soon learned, was a world dominated by a constant fear of deportation.

The "Deportation Police"
In 2004, under Ariel Sharon's government, Israel established an immigration administration whose sole function has been arresting illegal migrant workers and expelling them from the country. A special task force of 400 policemen was put together and was named the "Immigration Police". I remember the day that the government announced that the goal set for Immigration Police operations was 50, 000 arrests and deportations per year. There was real panic in the streets around the central bus station. What had been loud and lively conversations turned into whispers. Questions were asked obsessively seeking optimistic news. Either way, the kids could feel something had gone terribly wrong.

In the course of the following years, the Immigration Police became famous for its violent arrests and harassment. Fathers, often being the sole providers of the family, were the preferred target of these arrests. It was assumed that the rest of the family would have no choice but to leave the country and follow them to their country of origin. In extreme cases, young children were left alone in Israel without any care after both their parents had been deported overnight. Mothers recounted to us how children were wetting their beds at night, fearing the Immigration Police would come at night and arrest them or their parents. Children would arrive late for school explaining they had seen a police car, and then hidden behind a garbage can. Even legal workers were arrested on a daily basis, and their children would have to go to the police station again and again to identify their parents and have them released. In other cases, high school students themselves would be arrested, and would have to prove they were still minors and therefore could not be subject to deportation. Quite understandably they felt, hunted. Community leaders and activists were the first ones to get deported, so that the strong solidarity networks that had existed tended to collapse. Soon enough it was hard to spot an immigrant worker on the streets. They had all gone underground.

Projects with Migrant Workers

The crisis of the migrant workers in Israel gave rise to various civil society projects. Some organizations committed themselves mainly on the basis of a critical "human rights" perspective, while others took part with a more radical *political* perspective. Organizations like *Mesila* (The Help Center for Foreign Workers), *Kav LaOved* (Workers Hotline), Hotline for Migrant Workers, Physicians for Hunan Rights, and *La Escuelita* (a learning center for migrant workers from the Latin community) all did important work in extremely difficult conditions.

In some cases, like in the jointly organised public campaign for the granting of Israeli citizenship to all migrant workers' children, the logic of the struggle was that all organisations working in this field should cooperate. For us, involved in educational work in the local school, participation in the campaign had an extra pedagogical value. It has to do with what radical educators refer to as "pedagogy of solidarity".

In times of social crisis, students tend to direct their rage at their school (for example, through acts of vandalism or through refusal to learn), because for them school symbolises the system that oppresses them and their community. For me as one of their teachers, it was often hard to understand my position as an object for their social frustration, and to work with them through their rage. Their violence touches our body. We often get hurt; we often get angry. It is only with the right supervision that we can figure out what our duty is in regards to the aggression of our students. In the case of the migrant workers' children, we discovered our best practice to be showing those students the real social conditions that oppress them, and showing them ways to act against those conditions.

This process led to a series of demonstrations by the students together with us in front of the Knesset (Israeli Parliament). The children appeared on the special parliamentary committee concerning migrant workers, told their stories and received standing ovation from the audience. They became very active in the campaign for citizenship for all migrant workers' children and took a major role in it. Only through helping the students to direct their rage at the right address, and only through solidarity with their struggle, could we regain their trust and reduce self destructive behaviour in school.

"Our Place"

The next thing we did with the students we worked with was to establish an after-school club-house. The main goal of the project was to get the kids off the streets of the central bus-station area after school hours. The name of the club, its styling and its activities were created by the students themselves. The name they picked for the club was "Our Place"[4], a name that would bear witness to their feeling of lacking a place they could call their own and be accepted at[5]. The main activity they picked was break-dance lessons given by friends of theirs, themselves illegal migrant workers.

Another pedagogic challenge we encountered at the club was working with the racism of Mizrachi teenagers from the other neighborhoods against the immigrant students. Like other oppressed communities, the Mizrachi kids internalized the ruling, social logic of suppression of those who are weaker, and chose the migrant workers' children, the weak Other of their community, as a target of their suppression. For us it was an important lesson about racism among the discriminated communities. Only after confronting their racism, through a series of meetings closed only to the Mizrachi students, did they start to show up at the club.

As time went by, Our Place became a place that served wider parts of the community: Parents came for meetings to get information about immigration laws or to receive flyers with information about their rights during police arrests. School teachers used the place to hold meetings with the students, their parents, and with human rights organizations.

"Twists in National Memory" and Migrant Workers

The campaign for citizenship for all migrant workers' children was a partial success: only children who had been born in Israel, and were over ten years old, were entitled to an Israeli passport. There were also other, more peculiar conditions for citizenship: the children's parents had to prove they had entered the country legally, and the children had to prove they had no previous police convictions, although clearly there could be no connection between these criteria and citizen rights in principle. The most interesting condition for citizenship was that the children had to commit to serve in the Israeli Army. It is at this point that the case of migrant workers' children touches on the theme of the colonial disposition of the Zionist project. The eligibility for Israeli citizenship, as the point of intersection of the two, reveals that Israeli nationality today has less to do with being a Jew, and much more with the consent to its colonial acts against the Arabs.

---

4   Because the immigrant workers come from diverts countries English is the language most of them speak with their employers and often between them. The children, though they know Hebrew very well, would often speak amongst themselves English, as if it was their own "privet language". For that reason, I believe, they picked an English name for their club.
5   And, more generally speaking, bearing witness to the way in which the migrant worker functions as the inherent inverse position to the globalized position of the "citizen of the world".

Moreover, Israel's willingness to make an exception in its strict migration policy for the migrant worker's children, enables the Israeli regime to sustain its interests: providing a cheap workforce, serving the interests of wealthy Israeli employers, filling in the lack of workers doing the dirty unrewarding jobs etc.: at the same time, the government sustains a paranoid, racist position regarding the Palestinian, immigrant etc. Other. Accepting a small number of children from the immigrant community like the few Muslim refugees from Sudan, enables Israelis to maintain their position of being (potential) victims of anti-Semitic persecution which makes the strict immigration laws necessary to maintain Jewish demographics, while simultaneously holding the position of a moral nation (i.e. one that has learnt the "universal lesson" of the Holocaust), as well as a position of being a powerful nation (reaching out to help refugees of any genocide from around the world regardless of their race and religious views). Reflecting now on the campaign for citizenship for the children of the migrant workers, I believe the campaign failed to change the fundamental injustice underlying the Israeli discourse in that deeper sense.

Being an Educator in Times of Occupation and Deportation:
A critical pedagogue who was once my supervisor hung in his office a saying by Mark Alter from Warsaw Ghetto: "Being Jewish means always being on the side of those being beaten and never on the side of those beating". He told me he had often been criticised for hanging it there. I think hanging it next to his desk was a courageous act of re-appropriation of the universal humanist meaning of the saying: unconditional political identification with those being beaten. Only with that ethical stance could the political struggle – that of defining the border-lines between the beater and the beaten – be engaged in. It is also the only way to dismantle the discourse dividing good Jews (ones that do not object to aggressive privatization reforms and are against the Arabs) and bad Jews, between good Arabs (those who collaborate with, or do not protest against, Israeli colonialism) and bad Arabs. The position of migrant workers – not being Jewish, not being a "Third generation of Zionism", and not being legal citizens – can illuminate what being an educator in the occupying Israel is. By identification with the victims of the cruel logic of the social conditions i.e. the refugees, the women, the poor, gays, the Palestinians etc. we redefine the frontiers of the political struggle.

A colleague of mine once told me that loving a child is perhaps the most radical act an educator can perform. Today, looking back at the work we did with those students, I believe the most important thing was simply being with them, being on their side. Our moral stance as radical pedagogues is measured by the decision to be responsible for *all* children, without an exception, without giving in to pragmatic or institutional racist considerations. If a child has to be deported, at least let us give him a farewell party so s/he knows s/he's going to be missed. As I have tried to argue, this is not a mere empathic position; it is a radical political stance, a stance that shows that an alternative reality to the vicious existing one is possible. It is a position that struggles with the beaten in a country claiming to be one of the formerly beaten.

Uri Ellis, born 1977 in Kefar-Sava, currently lives in Ramat-Gan. He has completed his MA studies in Philosophy on political subjectivation processes informed by psychoanalytic theory. He is currently a fellow at the Mandel School for Educational Leadership in Jerusalem. He is active in Hitchabrut-Tarabut, a movement dedicated to connecting various political struggles in Israel.

From Both Sides, Now

ELAD ORIAN

There is no denying it – I was nervous when we walked into the streets of the Palestinian village. We had just crossed over, by foot, from a Jerusalem suburb into the West Bank. It is only a subtle geographical distance but a huge human and political one. The moment of crossing over felt as if somebody had suddenly changed the film – after stepping over the fence surrounding a neat Jewish middle-class suburb of Jerusalem, we found ourselves walking across olive groves in rural Palestine. We were a small group of Israelis on our way to the village of Biddu in order to take part in a joint Israeli-Palestinian demonstration against the construction of the Israeli separation barrier[1] on the village's lands. By this time, the people of Biddu had already been at struggle for several months, in the course of which five of its inhabitants had been killed by the Israeli army's repression of the demonstrations.

For me, it was the first time to participate in a joint Palestinian–Israeli protest against the separation barrier. My decision to join was based on a long-felt feeling of moral indignation at the Israeli occupation regime, and an understanding that not engaging in resistance would actually mean complicity. The turning point came for me when an Israeli demonstrator was shot by an Israeli army sniper.[2] Although Palestinians had been shot in such situations many times, even been killed, there was something much closer

---

1 The separation barrier is a complex of electronic fences, trenches and security roads, which is over 700 km long. It has been built – mostly on confiscated Palestinian land – to stop terrorist attacks, but more importantly to control the Palestinian territories and include Jewish settlements into the Israeli territory. For more details see: //www.btselem.org/English/Separation_Barrier/.
2 Gil Naamati was shot in both legs by an Israeli sniper while taking part in a direct action that tried to open a gate in the fence near the village of Mas'ha on the December 26, 2003. For more information see: www.awalls.org/topics/gil_naamati.

when it was an Israeli. Anyway it was a wake-up call: I could not go on living my life in Tel Aviv as if all this was not happening half an hour away from my house.

After our arrival to Biddu though, my problem was that the only reference I had for this situation – that of walking through a Palestinian village – was what I had learnt in the army. The narrow streets, the smells, the unpainted houses and abundant graffiti in Arabic, everything fit the image, familiar to every Israeli soldier, of a generic Palestinian village. A village without character or distinct qualities and obviously without familiar places or faces – a target. My instincts were screaming for a completely different set of reactions. Going into the village should be done at night, with a sniper covering our backs and night vision scopes, not like this in broad daylight. I knew this was an entirely wrong set of intuitions there and then, but I could not shake it away, nor could I get rid of the sensation of being out of place. I had a lot to overcome; after all, the whole point of being there was to resist this whole mechanism of repression, the obvious and violent one that is exerted on Palestinians, as well as the gentler one which is acting on Israeli citizens in the context of a permanent state of war.

As we approached the centre of the village, we met with the demo. About one or two hundred people, many young and mostly man, had already gathered and were chanting and revving themselves up. As the march towards the building site of the separation barrier started organising, still in the centre of the village, an Israeli army jeep drove into the village and threw some stun grenades[3] at the crowd: an altogether confusing and frightening experience, but quite futile as it did not send even a single demonstrator home. I never did any 'riot control' – the Israeli army jargonism for the repression of demonstrations – so I had no clue how these things work or what are the dynamics of the interaction between the soldiers and the Palestinian civilians. On top of that I never had stun grenades thrown at me. I was rather shaken by all that was going on around me. For the vast majority of Israeli Jews the idea of standing in the middle of an angry Palestinian crowd chanting "Allah – hu – akbar!" (Allah is great!) is one of the worst nightmares that one can think of. It is quite synonymous to being lynched. Yet at that moment, I had placed myself in such a situation and, moreover, was supposed to feel safe mingling in the crowd and to be afraid from the soldiers. It was partly working, I was afraid of the soldiers, but not feeling, at all, at ease among the Palestinian crowd demonstrating around me.

---

3   Stun grenades explode with a very loud blast and a glaring flash, a combination that for a moment cause severe disorientation on the part of the people affected by them.

When the demo got further away from the village and closer to the lands that were actually confiscated for the construction of the fence, a stand-off with the army was reached. We were standing on one hill and the army on the other, facing each other. At this point some foreign journalist started talking to me asking about how I was feeling and what it meant to be there as an Israeli Jew. To illustrate the strangeness of the position I was in, I told him it feels very odd standing in the "wrong" side of the Israeli snipers' sights, to which he responded that there were no snipers, only soldiers in riot control positions. I pointed out to him that what seemed like a bush on a terrace on the other hill was actually a camouflaged sniper.

I remembered how to look at those things. Although I would have classified myself as a lefty all my life and conceptually saw myself as far away from the Israeli mainstream, I was actually doing my bit within the framework of Jewish, middle-class Israeli citizenship. When the call came I went and did my army service like most everybody else. Even more, although I refused to serve in the West Bank during my compulsory three year service, I did combat duty in the south of Lebanon because once in the system I succumbed to its inner logic. The army exerts a very strong dynamic pushing towards its logical conclusion – it is not about protecting your country or yourself, let alone about being just, but about fulfilling this ultimate test of yourself: it's about being in combat. So despite my left wing, humanist – not to mention anti-militarist – upbringing, once in the system I wanted to test myself, to experience those extreme situations, to come out of it as a stronger person. Hence, at the bottom line, opinions aside, I became a regular combat soldier doing his regular combat duty, thus fulfilling the role set out for me by the Israeli state. However, the journey to release myself from this role started even while I was actively acting it.

A few months after that first excursion to Biddu I had a week-long training bout with my unit as at that time I was still doing active reserve duty.[4] I must confess it was not horrible, at times even enjoyable: orienteering, working with complex engineering systems, the physical challenge, spending time outdoors, are all things I liked doing since I was very young, and on top of that the guys with whom I was serving were good company. On the first day of the reserve duty I got a phone call from one of the activists who told me there were plans to remove a road block[5] later that week. I really wanted

---

4   In Israel every male who did regular army service continues to be a reserve soldier for many years and is called for service about once a year for a period of several weeks.

5   Restrictions on the movements of Palestinians are integral to the Israeli occupation of Palestine: hundreds of road blocks ranging from big, elaborate and manned complexes to simple concrete blocks criss cross the West Bank. Thereby, Palestinians are prevented from accessing Israel, but under the guise of

to take part in this action, since removing a road block is a very precise type of direct action. First, it corrects on the ground the wrongs of the occupation, removing an obstacle separating Palestinians from Palestinians and serving no security purpose whatsoever, only pure harassment. Second, while Israeli activists come for support, it is done by the people who actually suffer from it, allowing them to take control over their own life at least for a moment. It is a classic form of civil disobedience.

I could not, obviously, tell my commander that I wanted to go and remove a road block in the West Bank, so I told him I had an important meeting in the university that I would like to go and he approved. So I had two more days of army and after finishing an exhausting, but exciting, orienteering run in the middle of the night, I left my gear and rifle with the guys and hitchhiked my way back home. At seven in the next morning I was already on the bus to the action in the West Bank. It all went well, we managed to remove the roadblock but were stopped by the army on the way back. They surely knew who we were but probably had no proof of what we did. Even if they would have arrested us, it would probably have resulted in a couple of hours in a cell, nothing more. But for me this situation was actually pretty dangerous and profoundly stupid, because I was, formally, still a soldier that day, not having finished my reserve duty. I could have spent some serious jail time had they decided to charge me with anything.

It would be fair to say that this was the height of my schizophrenic existence as a soldier and activist at the same time. The ability to move, relatively freely, between these two worlds was so fundamentally confusing it left me detached from either of the two worlds. The freedom with which I was able to move between them made delimiting difficult, as they were both very clearly, the substance of my life – the army and activism, the mainstream and the margins of Israeli society, old friends and new ones. Nevertheless it became impossible to live these two, intertwined and contradictory, lives. They were incommensurable. I had to make a choice.

Although it took a lot of time to hatch and for me to realise what it was, the decision was clear, I left the army. However, even before this decision I had, for a long time, had a feeling that there was a lot I needed to forget in order to become a more complete activist, more true to the "cause", and a better person. The army had equipped me with a set of skills that were useful if I would have wanted to interact with Palestinians under the army's game plan: from the hand gestures that one is used to when dealing with

---

'security' Israel also imposes severe restrictions on movements of people and goods inside the West Bank. For more details see: www.btselem.org/English/Freedom_of_Movement/.

Palestinians at a check point to seeing every one and everything as targets and threats. So many things in me became excess baggage.

As time passed I realised that I could not really make memories disappear, they were with me for life. The only option open to me was learning new modes of thinking through action. Only by being with people, working and spending time together, could I transcend this notion of "targets" and "threats". Going a step further and jumping across this barrier, I started making real human connections with those formerly known as "targets" and "threats". We became friends, not only by protecting one another from the beating of an Israeli soldier during a demonstration, but also by chatting or enjoying a meal together. Friendships evolved, not trivial by any measure, that, however, need to confront some basic asymmetries: I can go visit my Palestinian friends, but not the other way around, just to mention a simple example. But by and large, these friendships manage to rise above this adverse context.

There is a lot of curiosity when I meet new people in Palestine, from both sides. They might have never met an Israeli under such circumstances, both at ease and on equal footing, sitting and drinking tea, and the questions start pouring out: what drives you to come here? Why? Do you think it makes a difference? And so on. At one point, almost inevitably, the issue of the army comes up: were you in the army? What did you do? Did you serve in Palestine? In one of my first visits to Bil'in,[6] a group of us was sitting together, some Palestinian and some Israeli, in a nice relaxed conversation. Then, however, one of the Palestinian men became very critical of the fact that I had done my army service. Another Palestinian replied to this by asking him which group he had belonged to at the age of eighteen: hadn't he been a member of the Islamic Jihad? And he told the guy that what really mattered is not where anyone of us had been before, but where we are *now*.

Indeed, neither of us can ditch his past, but we can try and create a personal and collective reality in which it is possible to remember and do not have to deny where we come from, but at the same time live beyond these memories. We can do this through working together in a concrete manner, taking action for changing our lives, our reality, the reality of Israelis and Palestinians alike – now.

---

[6] A village that has been one of the central points of joint Palestinian/Israeli resistance to the construction of the separation barrier during the last years. For more information see: http://www.bilin-village.org/index.htm.

Elad Orian, born 1974, lives in Jaffa and works in Israel and Palestine. He studied physics and upon failing to become a great physicist he moved on to environmental and political activism. His real passions are cooking and cycle touring. Check his work with Palestinian communities on: www.comet-me.org.

A Yid iz in Goles*.
"For three Transgressions of Israel, yeah, for four, I will not reverse it"

ELAZAR ELHANAN

Yesterday, while taking the subway with another Israeli friend voluntarily exiled in New York, we saw a man in long coat, a scarf and an old fashioned cap who bore an uncanny resemblance to the poet Nathan Alterman. This would have probably gone unnoticed except for the fact that earlier, while trying desperately to find a place to have coffee on a frozen Christmas day we saw a man that looked exactly like the late Yitzchak Rabin. That led us to consider the possibility that great Israelis of that generation, after they have died, move to this city, shake off the slim and unconvincing film of Israeliness and assume the other identity, the diasporic, Jewish one.

Israeli identity was constructed as an opposition to diasporic Jewish identity. An opposition, based on a lot of conflicting terms, an unstable mix of longing, guilt and self-hate. Trying to reconcile this conflict I, and I believe many others, was struck by the following paradox: apparently, as Israelis we have not gone far enough in order to cast away that old image of the Yiddish speaking Jew from "over-there"; as Jews, we have gone too far to ever genuinely to assume it again. It is this ambivalence that brought me to New York, where at the moment I am studying Yiddish..

I.

My experience of fashioning myself as a political "other" in Israel involves a series of ruptures with mainstream Israeli identity. I was born in Jerusalem in 1977, grew up during the first Intifada and the "peace process" following the

---

* *A yid iz in goles* (Yiddish): a Jew is in exile. This Hassidic saying means that a Jew is a Jew only in exile. Therefore an Israeli is not a Jew. Either that or the Zionist state is not the end of exile.

Oslo Accords. I joined the army in 1995 when I was 18. Having been raised on Zionist values of service and contribution to the greater good, I joined gladly. I have always held the commonplace belief of the Zionist left in dialogue and the possibility of peace with our neighbors if they would only accept our extended hand. At the same time I believed that in going to the army I was doing something important and right; that I was protecting my family and defending my country. Just as commonplace, I did not see a contradiction between serving the occupation and believing in peace; nor did I realize that our neighbors were actually our subjects, our serfs. I volunteered and did my service in the IDF's Special Forces and served for three years. However, the experiences I had, the things I saw and did, soon led me to the conclusion that as a soldier in that army I was not protecting anybody or defending anything. I was a fig leaf for the cowardice of politicians and a tool in the perpetuation of a political project I found objectionable, not to say criminal, namely the occupation and the settlement project in the West Bank and Gaza.

This realization however, had not translated itself to action until some time later. On the 4th of September 1997 my sister Smadar was killed by a suicide bomber in Jerusalem. She was 14-years-old and died several hundred feet from my house, which I was supposed to be protecting. After the tragedy all I heard around me, the support and advice I was given, was either the very dark silence of resignation and acceptance of fate, or the cry for revenge. I refused to accept either of the two options and decided to leave this game altogether. Not to kill for Israel and not die for it. To find another way.

For me, this other way was first of all in refusing to serve in the occupation army. Then as one of the founders of the joint Israeli-Palestinian, non-violent, solidarity movement Combatants for Peace[1]. Here, former fighters from both sides meet for dialogue and joint action. We are concentrating our efforts on building the movement and bringing Palestinians and Israelis combatants together, in dialogue meetings. We have held dozens of those, and brought together over 500 Israeli ex-soldiers and Palestinian ex-prisoners. We do that through our particular social capital in our respective societies – as fighters –which allows us to say things no one else would or could say, go into places where peace-activists could never enter before (such as high schools).

Our action in that respect is centered on our personal stories. We do not propose a solution or an answer. We don't pretend to be experts or scholars. We just tell a story that is very personal and at the same time integral to the collective experience in both societies. We tell people on both sides, with no shame and no fear: "That's what we did in your name. This is where it

---

1 See: www.combatantsforpeace.org

brought us. We believe that there is a better way". In the last couple of years we have talked in hundreds of venues, private houses, schools and universities. We spoke in the Israeli city of Sderot the day a child was critically injured by a Kassam rocket fired by Palestinians from the nearby Gaza Strip. We spoke in the West Bank village of Hussan on the same day the IDF perpetrated a massacre in Bet Hanun, a Palestinian city in the Gaza Strip. We always talk in pairs: A Palestinian and an Israeli, displaying physically that there is a partner to talk and listen to, showing "the other" to people that have never seen him other than through the lenses of fear and hate.

Similarly, the limits of my identity were tested by my membership in the Bereaved Families Forum,[2] which brings together Israeli and Palestinian bereaved families. They know loss and pain and they still struggle for peace. Through this group I had the possibility of meeting Palestinians, real ones, those a normal Israeli never meets, neither stereotypes nor caricatures. Not military targets, but human beings like Ali Abu Awwad who had spent four years in our jails, who was shot by a settler and whose brother was murdered by a soldier. Nevertheless Ali still wants peace. And there are many others like him. I had a chance to ask them if what we say about them is true: Do they really want to throw us in the sea? Do they really educate their kids to hate us? Is it true that we don't have anyone to talk to? And they answered me that for their part these things are not true, that in them we do have a partner to talk to – and that there is much to talk about. And I learned one other thing: If I can talk to these people, many of them former members of the Palestinian resistance movements, like the one that killed my sister, and that if they can talk to me after losing family members at the hands of soldiers like myself, if we can talk, then anyone can and no one has the excuse not to do so.

Breaking away from the game did not mean the effacing of the past but rather its integration in a performative discourse that charges it with new meaning. As a member of Combatants for Peace and the Bereaved Families Forum, my authority to speak out stems not only from my past as an active participant in the violence or as its victim but also from my wish to reject the manipulation of my personal loss and the rejection of the ongoing militaristic discourse. In acknowledging the pain of the other, in thereby refusing to participate or adhere to the prevailing doxa, a space is created that does not allow any coherence, any formation of an exclusive identity, in spite all of my efforts to stay in some way connected to the society I come from.

---

2   See: www.theparentscircle.org. In this group there are 500 families that have lost a family member in this conflict, Often more then one. 250 from Israel and 250 from Palestine

II.

But breaking with Israeli identity or rather: with the lack thereof is a painful disconcerting and surprisingly rapid process. The painful thing is rather that sense of lacking, the realization that Israeli identity is well confined and delineated but is devoid of a "center" Learned studies would claim otherwise: The law of return, enabling every Jew to become Israeli would expand that identity infinitely, the lack of officially defined borders would do the same etc. But actually there is a strong sense of what is Israeli and what is not. A sense that is based, one has to admit, on a common experience, that of being encircled by the impassable borders of the state, captured in the coarse, impoverished sound of the Hebrew language and marked by a strong desire to be somewhere else. Like prisoners, there is that sense also that other than the barbed wire around, the random idiom we grew into (since we could have been speaking any other language, since as secular Israelis, Hebrew does not hold the same place of sanctity in our hearts), and the misfortune that prevented us from leaving – or made us come to Israel in the first place –, there is nothing there. Israeli identity is devoid of essence, or a base.

Needless to say, the everyday identity-discourse in Israel is very different. The missing base is never questioned; its existence is taken for granted: we presume that we are part of a collective, that we are partners in a joint political and national venture that is run in good faith and for the general well-being of all the citizens, that our service for it, in the army and elsewhere, is warranted and worthwhile. However the very process of becoming a military refuznik immediately puts into question many of the foundations that constitute Israeli identity as such. Once I had examined them critically, the military, the sense of Jewish collective, of a joint social political project called Zionism, all these pillars turned to vapor. I came to realize that the national project is run for the good of the few at the expense of the many – be they Israelis or Palestinians.

That is where, for me, Yiddish came in. The experience of learning Yiddish, as an Israeli is not a simple one. The problematic relations between Jew and Israeli, Hebrew and Yiddish, Zionism and Diaspora all come into play. In fact, it pushes the limits of one's identity to its extreme. All the more so when one does it in New York, my current haven, where I study Yiddish at Columbia University. However, on the other hand this tension offers an identitary solution to that malaise: the dream of return to an origin, to an untainted, Jewish, diasporic identity.

For me, being "Israeli" is a binary opposition to being Jewish, a violent negation of the Diaspora. I look at it now as an archaic form of anti-Semitism that is preserved mainly in Israel and much more so, constitutes the creed of the Zionist left. As a way out of this entanglement I discovered the old, romanticized, mythologized image of the Yiddish speaker. The Yiddish speaker, the poor, the immigrant, the worker, self-educated, humanist, cosmopolitan, radical, burning with fervent belief and terrible naiveté that the world could change for the better, in spite of anti-Semitism, of pogroms and of nationalism – there is of course a terrible sense of dramatic irony embedded in the field – is something different. It is not the well-fed, contented, monolithic Jewish image propagated by mass-media of the Seinfelds[3], JAPs,[4] the Woody Allen-like bagel eating, funny, neurotic lawyers one would expect to meet in New York, nor is it the grounded, empty, forceful image of the Israeli. Being able to relate oneself to that sense of smallness, righteousness and justice, I find an intoxicating feeling.

III.

Delving into the world of Yiddish letters, the voices one hears are extremely compelling. In reading these old and oh so relevant texts, I was struck by the resemblance in tone and feeling between their experience and mine. They too had to deal with a conflicted and hated identity; they too had to decide for themselves what to salvage from the culture that bred them, what to bring to the new order and what to leave behind, or rather that they could not do without this culture that they could not bear.

The words of M.L . Halpern, one of the radical Proletpen[5] poets of the New York of the 1920s and 1930s, resonate with my own situation: *"Oh, Zlochov, you my home, my town / With the church spires synagogue and bath, / Your women sitting in the market place...Like life in spring awakened in me / My poor bit of longing for you--My home, my Zlochov.... But when steeped in longing, I recall...it's enough to extinguish in me / Like a candle, my longing for you–"* With remarkable poetic precision he writes of a world pregnant with chaotic violence: *"The peasant with the axe is my hatred in me / For my grandfather, and through him—for you--/ My home, My Zlochov"* and he goes on: *"But our world is full of wonders./ A horse and a cart over the fields / Will carry you out to a railway train...Till it brings you to a ship with a lower deck, / Which takes you away to NewYorkdowntown—"* . I can relate to these verses and feel as my own the frustration and longing even if I would hardly dare pronounce his conclusion: *"...And this, indeed, is my only consolation / That they will not bury me in you--/ My home, my Zlochov."*[6]

These words are available for me in ways that they, the old Yiddish poets paved, when they were as young as I am today. It is the experience of

---

3 See http://en.wikipedia.org/wiki/Seinfeld for details of this sitcom.
4 Short for: Jewish American Princess or Prince.
5 A group of proletarian writers who identified with the American Left from the 1920s to the early 1950s
6 Halpern M. L. "Zlochov my home" in: Harshav, Benjamin, Harshav, Barbara: American Yiddish poetry: a bilingual anthology. Berkeley 1986.

otherness that is found in the experience of immigration. Through that experience I want to relocate that mythical pintele yid, the Jewish dot, that irreducible Jewish essence that would have survived all the changes and social experiments. In 1921, Yankev Glatshteyn wrote in his poem '1919' (1921), against the backdrop of his recent immigration, the hopes following the end of WWI and the revolution and the despair brought by the red scare in the liberal West as well as the pogroms in Ukraine: *"Lately there is no trace left / Of Yankl, son of Yitskhok / But for a tiny round dot / That rolls crazily through the streets...Everywhere "Extras!" fall from above / And squash my watery head / And someone's long tongue / Has stained my glasses for good with a smear of red, / And red, red, red."*[7]

Indeed there is hope there of salvation. A possibility of a return, a chance to shed the burden of Israel and return to some old origin, warm, welcoming and just. The warm embrace of the mama-loshn, the tongue of the mother and the heart, could relieve me from the chains of Hebrew, the tongue of the father, the race and the blood (as the poet Uri Zvi Greenberg had put it). New York is filled with evidence of the rich and brave new world that was created here.

IV.

But of course this is all nonsense. A myth like every identity is and as such, not one that is actually available to me. For one, the path back to Jewishness is closed. Other than by remote affiliation, I do not share anything with those people of long ago. I, a child of the Zionist revolution, am the proof that the impossible can be made possible. The Jew can be undone; the irreducible dot got reduced to a mere racial difference. In the process of becoming a people like any other, the Israeli Jews lost that specificity. I do not share that culture; the Talmud and Mishna, the legend and the prayer have no part in my life. We read the Bible, and even that as a deed of ownership to the land; we do not have that sensibility or that unique place in society, of the marginal, the other, the minority. That unique sense of otherness, of quiet, proud difference is not really one I can feel. Today, the only place where I could sense that proud defiant otherness is in the presence of Palestinian communists, who rebel against everything, the general world and their own, with their insane naïve belief in humanity, in culture, in words, in spite of all evidence to the contrary.

But there is one more reason why I cannot inhabit this Yiddish space. Yiddishists, the proponents of Yiddish nationalism, were in many ways the antithesis of liberalism, they and their culture. Even if they rebelled against it, they never had taken part in the general evil. We, on the other hand, have. In

---

7   Glatstein Y. "1919" In: Ibd.

the course of Zionism, the Palestinian people have been expelled, occupied and repressed every day. As an Israeli I have participated in the violence, not only as a victim, as we would like to imagine, but as perpetrator. Assuming this identity of a refuznik, of a combatant for peace, means also coming to terms with the fact that the blood on our hands cannot be washed away by any symbolic act. Being a part of – even if rebelling against – a majority oppressive rule, sets us forever apart from these diasporic models. Alterman is buried in Tel Aviv, dreaming of the great Land of Israel. Rabin in Jerusalem.

People often love to lament the death of Yiddish and conflate it with the death of its speakers at the hand of Hitler and Stalin. But the truth is that modern secular Yiddish was not killed by the Holocaust but by liberalism, and the advent or modernity, the very things that made Zionism such an impressive force. I believe that in reality, many were happy to see Yiddish gone. It is a hard thing to say and there is no question that the actual death of Yiddish speakers was a real trauma but the notion was as early as the first years of the 19th Century', the first step of enlightenment in the Jewish East Europe, that in order for the Jew to be human, Yiddish has to die and with it its (sub)culture. Human is of course defined in liberal terms: as the white, bourgeois male. A fabricated identity Zionism could provide by embracing clear commonplace nationalism, based on language, blood and soil. One can draw attention to the anti-Semitic roots of Zionism and its Selbsthass (self-hatred) as well the shared ideas Zionism and National Socialism had in regard to the Ostjude,[8] to the fact that the very notion of Israel could be read as an anti-Semitic fantasy - rather then dealing with the 'other' just give it a state on someone else's land; hence the overwhelming international support? a notion that is in binary opostion to the Yiddishist formulation of "doikayt"– (hereness), that would perpetuate the position of the Jew as forever other, irremediably different but still entitled to equal rights. This notion was so much harder to digest. Interestingly the term for the Holocaust in Yiddish is *Der Khurban* (destruction) and it has been in use since the pogroms of 1905. As early as that it was clear for them that the modernization of East Europe, its crystallization into the reality of nation-states we know now, would come at the price of extermination of East European Jewry.

Walking in the streets of New York, one has to – if honest – take notice of the deafening silence of the absence of that Yiddish culture. Especially, as an Israeli, I can lament the loss and feel the longing but I can never go back.

---

8   This term introduced c.1900 by the Jewish writer Nathan Birnbaum denoted much less a geographical difference but rather a cultural one. Referring to the Jewish immigrants from Eastern Europe, the term quickly assumed a negative connotation. The designation combines two pejorative concepts: Jew and East. From it were derived other negatives such as *Ostjudengefahr* (eastern Jewish danger) and *Ostjudenfrage* (Eastern Jewish Question)(sub-editor's note).

However, inspired by their example, I can maybe think of formulating my own alternative identity that is not a part of, a way of having a non-identity, which might be a more "Jewish" one. Conflicted and torn, for ever changing and flexible, inclusive and exclusive, full of contradictions and paradoxes; it is a question of giving myself over to a volatile and fluid experience, that of the wonder and possibility of forming another identity, not in the terms of definition, structure and abstraction but in the ever changing terms of dialogue and negotiation. An inoperable identity, that by its very incapacity to work, would define the conditions of its existence, one that could aspire to be smaller, quieter, more modest and for once, defiant.

Elik Elhanan, born 1977 in Jerusalem, served as a soldier in an IDF combat unit from 1995-98 and then became a conscience objector. In 1997 his sister, Smadar, was killed by a Palestinian suicide bombing in Jerusalem. Elik is an activist with the Israeli-Palestinian Bereaved Families Forum since 1998. He is a founding member of Combatants for Peace, created in 2005, and served as its Israeli coordinator from June 2006 until June 2007. Elik now lives in New York. He is currently earning his PhD in Comparative Literature, Hebrew and Yiddish, at Columbia University.

GEGENWARTSBEW ÄLTIGUNG*.
Getting Drunk on the Past in Berlin and Sobering up in Yiddishland

DANIEL KAHN

TIME-BORDERLANDS

Decorating a wall of my Berlin apartment are maps of "disappeared countries," *meine "Wand der verschwundenen Länder"*. Czechoslovakia, Galicia, Palestine, the USSR, bombed and then divided Berlin, German occupied Europe, the GDR, Yugoslavia, East Prussia, Bessarabia, and so forth. Recently, when describing these maps to some friends, I asked them the German word for "ephemeral" or "temporary". They said it was *zeitbegrenzt*. I like this. "Time-bordered". I guess these maps are a reminder that even nations, appearing so immutable and absolute, are limited not only by the borders of space, but also of time.

Collecting these old maps of obsolete borders seems to me a related fetish to the study of Yiddish, the hybrid language and culture of 1,000 years of central and eastern European Jewish life. It is itself a kind of disappeared physical country, but one whose borders are now more imaginary than political. Yiddishland, as it has been called, is *zeitbegrenzt* as a geographical country. It is a kind of nation which crossed this time border-- or rather had this border thrust upon it. *Zeitbegrenzen* can also be a transitive verb. Now, for the most part, Yiddishland truly lives in *gules,* in exile, from history.

I did not move to Berlin, that city of ghostly borders, planning to make Jewish culture central to my work. I came for other reasons, not speaking a word of Deutsch or Yiddish, having been raised to think of Germans as Nazis

---

* In German discourse on the National Socialist past, *Vergangenheitsbewältigung* is a common term for 'coming to terms with the past'. The title *Gegenwartsbewältigung* ironically refers to this notion, meaning 'coming to terms with the present' (or their children), and interested mostly in the city's traces of Bertolt Brecht, David Bowie, and Nick Cave. But once I was in Germany, many questions about history, power, absence, irony, and memory kept haunting me. It wasn't long before I was getting drunk on the past and finding that I wasn't alone. Many Germans were drunk as well. But when you're drunk, the ground has a tendency to rush up on you and punch you in the face with its inconsistencies. Maybe I tripped on too many *Stolpersteine* ("stumbling blocks", golden plaques with names in front of the former houses of deported and murdered Jews). But somehow I found myself trying to sober up in Yiddishland.

THE KVETCH COMMODE
After visiting the gigantic Krakow Jewish Festival for the first time and studying Yiddish music in Weimar, I had a simultaneous overdose of both inspiration and complete depression and alienation. I felt like they were things I couldn't confront with any other language or culture than Yiddish. I decided to form a band to have a place to address some of my uncomfortable questions. One of the German terms for an accordion is a *Quetschkommode*, literally a "squeeze box." Well, in Yiddish, a kvetch is a complaint, and in English, a commode is slang for a toilet. So I like to tell people my accordion is just that: a toilet for my complaints. This became The Painted Bird.

The band is a mixture of musicians from Germany, Detroit, Sweden, New York, Philadelphia, and Russia. We took our name from the grotesque and controversial Jerzy Kosinski novel from the 60s about a boy who hides in various eastern European villages during WWII. A German friend asked me if I didn't think it was tasteless to name my band after a Holocaust book. I gave him the same answer Art Spiegelman gave when asked about the tastelessness of a Holocaust-themed comic ('Maus'): "Actually, I think the Holocaust was rather tasteless."

VERFREMDUNGS-KLEZMER
By exploring Yiddish on stage, I wanted to dive further into the misunderstanding and misconception; to really explore the alienation and enlightenment; to fight for "lost causes". Maybe I wanted to create situations where people would be at a concert and be forced to ask "Wait, what language is he singing?" or say, "That doesn't sound like Yiddish folk music," or just, "What is this?" I think all of these responses are more interesting and constructive than simply "positive" reactions. It's from these reactions that I first thought of using the term *Verfremdung* (alienation / estrangement), taken from Brecht's theatrical term *Der Verfremdungseffekt* ("The Alienation Effect"). The equation we concocted was *VerfremdungsKlezmer* = Radical Yiddish Song + American Gothic Folk + Punk Cabaret + Klezmer Danse Macabre = Alienation Klezmer Bund.

There is something equally compelling and problematic about the way performed Jewishness is produced and received in the world today, especially in Germany. But it creates a conversation I generally like to take part in. On another level, it's simply interesting to sing Yiddish, a Germanic language, for a German-speaking audience. They get the meaning of the songs somewhere between the Yiddish and the English translations, which I also sing. But being misunderstood has been a part of Yiddish culture for a long time.

YIDDISH CONTRABAND
Someone recently asked me if by getting into Yiddish I wanted to be some kind of cultural ambassador. I said no. There are far more qualified ambassadors than I: Michael Alpert, Adrienne Cooper, Michael Wex, to name a few, or Avrom Lichtenboym my teacher at YIVO (the Yiddish research institute in NY) from whom I learned about the *nayntsikers*. If anything, I said, I'd like to be a kind of *nayntsiker* -the 800 year-old Yiddish slang for a smuggler. It literally means a "ninety-er". Yiddish criminal jargon developed in the Rhine region of Germany where it was wise for criminals not be understood by the Germans or the French in the area. So *nayntsiker* was a Yiddish (Germanic) translation of the French word for ninety: *quatre-vingt-dix* (pronounced "katre-van-dees") – *Contrabandist*. Yiddish is full of little etymological bombs like this one. It comes from centuries of living in spite of borders, of smuggling words and ideas and making them one's own.

Unlike many Jewish artists who have become involved with this music, I didn't immediately have a feeling of "coming home". My first real encounter with the language and culture was from afar – as an outsider. Although I'm Jewish, I was raised in a thoroughly assimilated environment in which *yidishkayt* (Yiddishness) played a minimal and marginal role. Growing up in Michigan, I'd spent much of my life feeling hedged in by the narrow, religious, nationalistic and hypocritical definitions of Jewishness I was handed as a child.

For some reason, it seems that much of the world is somewhat obsessed with questions of "Jewish Identity". What exactly is it? Religious? Ethnic? Cultural? Linguistic? Racial? National? Dietary? The most convincing adjectival term I heard recently was *historical*. It is a *historical* identity. But what does that mean? It means it can mean what you mean it to mean.

But then I found that there is an international conspiracy of Jewish and non-Jewish Klezmorim and Yiddishists (Yiddish being one of the only languages with its own -ism) for whom "Jewish" means much more that what I was taught. This closely knit and wide-spread community of artists, musicians, and academics can be found in Moscow, Tel Aviv, Tokyo, Montreal, New York, Krakow, and in workshops like KlezKamp, Klez

Kanada and Yiddish Summer Weimar. But the scene in Germany is particularly vibrant and has been for decades.

*DEUTSCH*MER / KLEZMER

Across from my window on *Zionskirchstrasse* (Zion-church-street) is the cafe where they hold the monthly Klezmer *Stammtisch* (regulars' table) jam. People crowd around bottles and pass around the old street tunes and wistful ballads. Then they pump out *freylekhs* and *horas* on trumpets, clarinets, accordions, and guitars until closing time. In this group of Berliner Klezmorim, I made many good and lasting comrades. Their knowledge of the music, culture, and language is deep, and the Klezmer music they play is theirs. There's an old joke about Germans liking Klezmer because they can march to it. I think just the opposite is true: Klezmer music likes the Germans because it can march to them.

What drew me to Yiddish song and music culture in the first place was its dexterous ability to maneuver the muddier territories of folk and lyrical life. Klezmer music is angular, dissonant, heartfelt and complex. The songs are full of wicked humor, desperate love, serious drinking, prophetic morality, abundant poverty, evil kings, red flags, and drowned bridegrooms. Learning simultaneously about the sharp-toothed radicalism of Weimar-era, anti-fascist German cabaret, and the history of radical Yiddish folk culture, of the *Yidisher Arbeter Bund* (Jewish Labor Union), simply made sense to me as a natural outgrowth of my own background in punk, folk, theatre, political activism, as well as being a Jew. But many of the musicians who got me into this music are not Jewish at all. I am inspired by the sense of discovery, depth, openness and uncertainty I hear in many of the German Yiddish music projects.

DIASPORA UNTERNATIONALISM

Contrary to much vicious and persistent criticism in the conservative and quasi-liberal press (both Jewish and non-, German and non-), these artists are not engaging in a kind of shallow kitsch and clichés of "authentic Jewishness". If some Germans play kitschy Klezmer, it's not because they are "Goyim who don't get it." Plenty of Jews don't get it, either. And the reasons probably have more to do with talent and interest than with problems of cultural "ownership".

I have a friend in New York who wrote a manifesto of "Diaspora Nationalism" which claims, albeit ironically, that German Klez bands should pay a tax to the Jewish community for using and profiting from our culture. I say if we're going to keep cultural tabs like that, why not pay the Germans for exploring, and developing elements of "our" culture, which a lot of the Jewish community has little or no interest in? Then, by that logic, maybe I shall try to get the German government to pay me to sing their neglected *Volkslieder* (German folk songs).

No, the answer is not some kind of exclusion from "our Jewish cultural authenticity." What I love about this scene is the lack of clear "authenticity" which necessitates a sense of discovery and invention, even in the Frankenstein sense. What I like is that the continuum of "authenticity" has been broken. Furthermore, it is also important to take a critical view of the reasons that many Jews invest in this culture (myself included). Are we simply looking for a door into a Jewishness which does not necessarily have to do with Israel or religion, the two immovable pillars of the Jewishness so many of us were given as a "birthright"? Perhaps. But this, of course, is a distortion and a reduction of what can and should be a more nuanced cultural engagement. It is important to remember that this is, after all, a real living folk culture. It does indeed belong to everyone. We should not only encounter Yiddish for its folk-historical symbolism. The problem is that Yiddish, for Jews and Germans alike, has a giant *Stolperstein* in the way.

NOTES FROM THE *DENK' MAL LOUNGE*

There is of course a third pillar of Jewishness with which Yiddish finds itself inextricably linked. It is that part of the past which young Germans and Jews alike are taught to never forget a. It is part of who they are. It is *die Vergangenheit* (the past) which requires of us so much *Vergangenheitsbewältigung* ('coming to terms with the past'): what Yiddish calls *khurbn* (destruction), Hebrew *shoah,* everyone else Holocaust. German *Erinnerungspolitik* (memory politics), though, all too often becomes a rather neurotic and quite closed conversation between Germans and Germans about things the Germans did to Germans and non-Germans some two or three generations ago. And it is far from a comfortable process to go into the middle of.

The *Denk Mal Lounge* on Hannah Arendt Strasse in Berlin, yet another kind of *Stolperstein.* It is just around the corner from the giant Holocaust memorial in the center of Berlin, the *Denkmal für die ermordeten Juden Europas* (Memorial to the Murdered Jews of Europe). So someone opened a bar close that is called *Denk Mal Lounge.* It's a play on the German word for memorial, which includes the verb *denken* (to think). "Think for a moment!" But given the context here, a very loose translation might be "Never Forget...to have a good time!" Maybe they should call it the *Denk Mal Nicht*: "Stop thinking for a moment." Have a pilsner. Forget about the Holocaust. The bar is full of standard American 1950s kitsch deco. I think it's amazing. Google it! This pub might just be the final proof of the absolute idiocy and bankruptcy of *Vergangenheitsbewältigung* in the face of tasteless consumerism.

SIX MILLION GERMANS

But how can Yiddish, the culture of the so many of the victims of this apotheosis of bad-taste (the Holocaust, not the lounge), contribute to this discourse of *Erinnerungspolitik*? Why should it? Furthermore, is it only a culture of victims? The role in which Yiddish is usually cast is either a cartoon of a victimized mouse (again, all due respect to Art Spiegelman) or a cartoon of a vengeful, proto-Israeli partisan. Indeed it is this dichotomy which we aimed at addressing in our most recent record, *Partisans & Parasites*. The album features songs about biological and social parasitism, German anti-fascist cabaret songs and Yiddish ballads about Palestine and Hurricane Katrina, as well as a certain song called "Six Million Germans".

The song narrates the true account of Abba Kovner, a great partisan hero from Vilna who fought bravely against the Nazis, and then went on to become an honored poet and cultural figure in Israel. But these honors are not the focus of the song. Directly after the war, in 1945, certain members of his partisan group conspired to take full revenge for the systematic and indiscriminate extermination of their people and culture. They planned to kill six million Germans by poisoning the water of several major cities. They did not succeed. But the story is true, and simply reporting it (in rhyme, with a rather upbeat Klezmer polka melody) always makes people bit uneasy. Audience members who might start out dancing to the song often stop and get somewhat quiet and sullen when they start to hear the lyrics.

Mostly though, Germans find the song interesting and even funny. The song has even been translated into a wonderful rhyming German version and performed in left wing cabarets. I get more trouble from conservative Jews who do not like it that we're "airing our dirty laundry in front of the gentiles" (the Yiddish is: "*a shande far di goyim*"). There is also the problem that the song puts Israeli military aggression in this context of historical vengeance, suggesting the hate towards the Germans had been re-directed to the Palestinians. The song also questions this reading of the story, but many people have a "Don't Ask! Don't Ask!" policy when it comes to Palestine.

KLEZMER MACHT FREI?

This has been my experience of *Erinnerungspolitik* in action. Indeed, Yiddish needs to be seen as more than a culture of victims. I think it is equally valuable as a culture of, as Slavoj Žižek might call them, great lost causes. These causes were great not only in their internationalist, universalistic, humanist scope, but in their absolute eradication from today's discourse. Auschwitz may have "murdered the Enlightenment," but does that not in any way confirm that certain enlightenment ideals were worthwhile, since they were murdered by Fascists? Why must we believe that the murder of an idea disproves that idea? On the contrary, I believe it makes them all the more worth fighting for.

Some people like to claim (Jews and non-Jews alike) that by investing themselves in Jewish culture (or Yiddish, in particular), they are somehow defeating Hitler. While I certainly understand this impulse, it is one to be resisted. The fact is that Yiddish is not the culture or language of the Holocaust. Actually, there was nothing even remotely Jewish about the Holocaust. If anything, it had either to do with the Germans specifically or humans generally. Jews were its object, not its subject. While Yiddish songs and poetry written from the depths of that black hole are staggeringly moving and unjustly neglected, the essence of Yiddish culture was concerned with many other things until the black hole intruded. It had more to say than simply "*mir zenen do!*" ("We survive!") – from the Jewish partisans' hymn). Indeed, one of the greatest tragedies of the *khurbn* was the degradation of the vital multi-faceted life of a culture to the powerful but one-dimensional narrative of destruction and survival. The rich tapestry of a thousand years must not be completely obscured by the last five years of its life. We need to look closer at what was obscured and not mistake its murder for its essence.

Indeed, the essence of Yiddish culture lies not in what was lost, but what is still alive and relevant today. Since many of its native speakers – especially many secular Yiddishists, poets, musicians and Bundists – are aging and passing on, it is important for us to seek them out and learn from them now. But the question remains of how to use this culture in the future. Will there continue do be a Yiddishland, constructed out of a combination of memory and imagination? How will this resonate with our world? There still is the compelling relevance of a "national" language which developed without a "nation". The development of Yiddish has always depended on interconnectedness with other cultures and languages. For me, and many others as well, Yiddish is an excellent cultural model for anti-nationalist politics.

DISSIDENCE AND DISSONANCE
The Unternationale (the 'under-national') is a project which takes this internationalist engagement as its central theme and has fun with it. Born spontaneously out of a concert I played with Russian singer Psoy Korolenko in Moscow in winter 2007, it became an album with the Israeli Klezmer band Oy Division later that year in Tel Aviv. We did our Yiddish and Russian 'Sympathy for the Devil', Zionist and anti-Zionist songs from pre-revolutionary Russia, Chassidic drinking songs, Russian Jewish soldier songs, and an old tune with new Yiddish lyrics I wrote about the wall in Israel/Palestine. For bands like Oy Division, performing traditional Yiddish music in Israel is an act of defiance in itself, as it goes against 60 years of official Zionist repression of Yiddish in Israel. But for many young Israelis

today, the phantom limb of their Ashkenaz (European Jewish) cultural history is starting to itch. This itch is not only a longing for the past, but for a way forward.

I am convinced that the dichotomy between the "traditional" and the "progressive" is a false one: Thousands of years of radical traditions are relegated to the dustbin of innocuous nostalgia while the consumerscape is bombarded with constant news of "revolutionary" new products to buy. What of our traditions of subversion? What of our subversive traditions? Is it not a kind of radical patriotism to identify with and honor proudly the long line of satirists and dissidents? The naysayers and partisans of lost causes? Do they not form a nation of sorts? Do they not already comprise the great bulk of those whom history has canonized (after ignoring or martyring them)? And is it somehow conservative to sing a song from 100 years ago, if the song speaks about struggles which are all too relevant today. I wish some of these songs would get old. But they don't. I wish we did not have to sing about crippling poverty and sweatshops and imperialist war anymore. But we do. These old songs remind us that the problems we face today are nothing new. We can learn much from those who struggled with them before us.

MARCHING BACKWARDS INTO THE FUTURE
No, Yiddishland was not entirely *zeitbegrenzt*. It will probably outlive us all. A German recently asked me if Yiddish is *eine verlorene Sprache* - a lost language. I told him, "No. It's not lost. Just a bit lonely." The old songs, the old ideas, the old words, and poems, they're lonely not being read and sung and considered. They have a lot to tell us about who we are and where we came from. History repeats itself whether we learn from it or not. It is only a question of which history we want to take part in repeating. Ultimately, perhaps what Germans and Jews - both Israeli and *gulesdik* (diasporic) alike - can learn most from Yiddish is that folk culture need not be *Volkskultur* (the word so abused and tainted by the National Socialists: a nationalistic, racist, chauvinistic "People's Culture"). Indeed, a national culture can and should defy the borders of a nation. At least any nation which might one day end up hanging on my wall.

So let us march boldly backwards into the future. This watchword speaks to the central paradox in what I want to do with bands like The Painted Bird and The Unternationale. It could be a reference to the revived ritual at Klez Kanada of the whole community walking backwards up a hill, playing a *nign* (a wordless Jewish tune), with our eyes on the setting sun to greet the Sabbath. It could also be about keeping our eyes on the past while entering the future. And perhaps this is the best way to move forward, consciously. Maybe the real problem is this engagement with the *Vergangenheit*, with the past, as the past. I am not interested in the past, per se. Maybe what was lost wasn't the past at all. It was the future. An infinite number of futures were what was killed. Not the past. As one of our songs says: "yesterday is buried" (my translation of the old song "*S'iz Nito Keyn Nekhtn*"). What's worth exploring, then, is the lost territory of the alternate futures of the Yiddish past. This might be where the most progressive cultural path lies. It could maybe lead us to a kind of *Gegenwartsbewältigung* a final coming-to-terms-with-the-present.

Daniel Kahn, born in Detroit in 1978, currently lives in Berlin. He studied theatre and writing at the University of Michigan. He won awards for his poetry, plays, musical composition and acting. He lived and worked as a director, musician, and union/community organizer in New Orleans. After releasing four solo CDs of his own song-writing, he moved to Berlin in 2005, where he plays in several bands and founded projects including The Unternationale and The Painted Bird, which released its second album 'Partisans & Parasites' in 2009.

Outlook

Easy-going Uneasiness

CHARLOTTE MISSELWITZ

"I'm a Holocaust freak... Well, I was, until the project." Irit smiles while shaking her head. Two years after our participation in the German-Israeli exchange project Beyond Memory, we are sitting on her terrace in Haifa. Blending in to her view of the sea images of group sessions in Berlin, she says something has changed. Ever since she can think, the Holocaust has played a central role in her life. She was brought up by her grandma who as a child had escaped the Warsaw ghetto. She knows about her grandma's "survival guilt" because all the other family members died. She dealt with her own Second Generation status because her childhood nightmares were soothed by someone who had seen them for real. The 30-year-old had been preoccupied with all this constantly. Moreover, in Israel she was born into a culture that has been remembering the Holocaust more than six decades long. Then she went on an exchange project with Germans. Today, she sounds somewhat sarcastic.

This collection of essays mirrors various dissonances within the post-Holocaust societies in Israel and Germany. Irit's black humour is maybe an extreme expression. But many other essays display a noticeable number of quotation marks. They manifest their distance to mainstream terminology; they twist their narratives and simultaneously signal the lack of an adequate language for a somewhat post-discourse: post-traumatic, post-guilty, post-nationalist, post-identitarian. So one may ask: pre-what?

The broken memory positions in this book create questions rather then answers. They do not ask for obvious "lessons to be learned from the past". Nor do they proclaim the dissonances as models. Even the ambivalence behind these dissonances leaves a question mark: no longer being a "Holocaust freak" sounds cool, like the cure from some obsession. It sounds easy. At the same time the sarcasm involved in Irit's statement contains an uneasiness concerning her former self as well as her society. Likewise, many dissonances in the book oscillate between emancipation from prevailing memory narratives and deep concern for the past. Sixty years after the Holocaust the discourse seems to be full of both easy and uneasy fragments.

Twisting terminologies of a "shared past"

"You got Berlin, we only have Jerusalem. That's unfair!" Quite a popular joke told by young Israelis. Sitting with them in one of the city's many cafes, I - with a grandmother in the Bund Deutscher Mädel[1] - can only nod. The mellowness of the German capital seems like paradise compared to the conflictive reality in the Middle East. Outside the café, we may find one of these little plaques, a so-called Stolperstein (stumbling stone), memorizing Jews who were deported to Auschwitz. It seems like most Germans only 'stumble' over the country's Nazi past now and then. In Israel however, the Shoah still informs many people's everyday lives as well as popular perceptions of present realities – be it the ongoing Israeli-Palestinian conflict, or the imperative to maintain a genuinely Jewish state. It is indeed unfair.

However, the joke works well along official narratives. Once one has looked behind Germany's memory facades, reality gets more complicated. Phenomena like racism or Neo-Nazism derived from the country's past come to the surface. What first was a joke about historical injustice quickly blots out the shadows cast by contemporary claims "to have learned from history". And it is about continuing from here: the joke implies comprehension by the German counterpart. It plays with suggested realities, indicating who are "we" and who are the "others". Between our parents, let alone grandparents, this humour was still impossible. A communication emerges playful and worrying at the same time: Have we finally arrived in the aftermath of a shared past joking about official narratives and twisting their terminology?

At least for young Germans, the term of a 'Third Generation' seemed to be helpful in order to initiate a critical discourse concerning previous German attitudes towards the National Socialist past.[2] Yet in the exchange project Beyond Memory the therapeutic question was soon on the table: did the term maybe help to distance oneself from the grandparent's guilt? I started confronting my grandmother. Somehow paradoxical to this, I wanted to spot the guilt of the 'German people' engraved in my own genes. At the same time, I found out my grandfather, the very husband of the demonized grandmother, had been a member of Bekennende Kirche, a movement against the Nazis... According to the original suspicion, a twisted outcome, a post-narrative effect per se. By distancing or adopting, the 'Third Generation' term implied derivative guilt indeed. And the conclusion seemed easy: What do my

---

1   The section of the *Hitlerjugend* (Hitler Youth) for girls.
2   Cf. Jens Pyper (Ed.): Uns hat keiner gefragt. Positionen der dritten Generation zur Bedeutung des Holocaust, Berlin. 2002.

grandparents, whether National Socialist or oppositional, have to do with my own standing in today's society? Only, once stepping out of the discourse the new surroundings look deeply fragmented. If Irit originally had been a Holocaust freak, then I was a "guilt detective".

And yet another twist followed. As opposite and strangely connected effects, they render a spiral. While I began questioning the notion of a 'Third Generation', Irit took it up. The mix of the historical facades of Berlin mirroring also her Israeli identity made her switch tracks. She took up the term in order to delimit herself from a 'victim' status: "I wanted to have a discussion similar to yours in Israel, about dealing with history from a perspective of responsibility rather than trauma or guilt..."

A communication emerges, embracing glimpses of hypocrisy. Such as a German with a grandfather in the Wehrmacht[3] asking an Israeli if he or she had killed someone in the army. It tries to cross the lines of collective perceptions with terms like Third Generation. Or mockingly walk the path of well paved German-Israeli narratives as in the joke about Berlin. Whereas our parents and grandparents were still holding on to narratives, we are increasingly confronted with their exclusions and subdued continuities. Experiences by migrants or Palestinians today make the spiral of the aftermath drill into an abyss. They leave no choice but to break out, deconstruct narratives and communicate the absurd. And the growing confusion provokes defiance. Hence – seemingly easy - we put the shared past, the aftermath of the Holocaust and National Socialism, in quotation marks.

Uneasiness

And sitting on Irit's terrace, the mixing of collective memories with present moments could continue forever. For her, the 'twisted Holocaust freak' and me, the 'twisted Third Generation guilt detective', the new tasks seem well distributed. We criticize our societies, exchange memory narratives, crack them and patchwork them together. A new puzzle to get lost in. We give each other a high five. Likewise, all authors speak the twisted language. They all travel. A transnational discourse emerges, producing broken tones. So is this post-narrative attitude the pre-condition for future easiness?

There is no final definition for travelogues. And there had better be none. In this book, young academics, journalists, artists or activists tried to emancipate themselves from monolithic memory discourses without discarding remembrance as such. But they did not find the umbrella of the so-called "globalized memory discourse". Neither did memory get "decontextualized"[4],

---

3 German Army during World War II.
4 Sznaider, Natan and Daniel Levy: The Holocaust and Memory in the Global Age. Temple University Press. 2005

nor did the victim experience become "universalized". And even the transnational positions or dissonant tones cannot provide a model for future memory. They remain individual disruptions, reports of different journeys. Black humour, broken self-references are their glimpses of an uneasy process in the present.

Yet, one might say, the readiness to encounter the other narrative and to transcend ones own boundaries works better than any well-kept archive. One learns to endure contradictions, the ghosts of the past. None of the German essays speaks about the Wiedergutmachtung (reparations) for the Holocaust any longer. Nothing can really heal it. Even the idea of reconciliation through exchange becomes thus irrelevant.

It creates a sustaining of different narratives which again, might sound playful and easy. An Israeli linguistics student in Berlin described the encounter as: "Between Israelis and Americans it usually takes ten years of intimacy to be able ask certain questions. With the Germans however, not more than ten minutes." The Middle East Conflict, Holocaust, National Socialism, it gets right at the heart of the matter. And along the way, the exchange of stories creates a dissonant terminology. It becomes a game that people improve in playing with each new encounter. Like accelerated nut-cracking in which narratives are acted out. "Sorry for the Holocaust," says the German. "Forget about it," says the Israeli. "Ok," says the German, a little too fast... Post-narrative and playful indeed.

Still, the nuts are hard nuts. Cracking your own or the other narrative is even harder. If the game produces sarcastic tones, they express a complicated process, no easiness. All of the writers here read their Imre Kertesz or Primo Levi. We visited various concentration camps and memorial sites. And everyone faced the danger of getting lost in the past. We know, just one narrative is like sticking to a nut without cracking it. So the decision to deal with the present is a desperate act to take on responsibility. Our dissonant language expresses neither transnational "wisdom", nor post-narrative emancipation, nor capacities for encounter. In each of the frames it expresses uneasiness. And it is this uneasiness which provoked our escapism into the present full of memory traces, guilt detectives and Holocaust freaks.

Charlotte Misselwitz, born 1975 in East Berlin, studied Philosophy and Literature in Berlin and was one of the coordinators of *Beyond Memory*. Subsequently she went with a grant for Foreign Journalism for one year to Israel. Currently, she is freelancing for several newspapers and radio and just about to begin her PhD about Mediating the Muslim World in Western Media.